TEACHER'S GUIDE

CONNECTED  MATHEMATICS®3

Data About Us

Statistics and Data Analysis

Glenda Lappan, Elizabeth Difanis Phillips,
James T. Fey, Susan N. Friel

PEARSON

Boston, Massachusetts • Chandler, Arizona • Glenview, Illinois • Hoboken, New Jersey

Connected Mathematics™ was developed at Michigan State University with financial support from the Michigan State University Office of the Provost, Computing and Technology, and the College of Natural Science.

This material is based upon work supported by the National Science Foundation under Grant No. MDR 9150217 and Grant No. ESI 9986372. Opinions expressed are those of the authors and not necessarily those of the Foundation.

As with prior editions of this work, the authors and administration of Michigan State University preserve a tradition of devoting royalties from this publication to support activities sponsored by the MSU Mathematics Education Enrichment Fund.

Acknowledgments appear on page 304, which constitutes an extension of this copyright page.

Authors

A Team of Experts

Glenda Lappan is a University Distinguished Professor in the Program in Mathematics Education (PRIME) and the Department of Mathematics at Michigan State University. Her research and development interests are in the connected areas of students' learning of mathematics and mathematics teachers' professional growth and change related to the development and enactment of K–12 curriculum materials.

Elizabeth Difanis Phillips is a Senior Academic Specialist in the Program in Mathematics Education (PRIME) and the Department of Mathematics at Michigan State University. She is interested in teaching and learning mathematics for both teachers and students. These interests have led to curriculum and professional development projects at the middle school and high school levels, as well as projects related to the teaching and learning of algebra across the grades.

James T. Fey is a Professor Emeritus at the University of Maryland. His consistent professional interest has been development and research focused on curriculum materials that engage middle and high school students in problem-based collaborative investigations of mathematical ideas and their applications.

Susan N. Friel is a Professor of Mathematics Education in the School of Education at the University of North Carolina at Chapel Hill. Her research interests focus on statistics education for middle-grade students and, more broadly, on teachers' professional development and growth in teaching mathematics K–8.

With... Yvonne Grant and Jacqueline Stewart

Yvonne Grant teaches mathematics at Portland Middle School in Portland, Michigan. Jacqueline Stewart is a recently retired high school teacher of mathematics at Okemos High School in Okemos, Michigan. Both Yvonne and Jacqueline have worked on all aspects of the development, implementation, and professional development of the CMP curriculum from its beginnings in 1991.

Development Team

CMP3 Authors

Glenda Lappan, University Distinguished Professor, Michigan State University

Elizabeth Difanis Phillips, Senior Academic Specialist, Michigan State University

James T. Fey, Professor Emeritus, University of Maryland

Susan N. Friel, Professor, University of North Carolina – Chapel Hill

With...

Yvonne Grant, Portland Middle School, Michigan

Jacqueline Stewart, Mathematics Consultant, Mason, Michigan

In Memory of... **William M. Fitzgerald,** Professor (Deceased), Michigan State University, who made substantial contributions to conceptualizing and creating CMP1.

Administrative Assistant

Michigan State University
Judith Martus Miller

Support Staff

Michigan State University
Undergraduate Assistants:
Bradley Robert Corlett, Carly Fleming,
Erin Lucian, Scooter Nowak

Development Assistants

Michigan State University
Graduate Research Assistants:
Richard "Abe" Edwards, Nic Gilbertson,
Funda Gonulates, Aladar Horvath,
Eun Mi Kim, Kevin Lawrence, Jennifer Nimtz,
Joanne Philhower, Sasha Wang

Assessment Team

Maine
Falmouth Public Schools
Falmouth Middle School: Shawn Towle

Michigan
Ann Arbor Public Schools
Tappan Middle School:
Anne Marie Nicoll-Turner

Portland Public Schools
Portland Middle School:
Holly DeRosia, Yvonne Grant

Traverse City Area Public Schools
Traverse City East Middle School:
Jane Porath, Mary Beth Schmitt

Traverse City West Middle School:
Jennifer Rundio, Karrie Tufts

Ohio
Clark-Shawnee Local Schools
Rockway Middle School: Jim Mamer

Content Consultants

Michigan State University
Peter Lappan, Professor Emeritus,
Department of Mathematics

Normandale Community College
Christopher Danielson, Instructor,
Department of Mathematics & Statistics

University of North Carolina – Wilmington
Dargan Frierson, Jr., Professor,
Department of Mathematics & Statistics

Student Activities
Michigan State University
Brin Keller, Associate Professor,
Department of Mathematics

Consultants

Indiana
Purdue University
Mary Bouck, Mathematics Consultant

Michigan
Oakland Schools
Valerie Mills, Mathematics Education Supervisor

Mathematics Education Consultants:
Geraldine Devine, Dana Gosen

Ellen Bacon, Independent Mathematics Consultant

New York
University of Rochester
Jeffrey Choppin, Associate Professor

Ohio
University of Toledo
Debra Johanning, Associate Professor

Pennsylvania
University of Pittsburgh
Margaret Smith, Professor

Texas
University of Texas at Austin
Emma Trevino, Supervisor of
Mathematics Programs, The Dana Center

Mathematics for All Consulting
Carmen Whitman, Mathematics Consultant

Reviewers

Michigan
Ionia Public Schools
Kathy Dole, Director of Curriculum
and Instruction

Grand Valley State University
Lisa Kasmer, Assistant Professor

Portland Public Schools
Teri Keusch, Classroom Teacher

Minnesota
Hopkins School District 270
Michele Luke, Mathematics Coordinator

Field Test Sites for CMP3

Michigan
Ann Arbor Public Schools
Tappan Middle School: Anne Marie Nicoll-Turner*

Portland Public Schools
Portland Middle School: Mark Braun,
Angela Buckland, Holly DeRosia, Holly Feldpausch,
Angela Foote, Yvonne Grant*, Kristin Roberts,
Angie Stump, Tammi Wardwell

Traverse City Area Public Schools
Traverse City East Middle School:
Ivanka Baic Berkshire, Brenda Dunscombe,
Tracie Herzberg, Deb Larimer, Jan Palkowski,
Rebecca Perreault, Jane Porath*, Robert Sagan,
Mary Beth Schmitt*

Traverse City West Middle School:
Pamela Alfieri, Jennifer Rundio,
Maria Taplin, Karrie Tufts*

Maine
Falmouth Public Schools
Falmouth Middle School: Sally Bennett,
Chris Driscoll, Sara Jones, Shawn Towle*

Minnesota
Minneapolis Public Schools
Jefferson Community School:
Leif Carlson*,
Katrina Hayek Munsisoumang*

Ohio
Clark-Shawnee Local Schools
Reid School: Joanne Gilley
Rockway Middle School: Jim Mamer*
Possum School: Tami Thomas

*Indicates a Field Test Site Coordinator

Contents

Data About Us
Statistics and Data Analysis

▼ Unit Overview

Unit Description

In *Data About Us*, your students will learn about the process of statistical investigations. They will also construct and analyze distributions of data. They will compare data distributions by using what they know about measures of center and spread.

Statistical investigations involve a set of four interrelated components (Alan Graham, Statistical investigations in the secondary school [Cambridge: Cambridge University Press, 1987]).

- Posing a question: Formulate key question(s) to explore and decide what data to collect in order to address the question(s).

- Collecting the data: Decide how to collect the data and then collect it.

- Analyzing the data: Organize, represent, summarize, describe, and identify patterns in the data.

- Interpreting the results: Based on the analysis, predict, compare or identify relationships among the data, and use the information to make decisions about the original question(s).

Data are provided in many of the Problems in this Unit. If your students have not had much experience with working through the process of statistical investigations, you may have them collect their own data for some of the Problems. The Questions in the Problems can be applied either to the data in the Student Edition or to data collected by students.

Even if your students have already had experience collecting data, they may be interested in investigating questions that are relevant to them. Keep in mind that collecting data is time consuming, so carefully choose the Problems for which your students collect data.

Note: There are two Labsheets that you can have your students use when working on the Looking Back. One is an exact copy of the six graphs displayed in the Student Edition. The other gives all dot plots, histograms, and box plots for all three candles. Your students can use whichever Labsheet you deem more appropriate when working on the Looking Back.

Summary of Investigations

Investigation 1: **What's in a Name? Organizing, Representing, and Describing Data**

Investigation 1 presents introductory statistical material that will be used throughout *Data About Us*. It focuses on describing, interpreting, and comparing distributions of data. It is intended both as a preassessment of what students might already know and as a way to build understanding related to foundations of data analysis. Students are introduced to the process of statistical investigation. They also review and/or develop background in working with frequency tables, line plots, and bar graphs. Anticipating and recognizing how data vary are two key components of data analysis introduced in this Investigation. Selected measures of center (median and mode) and variability or spread (range) are explored.

Investigation 2: Who's in Your Household? Using the Mean

This Investigation focuses on developing the concept of *mean*. The average number of people in students' households provides the setting. The notion of "evening out" the distribution at a point (the mean) located on the horizontal axis is modeled by using cubes, ordered-value bar graphs, and line plots. The models support development of an algorithm for finding the mean: adding up all of the numbers and dividing by the total number of numbers. Students distinguish between categorical data and numerical data. They also make connections between data types and choice of measures of center and variability (or spread).

Investigation 3: What's Your Favorite. . .? Measuring Variability

Investigation 3 focuses on two measures of variability: interquartile range (IQR) and mean absolute deviation (MAD). Students are introduced to the IQR in the context of deciding how well a group of students estimate cereal portions for two different cereals. Students apply their knowledge of the IQR as a tool to analyze a database of 70 cereals and their sugar content. Finally, students are introduced to the MAD as a way to describe the differences in variation in wait times at an amusement park.

Investigation 4: What Numbers Describe Us? Using Graphs to Group Data

In Investigation 4, students extend their skills in working with data by comparing data sets using measures of center and spread. Students compare two or more distributions by looking at *outliers* (a new concept), how data vary, and which measures of center are appropriate to use as comparisons.

Students begin to notice that representations such as line plots and bar graphs are not suitable for displaying some data sets; larger patterns within the data sets can only be seen when the data are grouped. Additionally, it is time consuming to graph individual cases of data sets when the sets are so large.

Students learn to construct and analyze histograms and box-and-whisker plots in this Investigation. Box-and-whisker plots and histograms are representational tools that permit grouping data in intervals. They are more efficient and allow for more patterns to be seen when working with large data sets. In box-and-whisker plots, the data are grouped into four quartiles, each of which includes one fourth of the data values. In histograms, students can choose which interval size to use; the interval size remains constant throughout the graph.

Unit Vocabulary

- attribute
- box-and-whisker plot (box plot)
- categorical data
- cluster
- data
- distribution
- frequency table
- gap
- histogram
- interquartile range (IQR)
- interval

- line plot
- lower quartile
- maximum value
- mean
- mean absolute deviation (MAD)
- median
- minimum value
- mode
- numerical data
- ordered-value bar graph
- outlier

- quartile
- range
- scale
- shape of a distribution
- skewed distribution
- symmetric distribution
- summary statistic
- table
- upper quartile
- variability

Planning Charts

Investigations & Assessments	Pacing	Materials	Resources
Unit Readiness	Optional		• Unit Readiness*
1 What's in a Name? Organizing, Representing, and Describing Data	3 days	**Labsheet 1.1A** Name Lengths Table 1 **Labsheet 1.1B** Frequency Table: Lengths of Chinese Names **Labsheet 1.1C:** Frequency Table: Lengths of U.S. Names (accessibility) **Labsheet 1.2** Name Lengths Table 2 **Labsheet 1ACE** Exercises 1–4 **Labsheet 1ACE:** Exercise 17 (accessibility) **Labsheet 1ACE:** Exercise 20 (accessibility) • Half-Inch Grid Paper	• Data and Graphs • Expression Calculator

continued on next page

Planning Charts *continued*

Investigations & Assessments	Pacing	Materials	Resources
Mathematical Reflections	½ day		
Assessment: Check Up 1	½ day		• Check Up 1 • Spanish Check Up 1
2 Who's in Your Household? Using the Mean	4½ days	**Labsheet 2.1** Household Size 1 **Labsheet 2.3A** Skateboard Prices **Labsheet 2.3B** Dot Plots of Skateboard Prices **Labsheet 2ACE:** Exercises 4–7 (accessibility) **Labsheet 2ACE:** Exercise 27 (accessibility) • Blank Grid and Number Line • Half-Inch Grid Paper calculators 2-cm colored wooden cubes	**Teaching Aid 2.1A** Distribution of Household Size Table 1 **Teaching Aid 2.1B** Mean Distribution of Household Size 1 **Teaching Aid 2.2** Mean Distributions of Household Sizes **Teaching Aid 2.3** Symmetric and Skewed Distributions • Data and Graphs
Mathematical Reflections	½ day		
Assessment: Partner Quiz	1 day		• Partner Quiz • Spanish Partner Quiz

continued on next page

Planning Charts *continued*

Investigations & Assessments	Pacing	Materials	Resources
3 What's Your Favorite. . .? Measuring Variability	4½ days	**Labsheet 3.1** Serving–Size Estimates **Labsheet 3.2A** Distribution of Sugar in Cereals **Labsheet 3.2B** Cereal Distributions by Shelf Location **Labsheet 3.3A** Wait-Time Distribution for Scenic Trolley Ride **Labsheet 3.3B** Wait-Time Distributions for the Carousel and Bumper Cars **Labsheet 3ACE** Exercise 4 **Labsheet 3ACE:** Exercises 14–16 (accessibility) **Labsheet 3ACE:** Exercises 17 and 18 (accessibility) empty cereal boxes with different serving sizes (optional)	
Mathematical Reflections	½ day		
Assessment: Check Up 2	½ day		• Check Up 2 • Spanish Check Up 2

continued on next page

▶ UNIT
OVERVIEW
GOALS AND
STANDARDS
MATHEMATICS
BACKGROUND
UNIT
INTRODUCTION
UNIT
PROJECT

Planning Charts *continued*

Investigations & Assessments	Pacing	Materials	Resources
4 What Numbers Describe Us? Using Graphs to Group Data	4½ days	**Labsheet 4.1** Students' Travel Times to School **Labsheet 4.2A** Jumping-Rope Contest Data **Labsheet 4.2B:** Mrs. R's Class Data (accessibility) **Labsheet 4.2C** Mr. K's Class Data **Labsheet 4.3** 2nd- and 6th- Grade Heights **Labsheet 4ACE:** Exercises 10–12 (accessibility) **Labsheet 4ACE** Exercises 17–19 **Labsheet 4ACE** Exercise 31 • Graph Paper • Quarter-Inch Grid Paper	**Teaching Aid 4.1** Student Travel Times—Dot Plots and Histograms **Teaching Aid 4.2A** Making a Box-and-Whisker Plot **Teaching Aid 4.2B** Mrs. R's Class Data—A Box-and-Whisker Plot
Mathematical Reflections	½ day		
Looking Back	1 day	**Labsheet** Looking Back—6 Graphs **Labsheet** Looking Back—9 Graphs	
Assessment: Unit Project	Optional		• Sample Student Work 1 • Sample Student Work 2
Assessment: Self-Assessment	Take Home		• Self-Assessment • Notebook Checklist • Spanish Self-Assessment • Spanish Notebook Checklist
Assessment: Unit Test	1 day		• Unit Test • Spanish Unit Test • Unit Test Correlation
Total	22½ days	**Materials for All Investigations:** calculators; student notebooks; colored pens, pencils, or markers	

*Also available as an assignment in MathXL.

Block Pacing (Scheduling for 90-minute class periods)

Investigation	Block Pacing
1 What's in a Name: Organizing, Representing, and Describing Data	2½ days
Problem 1.1	1 day
Problem 1.2	½ day
Problem 1.3	½ day
Mathematical Reflections	½ day
2 Who's in Your Household? Using the Mean	3½ days
Problem 2.1	1 day
Problem 2.2	1 day
Problem 2.3	½ day
Problem 2.4	½ day
Mathematical Reflections	½ day

Investigation	Block Pacing
3 What's Your Favorite. . .? Measuring Variability	3½ days
Problem 3.1	1 day
Problem 3.2	1 day
Problem 3.3	1 day
Mathematical Reflections	½ day
4 What Numbers Describe Us? Using Graphs to Group Data	3½ days
Problem 4.1	1 day
Problem 4.2	1 day
Problem 4.3	1 day
Mathematical Reflections	½ day

Parent Letter

- Parent Letter (English)
- Parent Letter (Spanish)

UNIT
OVERVIEW

▶ GOALS AND
STANDARDS

MATHEMATICS
BACKGROUND

UNIT
INTRODUCTION

UNIT
PROJECT

Goals and Standards

Goals

Statistical Process Understand and use the process of statistical investigation

- Ask questions, collect and analyze data, and interpret data to answer questions

- Describe data with respect to its shape, center, and variability or spread

- Construct and use simple surveys as a method of collecting data

Attributes of Data Distinguish data and data types

- Recognize that data consist of counts or measurements of a variable, or an attribute; these observations comprise a distribution of data values

- Distinguish between categorical data and numerical data, and identify which graphs and statistics can be used to represent each kind of data

Multiple Representations for Data Displays Display data with multiple representations

- Organize and represent data using tables, dot plots, line plots, ordered-value bar graphs, frequency bar graphs, histograms, and box-and-whisker plots

- Make informed decisions about which graphs or tables can be used to display a particular set of data

- Recognize that a graph shows the overall shape of a distribution, whether the data values are symmetrical around a central value, and whether the graph contains any unusual characteristics such as gaps, clusters, or outliers

Measures of Central Tendency and Variability Recognize that a single number may be used to characterize the center of a distribution of data and the degree of variability (or spread)

- Distinguish between and compute measures of central tendency (mean, median, and mode) and measures of spread (range, interquartile range (IQR), and mean absolute deviation (MAD))

- Identify how the median and mean respond to changes in the data values of a distribution

- Relate the choice of measures of central tendency and variability to the shape of the distribution and the context

- Describe the amount of variability in a distribution by noting whether the data values cluster in one or more areas or are fairly spread out

- Use measures of center and spread to compare data distributions

Standards

Common Core Content Standards

6.RP.A.3 Use ratio and rate reasoning to solve real-world and mathematical problems, e.g., by reasoning about tables of equivalent ratios, tape diagrams, double number line diagrams, or equations. *Investigation 3*

6.RP.A.3A Make tables of equivalent ratios relating quantities with whole-number measurements, find missing values in the tables, and plot the pairs of values on the coordinate plane. Use tables to compare ratios. *Investigation 3*

6.SP.A.1 Recognize a statistical question as one that anticipates variability in the data related to the question and accounts for it in the answers. *Investigations 1, 2, 3, and 4*

6.SP.A.2 Understand that a set of data collected to answer a statistical question has a distribution, which can be described by its center, spread, and overall shape. *Investigations 1, 2, 3, and 4*

6.SP.A.3 Recognize that a measure of center for a numerical data set summarizes all of its values with a single number, while a measure of variation describes how its values vary with a single number. *Investigations 1, 2, 3, and 4*

6.SP.B.4 Display numerical data in plots on a number line, including dot plots, histograms, and box plots. *Investigations 1, 2, 3, and 4*

6.SP.B.5A Summarize numerical data sets in relation to their context, such as by reporting the number of observations. *Investigations 1, 2, and 4*

6.SP.B.5B Summarize numerical data sets in relation to their context, such as by describing the nature of the attribute under investigation, including how it was measured and its units of measurement. *Investigation 2*

6.SP.B.5C Summarize numerical data sets in relation to their context, such as by giving quantitative measures of center (median and/or mean) and variability (interquartile range and/or mean absolute deviation), as well as describing any overall pattern and any striking deviations from the overall pattern with reference to the context in which the data were gathered. *Investigations 1, 2, 3, and 4*

6.SP.B.5D Summarize numerical data sets in relation to their context, such as by relating the choice of measures of center and variability to the shape of the data distribution and the context in which the data were gathered. *Investigations 2, 3, and 4*

6.NS.C.6 Understand a rational number as a point on the number line. Extend number line diagrams and coordinate axes familiar from previous grades to represent points on the line and in the plane with negative number coordinates. *Investigations 2, 3, and 4*

6.NS.C.7 Understand ordering and absolute value of rational numbers. *Investigations 2, 3, and 4*

UNIT
OVERVIEW
▶ GOALS AND
STANDARDS
MATHEMATICS
BACKGROUND
UNIT
INTRODUCTION
UNIT
PROJECT

Facilitating the Mathematical Practices

Students in *Connected Mathematics* classrooms display evidence of multiple Standards for Mathematical Practice every day. Here are just a few examples of when you might observe students demonstrating the Standards for Mathematical Practice during this Unit.

Practice 1: Make sense of problems and persevere in solving them.

Students are engaged every day in solving problems and, over time, learn to persevere in solving them. To be effective, the problems embody critical concepts and skills and have the potential to engage students in making sense of mathematics. Students build understanding by reflecting, connecting, and communicating. These student-centered problem situations engage students in articulating the "knowns" in a problem situation and determining a logical solution pathway. The student-student and student-teacher dialogues help students not only to make sense of the problems, but also to persevere in finding appropriate strategies to solve them. The suggested questions in the Teacher Guides provide the metacognitive scaffolding to help students monitor and refine their problem-solving strategies.

Practice 2: Reason abstractly and quantitatively.

In Investigation 4, students compare two data sets. They give an answer to a broad question by linking that question with quantitative data. They find measures of center and spread to find statistical answers to questions and support their ideas.

Practice 3: Construct viable arguments and critique the reasoning of others.

In Investigation 3, students are asked to assess the reports of two fictional characters. They determine the validity of each character's interpretation of the data and conclude which one is used appropriately in the context.

Practice 4: Model with mathematics.

Throughout the Unit, students represent data by constructing graphs and plots. These include line plots, dot plots, frequency tables, ordered-value bar graphs, histograms, and box-and-whisker plots. Additionally, in Investigation 2, students use manipulatives to model the "evening out" process associated with finding the mean.

Practice 5: Use appropriate tools strategically.

Throughout the Unit, students use number lines and grid paper to construct plots and graphs. They use these tools to accurately represent data values in a data set. They also use calculators to compute exact statistics.

Practice 6: Attend to precision.

Students must pay attention to precision in Investigations 2, 3, and 4. In these Investigations, students calculate measures of center and spread, including mean, median, range, IQR, and MAD. Because these numbers are used to represent sets of data, students focus on exact calculations.

Practice 7: **Look for and make use of structure.**

Students use manipulatives (such as sticky notes or grid paper containing ordered values) to find the median, upper quartile, and lower quartile. For all medians, they know to find the midpoint of the ordered values. Students discuss algorithms for other statistical measures as well, and use the same algorithms and strategies to find summary statistics for a variety of problem situations.

Practice 8: **Look for and express regularity in repeated reasoning.**

Throughout the Unit, students look at graphs and their shapes. In Investigation 4, they revisit the vocabulary words *symmetric* and *skewed* when analyzing box plots. They apply the same reasoning to describe the box plots as they had earlier in the Unit.

Students identify and record their personal experiences with the Standards for Mathematical Practice during the Mathematical Reflections at the end of each Investigation.

Mathematics Background

The Process of Statistical Investigation

Statistics is the science of collecting, analyzing, and interpreting data to answer questions and make decisions. Statistical reasoning is a crucial part of science, engineering, business, government, and everyday life. Because of this, statistics has become an important strand in school curricula.

Understanding variability—how data vary—is at the heart of statistical reasoning. Variability must be considered within the context of a problem. There are several aspects of variability to consider, including noticing and acknowledging, describing and representing, and identifying ways to reduce, eliminate or explain patterns of variation.

Components of Statistical Investigation

Statistics is a process of data investigation, which involves four interrelated components (Alan Graham, Statistical investigations in the secondary school [Cambridge: Cambridge University Press, 1987]).

- Pose the question(s): formulate the key question(s) to explore and decide what data should be collected in order to address the question(s)

- Collect the data: decide on a method of data collection, and then collect the data

- Analyze the distribution: organize, represent, summarize, describe, and identify patterns in the data

- Interpret the results: predict, compare, and identify relationships, and use the results of the data analysis to make decisions about the original question(s)

A statistical investigation is a dynamic process that involves moving back and forth among the four interconnected components. For example, after collecting data and completing some analysis, statisticians may decide to refine the original question and gather additional data. The process may involve spending time working within a single component. For example, a statistician might form several different representations of the data at various stages of the process before selecting the representation(s) to be used in a final presentation of the data.

continued on next page

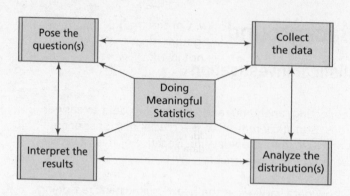

In *Data About Us*, several big ideas about statistics are explored, including the use of analytical tools and the reasoning involved when analyzing data. The concept map below illustrates relationships among these big ideas and other important concepts.

Doing Meaningful Statistics

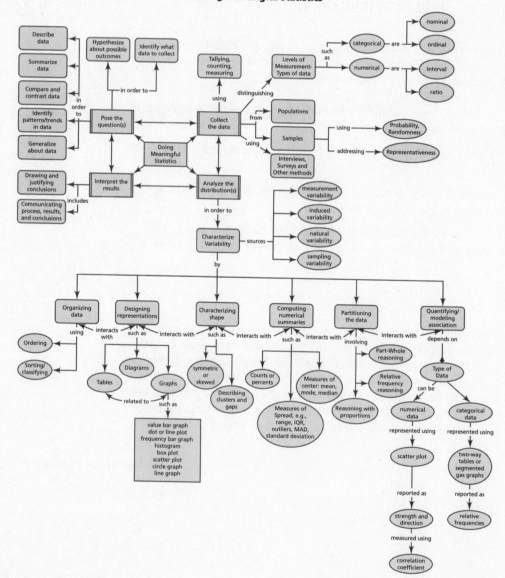

Enlarged sections of the concept map appear below. Consider having students use concept maps, such as the one above, to link together ideas that they explore during this Unit. Of course, their concept maps will not involve as many parts as the concept map above.

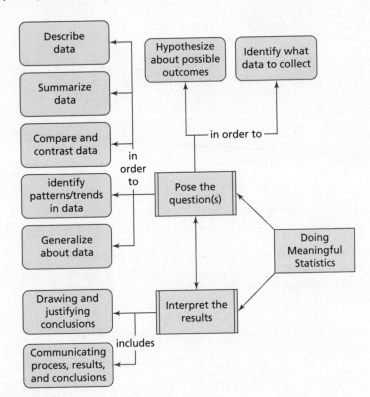

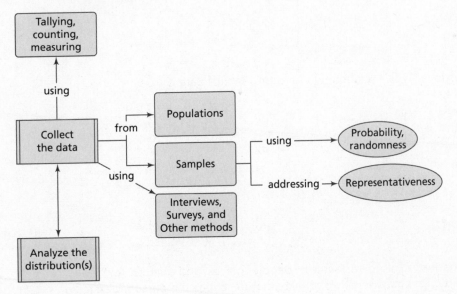

continued on next page

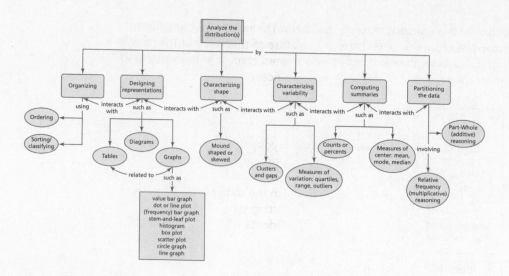

Posing Questions

Statisticians need to decide upon what questions to ask. The questions asked
impact the rest of the process of statistical investigation. A statistical question
is posed when the investigator anticipates that the answers will vary; answers of
these questions are not predetermined.

In this Unit, students will answer questions that may be classified as summary
questions or comparison questions.

Summary questions focus on descriptions of a single data set.

Example

What is the class's favorite kind of pet?

How many pets does the typical student have?

Comparison questions involve relating two (or more) sets of data across a
common attribute.

Example

How much taller is a sixth-grade student than a second-grade student?

*How much heavier is a sixth-grade student's backpack than a second-grade
student's backpack?*

Collecting Data

Statistical investigations explore attributes of people, places, and objects. An
attribute is a particular characteristic or quality that describes the person, place,
or thing about which data are being collected. The **data values** (or **observations**)
associated with those attributes are collected during the study.

For example, height is an attribute of NBA players. The height 6 feet 9 inches might be a data value collected for an individual *case* of that attribute. If there were three NBA players that measured 6 feet 9 inches, then the frequency of the observation *6 feet 9 inches* would be three occurrences.

In many Problems in this Unit, data are provided. If your students have not had much experience with collecting data as part of statistical investigations, it is important that your class collect their own data for some of the Problems in *Data About Us*. The Problems can be explored either with the data provided or with data collected by students. Keep in mind that collecting data is time-consuming, so carefully choose the Problems for which your students with gather data.

Problem Number and Title	Attributes to Investigate
Problem 1.2: Describing Name Lengths	name lengths in your own classroom
Problem 2.1: What's a Mean Household Size?	household sizes of your students
Problem 2.3: Making Choices	prices of favorite games
Problem 3.2: Connecting Cereal Shelf Location and Sugar Content	amounts of a particular nutrient in a variety of snacks
Problem 4.1: Traveling to School	time spent doing a certain task (such as traveling to school or doing homework)

Types of Data

Statistical questions in real life typically involve one of two general kinds of data: *categorical data* or *numerical data*. Knowing whether the data are numerical or categorical helps determine which representations and measures of center and spread are appropriate to report.

Numerical data are data that are numbers, such as counts, measurements, and ratings. In *Data About Us*, students work with two types of numerical data: counts and measurements.

continued on next page

Categorical data have values that represent discrete responses within a given category. There is no consistent scale involved. In this Unit, students experience two types of categorical data. One type, nominal data, has no order. Any link to a numbering system is arbitrary. The other type, ordinal data, has a numerical order, but the intervals between the data may be uneven. For both types of categorical data, it is impossible to perform numerical operations on the data.

Examples of Numerical Data

- Household size, which can be organized by displaying frequencies of households with one person, two people, and so on

- Student heights, which can be organized into intervals of observations on a bar graph from 40 to 44 inches, 45 to 49 inches, and so on

Examples of Categorical Data

- Birth years, which can be organized by displaying frequencies of people born in 1980, 1981, 1982, and so on

- Favorite types of books, which can be displayed by observations of people's preferences for mysteries, adventure stories, science fiction, and so on

Some categorical data seem to be similar to numerical data. For example, a bar graph of birth months may use numbers to represent months: 1 is used for January, 2 is used for February, 3 is used for March, and so on. You cannot, however, perform numerical operations using months of the year. For example, 1 is not half of 2 when 1 represents January and 2 represents February. Months represented numerically are actually categories labeled by numbers.

Generally, in *Data About Us*, students will tally, count, or measure data. The data are often recorded in tables organized by categories and values, such as the class lists of names in which counts of the letters in each name are used to analyze name lengths.

Analyzing Individual Cases vs. Overall Distributions

The primary purpose of statistical analysis is to describe aspects of variability in the data. Because of this purpose, data should be displayed, and their patterns should be examined. The distribution of data refers to the way the data in a set appear overall, highlighting how data cluster or vary. The patterns in the data require the aggregate features of the set be analyzed.

When students work with data, they are often interested in individual cases, particularly if the data are about themselves. Statisticians look at the overall distribution of a set of data, however, and are generally not interested in individual cases. Distributions, unlike individual cases, can be described by measures of central tendency (i.e., mean, median, and mode), spread (e.g., range, interquartile range, outliers, and mean absolute deviation), and shape (e.g., clusters, gaps, symmetry, and skew).

UNIT
OVERVIEW

GOALS AND
STANDARDS

▶ MATHEMATICS
BACKGROUND

UNIT
INTRODUCTION

UNIT
PROJECT

Students can think about data in a number of ways. Statisticians often use graphs to clarify a distribution of data. The graphs below help to illustrate how students may think about data. The following progression suggests growth in statistical thinking.

Individual Cases Students may focus on each data value. For example, they may focus on name lengths of individual cases rather than noticing that a group of cases may be related (e.g., several name lengths cluster around 11 to 15 letters). This kind of thinking is characteristic of young children.

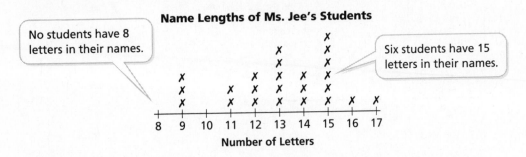

Name Lengths of Ms. Jee's Students

No students have 8 letters in their names.

Six students have 15 letters in their names.

Number of Letters

Middle Stage Students may focus on subsets of data values that are the same or similar, such as a category or a cluster. This may be more obvious when analyzing categorical data (e.g., a majority of students choose dogs as their favorite kind of pet). If students are working with numerical data, they might notice clusters (e.g., a group of students takes 8.9 to 9.6 seconds to complete a shuttle run).

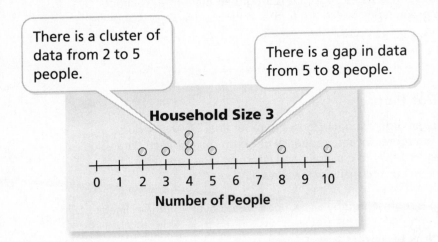

There is a cluster of data from 2 to 5 people.

There is a gap in data from 5 to 8 people.

Household Size 3

Number of People

continued on next page

Overall Distributions Students may view the set of data values as one distribution. Students look for features of the whole distribution that are not features of any of the individual cases (e.g., shape, center, spread). For example, in the distribution below showing the number of pets students have, the data cluster at one end but trail off to the right for several cases in which students have more than six pets.

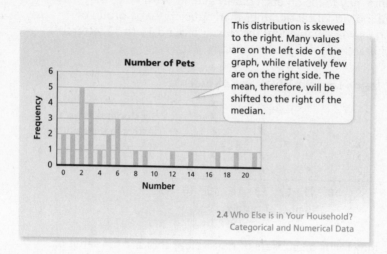

This distribution is skewed to the right. Many values are on the left side of the graph, while relatively few are on the right side. The mean, therefore, will be shifted to the right of the median.

2.4 Who Else is in Your Household? Categorical and Numerical Data

Choosing Representations for Distributions

Students learn about various types of graphs during their Elementary School experiences. These graph types, which are further addressed in *Data About Us*, include the following:

Line Plots and Dot Plots

Line plots and dot plots organize data along a number line. The Xs or dots above the number line represent the frequency of occurrence of each data value. Students find these plots easy to construct and interpret. They are useful first displays when there are not too many data values.

Line Plot Each case is represented by an "X" positioned over a number line.

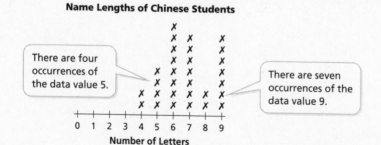

There are four occurrences of the data value 5.

There are seven occurrences of the data value 9.

UNIT
OVERVIEW

GOALS AND
STANDARDS

▶ MATHEMATICS
BACKGROUND

UNIT
INTRODUCTION

UNIT
PROJECT

Dot Plot Each case is represented by a circle or a dot positioned over a number line.

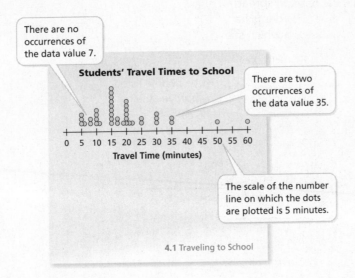

There are no occurrences of the data value 7.

Students' Travel Times to School

There are two occurrences of the data value 35.

Travel Time (minutes)

The scale of the number line on which the dots are plotted is 5 minutes.

4.1 Traveling to School

Ordered-Value Bar Graphs

In an ordered-value bar graph, the lengths of bars show the magnitude of individual data values. Each bar's length or height is the measure of an individual case. In *Data About Us*, the bars are generally displayed horizontally and are ordered by magnitude of data values. Students can mark up these graphs as they explore the concept of *mean*. They can even out the bars to locate the mean.

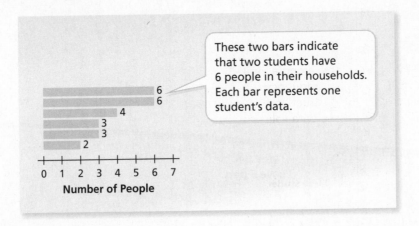

These two bars indicate that two students have 6 people in their households. Each bar represents one student's data.

Number of People

Frequency Bar Graphs

In a frequency bar graph, the length of each bar indicates the number of occurrences of that data value in the set. The height of a bar is not the value of an individual case; rather, it is the number of cases (frequency) that have that value. The bars can be drawn either vertically or horizontally. Students find these

continued on next page

graphs helpful when identifying the most frequently occurring data value (mode). Frequency bar graphs are very useful when displaying categorical data. They may be also be used with numerical data.

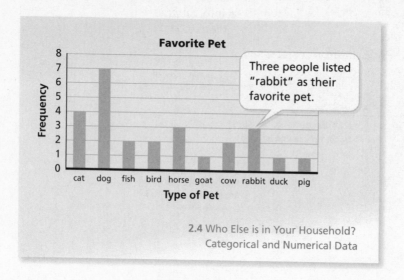

2.4 Who Else is in Your Household?
Categorical and Numerical Data

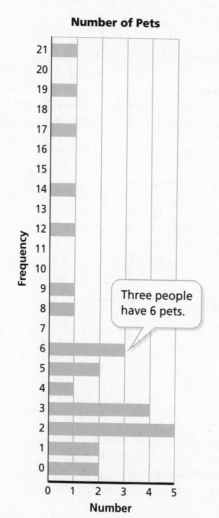

Histograms

Histograms display the distribution of numerical data using intervals. The vertical axis is labeled with either number counts or percents. So, the height of the bar indicates the frequency of data values within an interval. Students can use histograms to group data into intervals. This allows them to see patterns in the data distribution and identify the overall shape of a distribution.

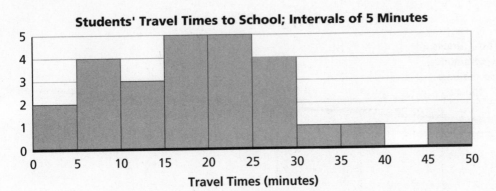

Students' Travel Times to School; Intervals of 5 Minutes

Travel Times (minutes)

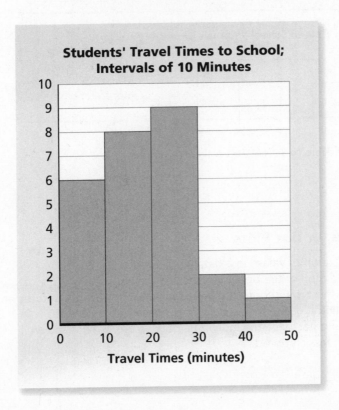

Students' Travel Times to School; Intervals of 10 Minutes

Travel Times (minutes)

continued on next page

Because data are organized by intervals, the bars touch. This shows the continuous nature of the number line. There are conventions that determine where entries whose data values occur at the end points of an interval will be placed. The animation below shows how to construct a histogram, paying particular attention to where points on the borders of intervals belong. Visit Teacher Place at mathdashboard.com/cmp3 to see the complete animation.

Making a Histogram

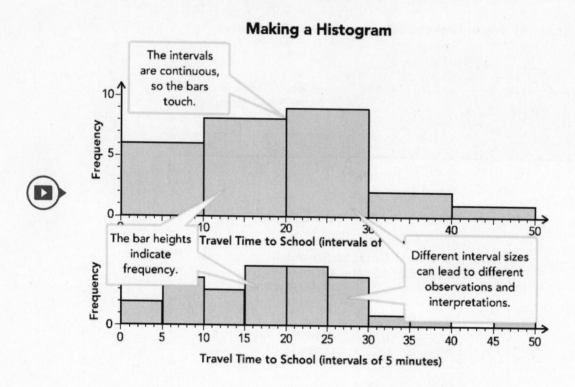

The intervals are continuous, so the bars touch.

The bar heights indicate frequency.

Travel Time to School (intervals of

Different interval sizes can lead to different observations and interpretations.

Travel Time to School (intervals of 5 minutes)

Box-and-Whisker Plots, or Box Plots

A box plot shows the distribution of values in a data set separated into four groups of equal size: each section of the box and each whisker represents 25% of the data. Students may use this type of graph to highlight a few important features of the data. They may also find it easier to use box plots to make comparisons among more than one set of data. Since the individual data values are not shown on the box plot, it can seem less cluttered.

UNIT
OVERVIEW

GOALS AND
STANDARDS

▶ MATHEMATICS
BACKGROUND

UNIT
INTRODUCTION

UNIT
PROJECT

A box plot is constructed from the five-number summary of the data stemming from the interquartile range (IQR): minimum data value, lower quartile (Q1), median (Q2), upper quartile (Q3), and maximum data value. Outliers can be identified using the IQR.

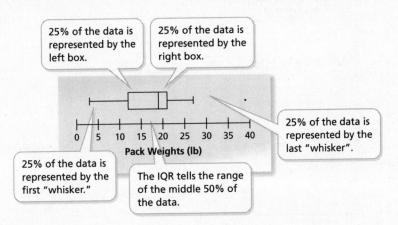

25% of the data is represented by the left box.

25% of the data is represented by the right box.

25% of the data is represented by the last "whisker".

Pack Weights (lb)

25% of the data is represented by the first "whisker."

The IQR tells the range of the middle 50% of the data.

Guiding Students to Construct and Read Graphs

Constructing Graphs

Graph paper is suggested as an optional tool for students to use when representing data distributions.

- When students draw bar graphs to represent categorical data, the bars may be drawn between the lines of the graph paper. Labels are placed below the bars.

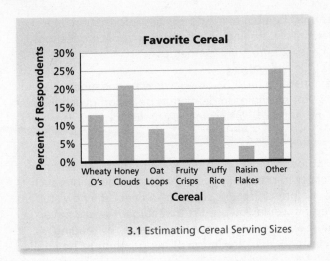

Favorite Cereal

Percent of Respondents

Cereal: Wheaty O's, Honey Clouds, Oat Loops, Fruity Crisps, Puffy Rice, Raisin Flakes, Other

3.1 Estimating Cereal Serving Sizes

continued on next page

• When students draw bar graphs to represent numerical data, the data
  values may be marked on the lines of the graph paper.

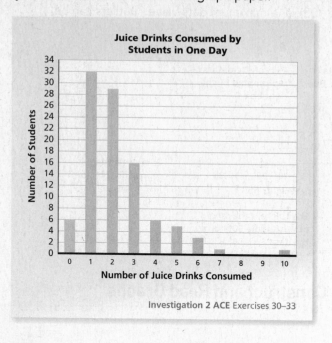

Investigation 2 ACE Exercises 30–33

Reading Graphs

Graphs are a central component of data analysis. The following three concepts
help students to understand and analyze graphs.

Reading the Data: Students must be able to locate specific information on a
graph. Understanding the data involves being able to answer explicit questions,
such as *How many students have 12 letters in their names?*

Reading Between the Data: Students must be able to answer questions relating
to subsets, or groups, of data. For example, students may be asked questions such
as *How many students have more than 12 letters in their name? or How many of
the students' name lengths cluster at 6–7 letters?*

Reading Beyond the Data: Students must be able to extend the information
they read from the graph in order to predict or infer when asked questions such
as *What is the typical number of letters in these students' names? If a new student
joined our class, how many letters would you predict that student would have
in his or her name?* These questions cannot be answered directly by reading
specific values on the graph. Instead, the knowledge of the graph must be applied
and extended.

Once students draw their graphs, they can use them in the interpretation phase of
the statistical-investigation process. The first two categories of questions, reading
the data and reading between the data, require basic skills in understanding
graphs. It is reading beyond the data, however, that helps students to develop
higher-level thinking skills, such as inference and justification.

UNIT
OVERVIEW

GOALS AND
STANDARDS

▶ MATHEMATICS
BACKGROUND

UNIT
INTRODUCTION

UNIT
PROJECT

Shapes of Distributions

The overall shape of a distribution can be described as symmetrical or skewed. A distribution's shape can also be described by noting other characteristics such as clusters, peaks, gaps, or outliers.

Symmetry is used to describe the shape of a data distribution. A **symmetric** distribution has a graph that can be divided at the center so that the halves are mirror images of each other. A **nonsymmetric** distribution's halves will not look like mirror images of each other.

Some graphs of data distributions have many more observations on one side of the graph than the other. Distributions with data values clustered on the left and a tail extending to the right are said to be **skewed right**. Distributions with data values clustered on the right and a tail extending to the left are said to be **skewed left**.

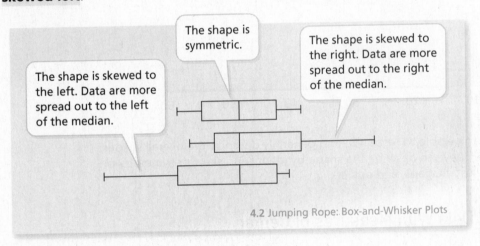

The shape is skewed to the left. Data are more spread out to the left of the median.

The shape is symmetric.

The shape is skewed to the right. Data are more spread out to the right of the median.

4.2 Jumping Rope: Box-and-Whisker Plots

This histogram is skewed to the left.

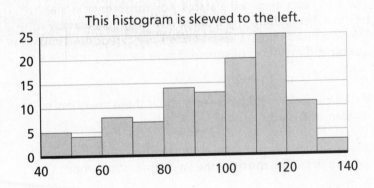

continued on next page

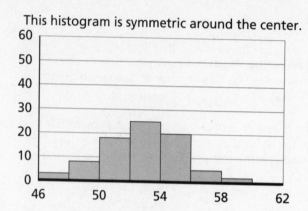

This histogram is symmetric around the center.

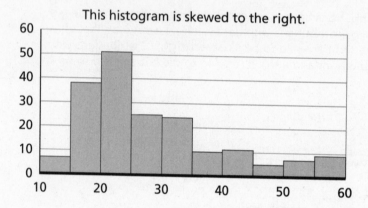

This histogram is skewed to the right.

Students need to be able to recognize and generally describe the overall shapes of distributions. They can describe the shape by identifying skew or symmetry or by identifying clusters, gaps, and outliers.

Describing Data With Measures of Center

The purpose of data analysis is to describe areas of stability or consistency in the natural variability that occurs in a distribution. There are several numbers that can be used to summarize values in a distribution. These numbers are categorized into two groups: measures of center and measures of spread. These summary numbers are essential tools in statistics.

In the *Connected Mathematics* curriculum, students learn about three measures of central tendency: *mean*, *median*, and *mode*.

The **mean** represents an equal sharing of values in a data set. The **median** marks the midpoint of a set of ordered data. The **mode** is the value that occurs most frequently in a set of data.

For example, consider the following situation.

Six students in a middle-school class use the United States Census guidelines to identify the number of people in their households.

This situation can be modeled using cubes. Each cube represents one person in a household. Each stack of cubes represents the number of people in a specific student's household.

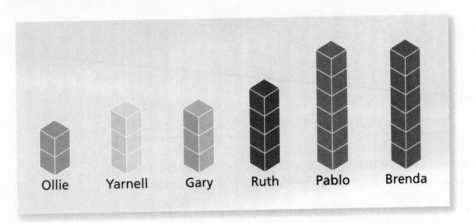

Measures of center can be used to identify a good estimate of the typical household size for all sixth-grade students.

Students might find it helpful to organize the data from smallest household size to largest household size.

Name	Number of People in Household
Ollie	2
Yarnell	3
Gary	3
Ruth	4
Pablo	6
Brenda	6

continued on next page

Mode

The *mode* is the data value that occurs most frequently in a set of data. There are two occurrences each of households with 3 people and with 6 people, whereas the other values only have one occurrence each. So, this data set is bimodal; for these data, there are two modes: 3 and 6.

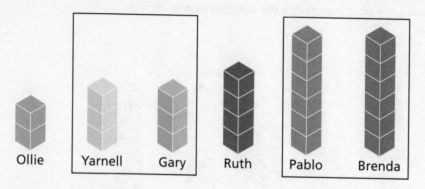

The mode sometimes has more than one value. A distribution may be unimodal, bimodal, or multimodal. It can also have no mode if there are no duplicate data values.

The mode is unstable because a change in just a few data values can lead to a change in the mode. Because of this, statisticians often use other measures of center to summarize numerical data.

Median

The *median* is the numerical value that has both a *position* and *value*. Its position marks the midpoint of a set of ordered data. The value of the median is the value of the midpoint (when there is an odd number of data values) or the average of the two middle data values (when there is an even number of data values).

In the data below, the median is $3\frac{1}{2}$ people.

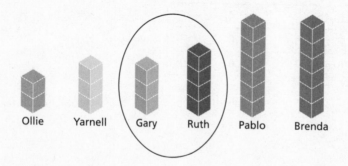

The value of the median is unlikely to be influenced by extreme data values. This makes the median a good measure to use as a summary number when working with skewed distributions. The median marks the location that divides a distribution into two equal parts.

Note that with an even number of data values, 50% (half) of the data values are less than or equal to the median and 50% (half) are greater than or equal to the median.

With an odd number of data values, roughly 50% (half) of the data values are less than or equal to the median and roughly 50% (half) are greater than or equal to the median.

Steps in identifying the median:

Even number of data values

1. Order the data from least to greatest (or greatest to least)
2. Locate the middle two data values.
3. Find the average of these two data values.

> **Example:** Household sizes: 2, 3, 3, 4, 6, 6
>
> The middle two data values are 3 and 4. The average of those two values is $3\frac{1}{2}$.

Odd number of data values

1. Order the data from least to greatest (or greatest to least)
2. Locate the middle data value.
3. The median is the value of the middle data value.

> **Example:** Household sizes: 2, 3, 3, 4, 5, 6, 6
>
> The middle data value is 4, so the median is 4.

Note: When repeated values span the midpoint, students might be able to more easily recognize the value of the median. In the example below, students may quickly notice that 4 is the midpoint of both data sets, as it occupies multiple middle-value positions.

Household sizes (odd): 2, 3, 3, 4, 4, 4, 5, 6, 6

Household sizes (even): 2, 3, 3, 4, 4, 4, 4, 4, 4, 5, 6, 6

continued on next page

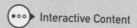

Mean

The word *average* usually refers to the mean. The *mean* is influenced by all values of a distribution of data, including extremes or outliers. It is a good measure of center to describe data distributions when working with distributions that are roughly symmetric. In the data shown below, the mean is 4 people.

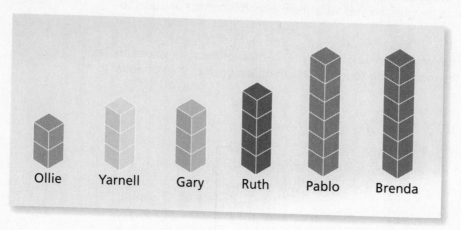

In *Connected Mathematics*, students are encouraged to think about the mean in a few related ways:

Evening Out

If everyone receives or has the same amount, what would that amount be? For example, suppose the members of the six households are rearranged so that each household has the same number of people. How many people are in each household?

Original distribution:

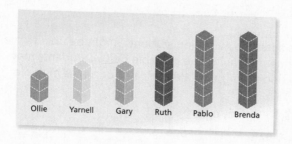

UNIT
OVERVIEW

GOALS AND
STANDARDS

▶ MATHEMATICS
BACKGROUND

UNIT
INTRODUCTION

UNIT
PROJECT

Evened-out distribution:

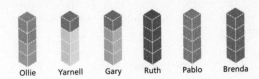

The same idea can be used to locate the mean of data displayed on an ordered-value bar graph.

Evened-out distribution—initial step:

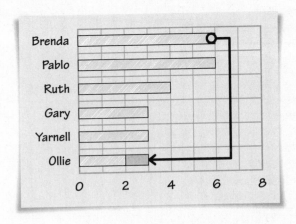

Evened-out distribution—final step:

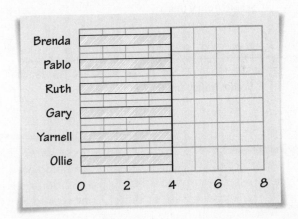

continued on next page

Balance model:

Differences from the mean balance out so that the sum of differences below and above the mean equal 0. When students find the mean absolute deviation (MAD), they consider this balance model.

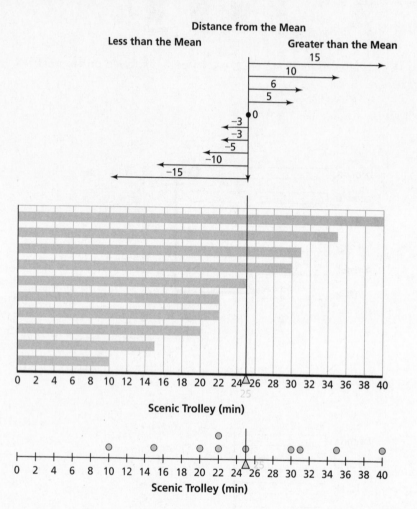

Distance from the Mean

Less than the Mean　　　Greater than the Mean

Scenic Trolley (min)

Scenic Trolley (min)

Typical value:

What is a typical value that could be used to characterize these data? This is a general interpretation used more casually when students are being asked to think about the three measures of center and which to use. Students should consider what values influence each measure of center. They should also think about what claim they are making with the measures they report.

Moving from models to algorithms—Computing with an algorithm:

The sum of all values is taken, and then it is divided by the number of observations. This is a computational version of the models described above. It groups all values together, and then partitions them into equal groups.

$6+6+4+3+3+2 = 24$	(1) Add all the data values together.
$24 \div 6 = 4$	(2) Divide the sum of the data values by the number of data values. (There are six data values.)
The mean number of people in a household is 4.	The quotient is the mean.

Note that Ollie has two people in his family. Yarnell and Gary each have three people in their families. Ruth has four people in her family. Paul and Brenda each have six people.

What is the average (mean) number of people in these six households?

Before		After	
Ollie	2 people	Ollie	4 people
Yarnell	3 people	Yarnell	4 people
Gary	3 people	Gary	4 people
Ruth	4 people	Ruth	4 people
Pablo	6 people	Pablo	4 people
Brenda	6 people	Brenda	4 people
Total	24 people	Total	24 people

In summary, to identify measures of center:

- Mode: Locate the most-frequent value from a graph or a table of data

- Median: List data values in order from least to greatest, and then identify the location that divides the data set in half (50%)

- Mean: Evenly distribute the quantities among the cases; to compute, add up all the data values and divide by the number of data values

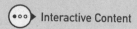

Describing Data With Measures of Spread

Other summary numbers that are used to describe data distributions are measures of variability.

Measures of variability, or **measures of spread**, describe the degree of variability of individual data values, as well as their distances from measures of center. In statistics, variability is a quantitative measure of how close together or spread out a distribution of data is. Several questions may be used to highlight interesting aspects of variation.

- *What does the distribution look like?*
- *How much do the data points vary from one another, or from the mean or median?*
- *Why might these data vary?*

In *Data About Us*, students identify three measures of variability, or spread. These measures of spread are helpful tools with which two or more data distributions can be compared.

The **range** is the difference between the maximum and the minimum data values. The **IQR (interquartile range)** is the range of the middle 50% of the data values. The **MAD (mean absolute deviation)** describes the average distance between each data value and the mean (the absolute value of the difference between each data value and the mean). The MAD and IQR are both connected to measures of center. In addition, students are encouraged to discuss where data cluster and where there are holes or gaps in the data.

Range

To find the range, identify the maximum and minimum data values in the distribution. Then, find the difference of those two values. In the distribution below, the range is 42 minutes (45–3).

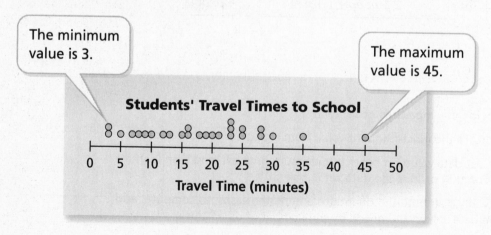

UNIT
OVERVIEW

GOALS AND
STANDARDS

▶ MATHEMATICS
  BACKGROUND

UNIT
INTRODUCTION

Interquartile Range (IQR)

The IQR (interquartile range) is the range of the middle 50% of the data values; it is often associated with the median. Because the IQR does not include the upper or lower quartiles (upper and lower 25% of the data values), it reduces the effect of any outliers. The IQR provides a numerical measure of how close to or distant from the data values in the second and third quartiles of a distribution are with respect to the median.

Consider the distribution of U.S. Name Lengths in a class of 30 students. The image below shows both the original data set, listed in order from least to greatest, as well as a dot plot representation of the data set.

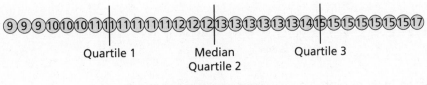

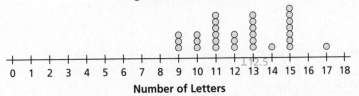

Lengths of U.S. Names

Number of Letters

Notice that the median of 12.5 letters is marked on the graph. Because there are 30 data values, the median partitions the name lengths into two equal-sized groups. In this example, fifteen of the name lengths are less than the median, and fifteen of the name lengths are greater than the median.

On the dot plot, the median and Quartiles 1, 2, and 3 are marked. The quartiles are determined by partitioning the ordered distribution into four parts, each containing one quarter of the data values. The median is the midpoint of the distribution, found between 12 and 13 letters. This is the same value as Quartile 2. Quartile 1 divides the lower half of the data set in half. In this case, Quartile 1 is located at the eighth smallest name length, 11 letters. Quartile 3 partitions the upper half of the data set in half. In this example, Quartile 3 is located at the eighth largest name length, 15 letters.

The IQR is the distance between the two values that mark Quartile 1 and Quartile 3—the range of the middle 50% of all the students' name lengths. In this example, the IQR is 15 − 11, or 4 letters. The middle 50% of the name lengths has a spread of 4 letters.

continued on next page

A similar process can be found for identifying the IQR for Japanese name lengths. The range between the greatest values of Quartile 1 and Quartile 3 is 2 letters. The middle 50% of the name lengths has a spread of 2 letters.

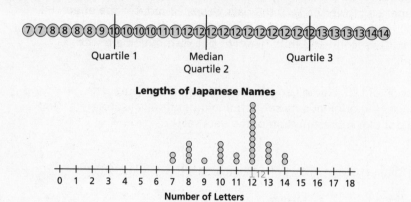

Quartile 1   Median   Quartile 3
                   Quartile 2

Lengths of Japanese Names

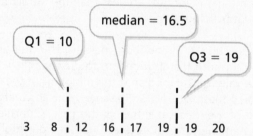

Number of Letters

From the analysis of the two dot plots, you can conclude that the middle 50% of U.S. name lengths are more spread out than the middle 50% of Japanese name lengths.

Note: In the Student Edition, students use the manipulative of folding pieces of paper to locate the lower quartile, median, and upper quartile. This manipulative works well when the ordered set of data can be evenly grouped into four groups. This manipulative becomes more difficult to work with when the data cannot be grouped in this manner. The images below show the process of finding the IQR for an even number of data values and for an odd number of data values.

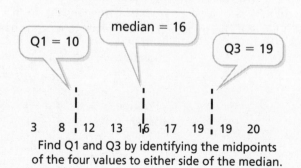

median = 16.5

Q1 = 10

Q3 = 19

3   8 | 12   16 | 17   19 | 19   20

Each partition contains two data values.
Find Q1 and Q3 by identifying the midpoints of the
four values to either side of the median.

median = 16

Q1 = 10

Q3 = 19

3   8 | 12   13   16   17   19 | 19   20

Find Q1 and Q3 by identifying the midpoints
of the four values to either side of the median.

UNIT
OVERVIEW

GOALS AND
STANDARDS

▶ MATHEMATICS
BACKGROUND

UNIT
INTRODUCTION

UNIT
PROJECT

Mean Absolute Deviation (MAD)

The MAD (mean absolute deviation) relates the variability of a distribution to the mean. It determines whether or not the data values in the data set are close to the mean. The MAD is the average distance between each data value and the mean.

Consider the representations below. Visit Teacher Place at mathdashboard.com/cmp3 to see the complete animation.

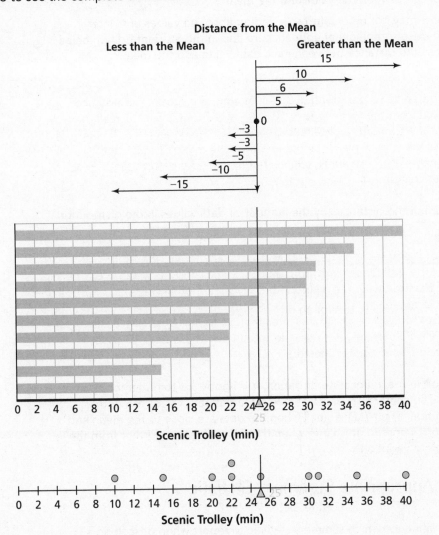

The ordered-value bar graph and the dot plot show ten different wait times that customers experienced while waiting to ride the Scenic Trolley. This information can be used to find out how much the data vary in relation to the mean of the distribution.

The mean of the data in this distribution is 25 minutes. Four people waited longer than 25 minutes, five people waited less than 25 minutes, and one person waited exactly 25 minutes.

continued on next page

The diagram above the ordered-value bar graph shows the distances of all the data values from the mean. The MAD is the number that summarizes these differences. It answers the question *On average, how much do the wait times for the Scenic Trolley differ from the mean wait time for the Scenic Trolley?*

To compute the MAD,

1. Add the distances of each value from the mean. (The distance is the absolute value of the difference between the value and the mean.)

   Note: Students may not be comfortable finding absolute values until later grades. The type of graphic that appears here and in the Student Edition helps students to see the distance between each data value and the mean.

   > **Example**
   >
   > For the ordered value bar graph in the animation, the sum of the distances of each value from the mean is $15 + 10 + 6 + 5 + 0 + 3 + 5 + 10 + 15$, or 72. Notice that the sum of the distances greater than the mean ($15 + 10 + 6 + 5$) is the same as the sum of the distances less than the mean ($3 + 3 + 5 + 10 + 15$), or 36 minutes. This is not a coincidence but is instead a pattern that will be seen in every data distribution.

2. Divide the sum of the distances by the number of data values in the distribution.

   > **Example**
   >
   > The MAD of the ordered value bar graph in the animation, therefore, is $72 \div 10$ (the sum of the differences between the data values and the mean $\div$ the number of data values in the distribution), or 7.2. So, on average, a person may wait 7.2 minutes more than or less than the mean wait time of 25 minutes. Recall, however, that the graph indicates that, while the MAD is 7.2 minutes and the average is 25 minutes, it is possible to wait anywhere from 10 minutes to 40 minutes to ride the roller coaster.

When considering the mean absolute deviation, it is important to remember that the MAD provides an average measure of how close the data values are to the mean of a distribution. The MAD is small when the data are close to the mean and show little variation or spread. It is large when the data values are further from the mean and show more variation.

Choosing an Appropriate Summary Statistic

Many factors can influence which summary statistic to report when describing a data distribution. No measure of center or spread is best to use in all situations. Instead, the context and the shape of the distribution affect which measure should be reported. It is important to choose statistics that represent data with as much integrity as possible. With that in mind, the following questions can help you choose which summary statistic to report.

What shape does the distribution have? Is it skewed or symmetric? Are there any outliers?

   If the data values of a distribution are arranged symmetrically around the median, then the mean and median usually have a similar value. Either measure of center will be representative of the typical value in a distribution. You can choose to report whichever measure is easier for you to compute.

UNIT
OVERVIEW

GOALS AND
STANDARDS

▶ MATHEMATICS
BACKGROUND

UNIT
INTRODUCTION

UNIT
PROJECT

When the distribution is skewed (not symmetric), however, then the mean and median will most likely be different. Extreme outliers on either end of the graph pull the mean toward that end of the distribution.

The median, on the other hand, is resistant to any extreme observations (outliers) in a data set. So, for skewed distributions, statisticians often choose to report the median as the representative statistic for a data set.

A distribution that is greatly skewed will have a greater difference between the mean and the median.

This histogram is skewed to the left.

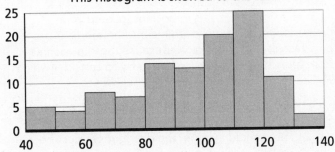

This histogram is symmetric around the center.

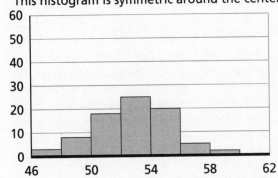

This histogram is skewed to the right.

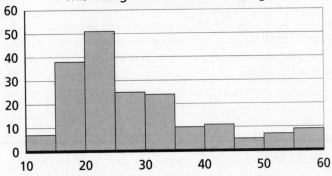

continued on next page

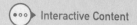

Which is easier to compute?

One of the benefits of reporting the mean is that the data can be tracked more easily. An investigator can keep a running total of the data as it is being collected. Additional values that are collected later can simply be added to the running total, and the new mean can be quickly calculated.

Identifying the median, on the other hand, can be difficult when there are either many data values or when additional values are collected later. The data values have to be rearranged with each additional value.

Which measure best answers your question or supports your intent?

When choosing a data measure to report, it is important to keep your question and purpose in mind. For example, both means and medians are measures of center. They describe what is typical. Because these measures can be very different from one another, however, you need to consider which measure supports your ideas or questions.

For example, suppose a city's mean household income is $70,000, and the median household income is $50,000. Since the median household income is less than the mean household income, the distribution must be skewed to the right. A reporter may choose one statistic over the other to make a particular point. In this case, the mean and median are substantially different, and each can be used to support different ideas.

Which measure of variability best represents the distribution?

The IQR is linked to the median, and the MAD is linked to the mean. Because of this, the measure of variability that best represents a data distribution depends on which measure of center best represents the distribution. Frequently, means, and therefore MADs, are chosen to represent symmetric distributions. For skewed distribution, medians and IQRs are often chosen as good representations. This is because medians and IQRs are less influenced by outliers or extreme data values.

Which measure might you choose to represent categorical data?

When the data distribution does not contain numerical values, the mode is used to represent the distribution. Mean and median cannot be calculated, so the mode is the only way to report a most popular or most frequent observation. For categorical data, there is no appropriate measure of spread. For example, if you investigate favorite pets, there are no "least" or "greatest" values. A range cannot be calculated.

Interpreting Results

The final stage of any statistical investigation is interpreting the results of the data collection and analysis. The initial question, or any questions that arose from the investigation's process, still need to be answered. Interpretations usually involve summarizing or comparing data distributions while keeping the variability in the data in mind. Suggested guidelines for describing are listed below. The responses to these prompts can help to summarize or compare data.

Guidelines for Describing Distributions

Use these prompts to help you think about describing data distributions.

A. Look at the collected data and their graph.

1. Is there anything surprising about the data or their distribution?

2. Are there any additional questions you want to consider after having looked at the distribution?

3. Do you want to make a different graph to display the data?

B. Describe the shape of the data.

1. Clusters and Gaps: Where do the data in the distribution cluster? Are there any gaps in the distribution?

 a. Consider the middle of the distribution.

 b. Consider each end of the distribution.

 c. Consider multiple instances of clusters and gaps in the distribution.

2. Spread: How spread out are the data?

 a. What are the maximum and minimum data values?

 b. Do the data on either side of the median (or the mean) look like mirror images? If so, the distribution can be considered *symmetric*.

 c. Are the data spread out more on one side of the median (or mean)? If so, the distribution can be considered *skewed*.

 d. Are there any outliers?

C. Are the data categorical or numerical?

1. If the data are categorical, which measures of center can you use to describe what is typical?

2. If the data are numerical, which measures of center can you use to describe what is typical?

D. Identify measures of center.

1. What is the mode of the data? Which data values occur more frequently or less frequently?

2. What is the mean of the data?

3. What is the median of the data?

4. How do the mean and median compare?

5. If the mean and median are different, why might this be so? (Consider your answers from part (B).)

continued on next page

E. Identify measures of spread.

1. How alike or different are the data values from one other?

2. How close together or spread out are the data values?

3. Identify the range. What information does the range provide? Is this an appropriate measure of spread for the distribution being analyzed?

4. Identify the IQR. What information does the IQR provide? Is this an appropriate measure of spread for the distribution being analyzed?

5. Identify the MAD. What information does the MAD provide? Is this an appropriate measure of spread for the distribution being analyzed?

F. Revisit the original questions.

1. Is there anything surprising about the data or their distribution?

2. Are there any additional questions you want to consider after having looked at the distribution?

3. Do you want to make a different graph to display the data?

UNIT
OVERVIEW

GOALS AND
STANDARDS

MATHEMATICS
BACKGROUND

▶ UNIT
INTRODUCTION

UNIT
PROJECT

Unit Introduction

Using the Unit Opener

The Looking Ahead contains questions that relate to concepts within the Unit. Read the Looking Ahead. Ask the students how they might go about answering the questions posed. How might they collect data to support their answers? How many people would they survey to answer those questions?

You can also introduce *Data About Us* by having a class discussion about the "typical" middle-school student. Ask students what they think the word typical means. Then ask them about characteristics of a typical middle-school student. What is the typical height? The typical favorite band? The typical number of siblings?

Discuss whether these typical characteristics of your class would be the same as the characteristics for a class in another part of town, another state, or another country. For example, would the typical favorite food for your class be the same as the typical favorite food for a middle-school class in Japan? After the discussion, refer your students to the Unit Project page at the beginning of the Student Edition.

Discuss the questions posed in the introductory paragraph of the Unit Project. Do not focus on finding the "correct" answers at this time. Your students will learn mathematical concepts throughout the Unit that will help them to answer these questions. Ask your students to keep these questions in mind, however, as they work through the Investigations. Have them think about how they might use the ideas they are learning to help them determine the answers.

Using the Mathematical Highlights

The Mathematical Highlights page in the Student Edition provides information to students, parents, and other family members. It gives students a preview of the mathematics and some of the overarching questions that they should ask themselves while studying *Data About Us*.

As they work through the Unit, students can refer back to the Mathematical Highlights page to review what they have learned and to preview what is still to come. This page also tells students' families what mathematical ideas and activities will be covered as the class works through *Data About Us*.

▼ Unit Project

Introduction

The *Is Anyone Typical?* Unit Project is an optional assessment for *Data About Us*. During this Unit Project, students gather and analyze data to find some "typical" characteristics of their classmates. Have students discuss what they would like to know about their classmates. Then, have them suggest questions they could ask to find this information.

Throughout the Unit, remind students to use the concepts they are learning to think about the questions they might ask their classmates. You may want to set aside a few minutes of class time every few days for students to write their questions. Some teachers have found it useful to have students designate one or two pages in their notebooks as "special data pages." They can record information about their questions on these pages. They should think about what data they want to collect and analyze at the end of the Unit to answer the question Is *Anyone Typical?*

Assigning

The *Is Anyone Typical?* Unit Project is introduced at the beginning of the Unit and is formally assigned at the end of the Unit. Students use what they have learned in Data About Us to conduct a statistical investigation and determine some typical characteristics of middle-school students.

Some schools may require administrative approval of surveys; check your school policies prior to assigning the Unit Project. If your students want to collect data from other classes or grade levels, you may want to coordinate the data collection so that classes from which data are collected are not disturbed several times.

The project can be assigned in a variety of ways. If you have several days available, you can have each group write and conduct a survey consisting of five to ten questions. Each group can collect, analyze, and interpret the data, and then prepare a report of their findings. If your time is limited, you may choose to work as a class to develop and conduct the survey. Each group can analyze and interpret the data for one question

Providing Additional Support

This project requires students to conduct a statistical investigation to determine some "typical" characteristics of students in their class or school. Each group can tackle their own complete investigation, or you can write a survey as a class and assign each group the task of analyzing and interpreting the results of one survey question.

When you assign the project, remind students of the question they are trying to answer: *What are some characteristics of a typical middle-school student?* Have your students recall some of the typical characteristics they have already determined by working through the Investigations, such as height and name length. Then have a class discussion about the four steps involved in a statistical investigation.

UNIT
OVERVIEW

GOALS AND
STANDARDS

MATHEMATICS
BACKGROUND

UNIT
INTRODUCTION

▶ UNIT
PROJECT

Step 1: Posing Questions

Before writing their surveys, students should decide what information they want to investigate. Tell them that an interesting survey will collect both categorical and numerical data. You will want to check each group's list of questions before allowing them to proceed with their survey. You should be vigilant about the kinds of questions your students ask. Questions that might embarrass students or make them feel uncomfortable should not be included.

Have your students consider the following to help them refine their survey questions.

- What will you learn from this question?
- How will this question help you learn about the typical middle-school student?

Have students brainstorm questions they might ask as a class or in groups. They can then work to narrow down the list.

After students have decided what they want to investigate, they should make sure their questions are precise and unambiguous. Discuss the types of questions that work best as open-ended questions.

- How old are you in months?

Discuss the types of questions that work best if choices are provided. Ask students why these might work best as questions with answer choices.

- What do you tend to do when you are bored? Check one response that best describes you:

    _____ watch TV

    _____ read a book

    _____ complain

    _____ listen to the radio

    _____ play with a pet

    _____ talk on the phone

Students can also ask questions with responses that have a rating scale. For example,

- Circle only one answer. 1 means strongly disagree, and 5 means strongly agree.

    Students should be allowed to wear hats in school.

    1 2 3 4 5

Step 2: Collecting the Data

Students should decide who they will survey—only students in their class or a larger group of students. They need to produce, duplicate, and distribute their survey. You may want to coordinate the data collection so that classes from which data are collected are not disturbed several times.

Step 3: Analyzing the Data

Once they have collected the data, students should organize and display the data. They should decide which displays and which measures of center and spread are best to report for each set of data.

Step 4: Interpreting the Results

After the data have been analyzed, students should interpret the results and present it in some way. They can write a report or make a poster to show their findings. The presentation should include their survey questions, information about how the data were collected, appropriate data displays and measures of center and spread, and concluding statements about what is typical about their survey population.

If you create the survey as a class and assign one question to each group, you will want to come together as a class to discuss the results and assemble the characteristics of a typical student.

Grading

A suggested scoring rubric and two sample projects with teacher comments follow. The first sample is a report; the second is a story.

Suggested Scoring Rubric

This rubric for scoring the project employs a scale that runs from 0 to 4, with a 4+ for work that goes beyond what has been asked for in some unique way. You may use the rubric as presented here or modify it to fit your district's requirements for evaluating and reporting students' work and understanding.

4+ Exemplary Response

- Complete, with clear, coherent explanations

- Shows understanding of the mathematical concepts and procedures

- Satisfies all essential conditions of the problem and goes beyond what is asked for in some unique way

4 Complete Response

- Complete, with clear, coherent explanations

- Shows understanding of the mathematical concepts and procedures

- Satisfies all essential conditions of the problem

UNIT
OVERVIEW   GOALS AND
STANDARDS   MATHEMATICS
BACKGROUND   UNIT
INTRODUCTION   ▶ UNIT
PROJECT

3 Reasonably Complete Response

- Reasonably complete; may lack detail in explanations
- Shows understanding of most of the mathematical concepts and procedures
- Satisfies most of the essential conditions of the problem

2 Partial Response

- Gives response; explanation may be unclear or lack detail
- Shows some understanding of some of the mathematical concepts and procedures
- Satisfies some essential conditions of the problem

1 Inadequate Response

- Incomplete; explanation is insufficient or not understandable
- Shows little understanding of the mathematical concepts and procedures
- Fails to address essential conditions of problem

0 No Attempt

- Irrelevant response
- Does not attempt a solution
- Does not address conditions of the problem

Sample Student Work

The samples that follow are from a class in which each group investigated one question. **Sample Student Work 1** shows states that students have visited. **Sample Student Work 2** displays data about the students' favorite radio stations.

A Teacher's Comments on Sample 1

Sample Student Work 1

I evaluated each step of the investigation separately, using a four-point scale for each step. These students received 10 of 16 possible points for their project. I would recommend that they redo the "Interpret the Results" section of their project.

Step 1: Posing Questions (3 Points)

These students asked interesting questions. However, they should have clarified what they meant by "been to." Did they mean visited or just traveled through?

Step 2: Collecting the Data (3 Points)

The students did not mention the number of students they surveyed. I can determine the number of students that were surveyed from the first graph by counting and adding the heights of the bars $(1 + 3 + 3 + 1 + 3 + 1 + 2 + 1 + 3 + 3 + 1 + 1 + 1 + 1 = 25)$.

Step 3: Analyzing the Data (3 Points)

The graphs are quite interesting. Students explored both categorical and numerical data. The first graph shows the numbers of states students have visited. No summary statistics are given for this graph. It is interesting to note that the spread in the number of states visited is from 3 to 25 and the median is between 8 and 9 states.

The other two graphs show categorical data. The first graph is a bar graph. The students used numbers on the horizontal axis to represent the states and provided a key to the right of the graph. The second graph was intended to be a line plot, but has a vertical axis like a bar graph. This vertical axis is not necessary, since the numbers of Xs indicate the frequencies. The students determined that the mode state is 40, South Carolina. (These students live in North Carolina, and so did not consider it a "state visited.") These students, correctly, did not include any other statistics for these two graphs. The mean and median are not appropriate measures for categorical data.

Step 4: Interpreting the Results (1 Point)

The students provided only one summary statement about their results—that the mode state is South Carolina. They could have discussed the fact that the mode state and the states close to the mode (Virginia, Georgia, Florida, and Tennessee) are neighboring states of North Carolina. They might also have mentioned that, in the first graphs, values of 23, 14, 17, and 18 are unusual values, and explored why these students had visited so many states.

A Teacher's Comments on Sample 2

Sample Student Work 2

I evaluated each step of the investigation separately, using a four-point scale for each step. These students received 13 of 16 possible points for their project.

Step 1: Posing Questions (4 Points)

The question was clearly stated.

Step 2: Collecting the Data (3 Points)

In their summary paragraphs, the students indicate that they surveyed 21 students, yet their graphs show data from only 19 students. Perhaps two students did not have a favorite station. Students should have mentioned this or included a "no favorite" category.

Step 3: Analyzing the Data (3 Points)

These students used four different displays. The line plot, the bar graph, and the circle graph are appropriate. The line graph is not appropriate because it is designed to show change over time. On the line plot, the Xs are not aligned, so the stack of Xs for 102.1 looks shorter than it should relative to the stack for 101.1.

Step 4: Interpreting the Results (3 Points)

These students included a summary statement. They acknowledge the inappropriateness of the mean, median, or range for categorical data. I would have liked them to talk a bit more about the radio stations. Stations 101.1 and 102.1 are far more popular than the other three choices.

Notes

UNIT

STUDENT PAGE

Looking Ahead

What is the greatest number of pets owned by the students in your class? How can you find out?

How much do the sugar contents of different kinds of cereals vary?

How can you determine which of two basketball teams has taller players? Older players?

Charlestown Spartans

Player	Age	Height (cm)	
#37	23	185	
#29	27	173	
#56	19	204	
#39	35	202	
#28	32	190	
#16	33	209	
#25	30	189	

Notes _____

_____

_____

Part of a biologist's job is to collect data on organisms, such as coral. They do this to understand the organism and its role in the world. Not all coral is the same, so biologists study many corals in order to learn more about the species as a whole.

In a similar way, the United States government gathers information about its citizens. They do this to learn more about the population as a whole. Collecting data from every household in the United States is a huge task. So, many surveys involve gathering information from much smaller groups of people.

People often make statements about the results of surveys. It is important to understand these statements. For example, what does it mean when reports say that the average middle-school student watches three hours of television on a weekday and has four people in his or her family?

In *Data About Us*, you will learn to collect and analyze data. You will also learn to use your results to describe people and their characteristics.

Looking Ahead   3

Notes

Mathematical Highlights

Data About Us

In *Data About Us,* you will learn different ways to collect, organize, display, and analyze data.

In this Unit you will learn to:

- Use the process of data investigation by posing questions, collecting and analyzing data, and interpreting the data to answer questions

- Organize and represent data using tables, dot plots, line plots, bar graphs, histograms, and box-and-whisker plots

- Describe the overall shape of a distribution and identify whether or not it is symmetrical around a central value

- Compute the mean, median, and mode of a data distribution, and use these measures to indicate what is typical for the distribution

- Describe the variability of a distribution by identifying clusters and gaps, and by calculating the range, Interquartile Range (IQR), and Mean Absolute Deviation (MAD)

- Identify which statistical measures of center and spread should be used to describe a particular distribution of data

- Distinguish between categorical data and numerical data, and identify which graphs and statistics may be used to represent each type of data

- Compare two or more distributions of data, including using measures of center and spread to make comparisons

When you encounter a new problem, it is a good idea to ask yourself questions. In this Unit, you might ask questions such as:

What question is being investigated to collect these data?

How might I organize the data?

What statistical measures will help describe the distribution of data?

What will these statistical measures tell me about the distribution of the data?

How can I use graphs and statistics to report an answer to my original question?

Notes _____

_____

_____

Common Core State Standards
Mathematical Practices and Habits of Mind

In the *Connected Mathematics* curriculum you will develop an understanding of important mathematical ideas by solving problems and reflecting on the mathematics involved. Every day, you will use "habits of mind" to make sense of problems and apply what you learn to new situations. Some of these habits are described by the *Common Core State Standards for Mathematical Practices* (MP).

MP1 Make sense of problems and persevere in solving them.

When using mathematics to solve a problem, it helps to think carefully about

- data and other facts you are given and what additional information you need to solve the problem;
- strategies you have used to solve similar problems and whether you could solve a related simpler problem first;
- how you could express the problem with equations, diagrams, or graphs;
- whether your answer makes sense.

MP2 Reason abstractly and quantitatively.

When you are asked to solve a problem, it often helps to

- focus first on the key mathematical ideas;
- check that your answer makes sense in the problem setting;
- use what you know about the problem setting to guide your mathematical reasoning.

MP3 Construct viable arguments and critique the reasoning of others.

When you are asked to explain why a conjecture is correct, you can

- show some examples that fit the claim and explain why they fit;
- show how a new result follows logically from known facts and principles.

When you believe a mathematical claim is incorrect, you can

- show one or more counterexamples—cases that don't fit the claim;
- find steps in the argument that do not follow logically from prior claims.

Notes _____

_____

MP4 Model with mathematics.

When you are asked to solve problems, it often helps to

- think carefully about the numbers or geometric shapes that are the most important factors in the problem, then ask yourself how those factors are related to each other;
- express data and relationships in the problem with tables, graphs, diagrams, or equations, and check your result to see if it makes sense.

MP5 Use appropriate tools strategically.

When working on mathematical questions, you should always

- decide which tools are most helpful for solving the problem and why;
- try a different tool when you get stuck.

MP6 Attend to precision.

In every mathematical exploration or problem-solving task, it is important to

- think carefully about the required accuracy of results; is a number estimate or geometric sketch good enough, or is a precise value or drawing needed?
- report your discoveries with clear and correct mathematical language that can be understood by those to whom you are speaking or writing.

MP7 Look for and make use of structure.

In mathematical explorations and problem solving, it is often helpful to

- look for patterns that show how data points, numbers, or geometric shapes are related to each other;
- use patterns to make predictions.

MP8 Look for and express regularity in repeated reasoning.

When results of a repeated calculation show a pattern, it helps to

- express that pattern as a general rule that can be used in similar cases;
- look for shortcuts that will make the calculation simpler in other cases.

You will use all of the Mathematical Practices in this Unit. Sometimes, when you look at a Problem, it is obvious which practice is most helpful. At other times, you will decide on a practice to use during class explorations and discussions. After completing each Problem, ask yourself:

- What mathematics have I learned by solving this Problem?
- What Mathematical Practices were helpful in learning this mathematics?

Unit Project

Is Anyone Typical?

What are the characteristics of a typical middle-school student? Does a typical middle-school student really exist? As you proceed through this Unit, you will identify some "typical" facts about your classmates, such as:

- The typical number of letters in a student's full name
- The typical number of people in a student's household
- The typical height of a student

After you have completed the Investigations in *Data About Us,* you will carry out a statistical investigation to answer the question,

"What are some of the characteristics of a typical middle-school student?"

These characteristics may include:

- Physical characteristics (such as age, height, or eye color)
- Family and home characteristics (such as number of siblings or number of computers)
- Behaviors (such as hobbies or number of hours spent watching television)
- Preferences, opinions, or attitudes (such as favorite musical group or choice for class president)

As you work through this Unit, make and refine your plans for your project. Keep in mind that a statistical investigation involves posing questions, collecting data, analyzing data, and interpreting the results of the analysis. As you work through each Investigation, think about how you might use what you are learning to complete your project.

Notes _____

_____

What's in a Name?
Organizing, Representing, and Describing Data

▼ Investigation Overview

Investigation Description

Investigation 1 presents introductory statistical material that will be used throughout *Data About Us*. It focuses on describing, interpreting, and comparing distributions of data. It is intended both as a preassessment of what students might already know and as a way to build understanding related to foundations of data analysis. Students are introduced to the process of statistical investigation. They also review and/or develop background in working with frequency tables, line plots, and bar graphs. Anticipating and recognizing how data vary are two key components of data analysis introduced in this Investigation. Selected measures of center (median and mode) and variability or spread (range) are explored.

Investigation Vocabulary

- attribute
- cluster
- data
- distribution
- frequency table
- gap

- line plot
- maximum value
- median
- minimum value
- mode
- range

- scale
- shape of a distribution
- summary statistic
- table

Mathematics Background

- The Process of Statistical Investigation
- Components of Statistical Investigation
- Posing Questions
- Collecting Data
- Analyzing Individual Cases vs. Overall Distributions
- Choosing Representations for Distributions
- Guiding Students to Construct and Read Graphs
- Shapes of Distributions
- Describing Data With Measures of Center
- Describing Data With Measures of Variability
- Interpreting Results

Planning Chart

Content	ACE	Pacing	Materials	Resources
Problem 1.1	1–4, 15–16	1½ days	**Labsheet 1.1A** Name Lengths Table 1 **Labsheet 1.1B** Frequency Table: Lengths of Chinese Names **Labsheet 1.1C:** Frequency Table: Lengths of U.S. Names (accessibility) **Labsheet 1ACE** Exercises 1–4 • Half-Inch Grid Paper	• Data and Graphs
Problem 1.2	5–8, 17–18, 24–28	½ day	**Labsheet 1.2** Name Lengths Table 2 **Labsheet 1ACE:** Exercise 17 (accessibility) • Half-Inch Grid Paper	• Data and Graphs • Expression Calculator
Problem 1.3	9–14, 19–23, 29–30	1 day	**Labsheet 1ACE:** Exercise 20 (accessibility) • Half-Inch Grid Paper sticky notes	• Data and Graphs
Mathematical Reflections		½ day		
Assessment: Check Up 1		½ day		• Check Up 1

▼ Goals and Standards

Goals

Statistical Process Understand and use the process of statistical investigation

- Ask questions, collect and analyze data, and interpret data to answer questions

- Describe data with respect to its shape, center, and variability or spread

- Construct and use simple surveys as a method of collecting data

Attributes Distinguish data and data types

- Recognize that data consist of counts or measurements of a variable, or an attribute; these observations comprise a distribution of data values

- Distinguish between categorical data and numerical data, and identify which graphs and statistics can be used to represent each kind of data

Multiple Representations for Displaying Data Display data with multiple representations

- Organize and represent data using tables, dot plots, line plots, ordered-value bar graphs, frequency bar graphs, histograms, and box-and-whisker plots

- Make informed decisions about which graphs or tables can be used to display a particular set of data

- Recognize that a graph shows the overall shape of a distribution, whether the data values are symmetrical around a central value, and whether the graph contains any unusual characteristics such as gaps, clusters, or outliers

Measures of Central Tendency and Variability Recognize that a single number may be used to characterize the center of a distribution of data and the degree of variability (or spread)

- Distinguish between and compute measures of central tendency (mean, median, and mode) and measures of spread (range, interquartile range (IQR), and mean absolute deviation (MAD))

- Identify how the median and mean respond to changes in the data values of a distribution

- Relate the choice of measures of central tendency and variability to the shape of the distribution and the context

- Describe the amount of variability in a distribution by noting whether the data values cluster in one or more areas or are fairly spread out

- Use measures of center and spread to compare data distributions

Mathematical Reflections

Look for evidence of student understanding of the goals for this Investigation in their responses to the questions in *Mathematical Reflections*. The goals addressed by each question are indicated below.

1. The process of carrying out a statistical investigation involves asking a question, gathering and analyzing data, and interpreting the results to answer the question. Choose a data set from this Investigation. Use the data set to answer each question below.

- What was the question asked?
- How were the data collected?
- How were the data analyzed and represented?
- How did the results from the analysis help you answer the question?

Goals

- Ask questions, collect and analyze data, and interpret data to answer questions
- Describe data with respect to their shape, center, and variability or spread
- Recognize that data consist of counts or measurements of a variable, or an attribute; these observations comprise a distribution of data values
- Construct and use simple surveys as a method of collecting data

2. You can represent a set of data using such displays as a data table, a frequency table, and a dot or line plot. Explain how these displays are related.

Goal

- Organize and represent data using tables, dot plots, line plots, ordered-value bar graphs, frequency bar graphs, histograms, and box-and-whisker plots

3. The median and mode are two measures of the center of a data distribution. The range is a measure of variability, or how spread out the data are.

a. What does each measure of center tell you about a data set?

b. Can the mode and the median for a data set have the same value? Can they have different values? Explain your answers.

c. How does the range tell you how much the data vary?

d. Suppose we add a new data value to a set of data. Does this new value affect the mode? The median? The range? Explain.

Goals

- Distinguish between and compute measures of central tendency (mean, median, and mode) and measures of spread (range, interquartile range (IQR), and mean absolute deviation (MAD))
- Identify how the median and mean respond to changes in the data values of a distribution

- Describe the amount of variability in a distribution by noting whether the data values cluster in one or more areas or are fairly spread out

4. What strategies can you use to make comparisons among data sets?

Goal

- Recognize that a graph shows the overall shape of a distribution, whether the data values are symmetrical around a central value, and whether the graph contains any unusual characteristics such as gaps, clusters, or outliers

Standards

Common Core Content Standards

6.SP.A.1 Recognize a statistical question as one that anticipates variability in the data related to the question and accounts for it in the answers. *Problems 1, 2, and 3*

6.SP.A.2 Understand that a set of data collected to answer a statistical question has a distribution, which can be described by its center, spread, and overall shape. *Problems 1, 2, and 3*

6.SP.A.3 Recognize that a measure of center for a numerical data set summarizes all of its values with a single number, while a measure of variation describes how its values vary with a single number. *Problems 2 and 3*

6.SP.B.4 Display numerical data in plots on a number line, including dot plots, histograms, and box plots. *Problems 1 and 2*

6.SP.B.5a Summarize numerical data sets in relation to their context, such as by reporting the number of observations. *Problem 3*

6.SP.B.5c Summarize numerical data sets in relation to their context, such as by giving quantitative measures of center (median and/or mean) and variability (interquartile range and/or mean absolute deviation), as well as describing any overall pattern and any striking deviations from the overall pattern with reference to the context in which the data were gathered. *Problem 3*

Facilitating the Mathematical Practices

Students in *Connected Mathematics* classrooms display evidence of multiple Common Core Standards for Mathematical Practice every day. Here are just a few examples of when you might observe students demonstrating the Standards for Mathematical Practice during this Investigation.

Practice 1: Make sense of problems and persevere in solving them.

Students are engaged every day in solving problems and, over time, learn to persevere in solving them. To be effective, the problems embody critical concepts and skills and have the potential to engage students in making sense of mathematics. Students build understanding by reflecting, connecting, and communicating. These student-centered problem situations engage students in articulating the "knowns" in a problem situation and determining a logical solution pathway. The student-student and student-teacher dialogues help students not only to make sense of the problems, but also to persevere in finding appropriate strategies to solve them. The suggested questions in the Teacher Guides provide the metacognitive scaffolding to help students monitor and refine their problem-solving strategies.

Practice 4: Model with mathematics.

Throughout Investigation 1, students represent data by constructing line plots and dot plots. They then use these models to work with the sets of data.

Practice 7: Look for and make use of structure.

Students use manipulatives (such as sticky notes or grid paper containing ordered values) to find the median in Investigation 1. This prepares them for finding the upper and lower quartile in Investigation 3. For all medians, students know to find the midpoint of the ordered values. They think about how to find the median when the number of data values is even and when the number of data values is odd.

Students identify and record their personal experiences with the Standards for Mathematical Practice during the Mathematical Reflections at the end of the Investigation.

▼ Problem Overview

> *Focus Question* What are "data"? How do you represent data using a frequency table or a line plot? How can you compare two distributions of data?

Problem Description

Students analyze name-length data for two different classes of students, one from the United States and one from China (with whom the U.S. class has a pen-pal relationship). Students focus on describing typical name lengths, describing distributions, and comparing distributions. Teachers can use this context to introduce frequency tables and to review using line plots to represent data.

Note: The Mathematics Background contains information about various kinds of graphs. It also provides general hints for use of graph paper. This information may be useful throughout the Unit, but particularly helpful for Investigation 1.

Problem Implementation

Have students work in pairs on this Problem.

Labsheet 1.1A: Name Lengths Table 1 is a copy of the table of Chinese and U.S. names in the Student Edition with genders included. Labsheets 1.1B and 1.1C are frequency tables that students can fill out for the Chinese and U.S. class data.

Materials

- **Labsheet 1.1A:** Name Lengths Table 1
- **Labsheet 1.1B:** Frequency Table: Lengths of Chinese Names
- **Labsheet 1.1C:** Frequency Table: Lengths of U.S. Names (accessibility)
- **Labsheet 1ACE:** Exercises 1–4
- **Half-Inch Grid Paper**

Using Technology

The **Data and Graphs** online tool contains the data of the Chinese, U.S., Japanese, and Korean classes from Investigation 1. If your students have access to computers, they can use this online tool to help them plot the data as well as find measures of center and spread.

Vocabulary

- attribute
- cluster
- data
- distribution

- frequency table
- gap
- line plot
- scale

- shape of a distribution
- table

Mathematics Background

- The Process of Statistical Investigation
- Components of Statistical Investigation
- Posing Questions
- Collecting Data
- Guiding Students to Construct and Read Graphs
- Shapes of Distributions
- Interpreting Results

At a Glance and Lesson Plan

- At a Glance: Problem 1.1 Data About Us
- Lesson Plan: Problem 1.1 Data About Us

▼ Launch

Connecting to Prior Knowledge

It is important to look back at the data analysis experiences students may have already had. Students in Kindergarten through Grade 5 should have learned to categorize data, compare data categories, and make picture graphs, bar graphs, and line plots. This prior experience will inform what they learn in Grade 6, although line plots (or dot plots) are the most visible displays in this Unit.

Use Problem 1.1 to assess what students appear to know and are able to do with respect to statistics. Identify what students know about using graphs. Review these representations with your students, and revisit or introduce these graphs, depending on students' background knowledge.

Problem 1.1 also introduces students to the idea of using data analysis to compare two data sets.

Suggested Questions

- Do you know anything interesting about how you were named or about the history behind your family's name? (Student responses will vary.)

- Do you use nicknames, full first names, middle initials, or full middle names? (Student responses will vary.)

Introduce the Problem context using the Launch questions in the Student Edition:

- What attribute is being investigated here? How do you determine the data values? (name lengths; count letters in the names)

- Once you have gathered your data values, how might you represent them? (Connecting to their prior experiences, students might respond with *bar graphs* or *line plots*. For every student suggestion, ask how the graph would be made. Your students will most likely suggest line plots. For example, students can make line plots by indicating the lengths of the various names with X's on the horizontal axis of a number line. If you choose, you can use the Chinese class data to review both line plots and bar graphs and discuss how each is made.)

Presenting the Challenge

Pose the opening challenge.

- How can you compare the name lengths of these two classes?

Take suggestions from the class without commenting on their suggestions. This is what students will explore in the Problem.

Note: If you use your own class data and you have 30 students, your data are easily integrated here. However, if you have a different number of students, you can include your class data when you are ready to identify summary statistics (for example, median and range in Investigation 1). Your students can compare different-sized data sets with the summary statistics.

▼ Explore

Providing for Individual Needs

Some students may need support in making and interpreting line plots. You may wish to do a mid-Problem Summarize after Questions A and B.

You can ask the following for Questions A and B.

Suggested Questions

- How do you locate the shortest and longest data values, or observations, for each set of data? (Have students scan the data or use the frequency table. For the Chinese names, 4 letters is the shortest length, and 9 letters is the longest length. For the U.S. names, 9 letters is the shortest length, and 17 letters is the longest length.)

- How can you use the shortest and longest name lengths to set up number lines for making the line plots? (Based on the two shortest name lengths, a number line should start at 4 letters; based on the two longest name lengths, a number line can end at 17 letters. In this situation, it is okay to begin the number line at 0; ending it at one value greater than 17 letters is also common practice.)

Since students will compare the two distributions of data, they should use the same scale for the two line plots. Students can make a scale for each line plot that begins with a value that is less than or equal to the shortest value from the two sets of data; likewise, the scale should end with a value one greater than or equal to the largest value from the two data sets. Ask them why having the same scale is helpful and give them an opportunity to amend their graphs before going on to Question C. Students can make their final plots so that one is below the other with scales aligned on the same piece of paper.

Students can sketch a first draft by numbering the line from the least to the greatest data values. They can plot the remainder of the data values, using an "X" for each, above correct locations on the line plot.

As you observe students making their line plots, you might check their understanding of how to read graphs. As a central tool for data analysis, graphs deserve special attention. Three components of graph comprehension are useful to consider when discussing distributions:

- Reading the data involves locating information from a graph to answer explicit questions. For example, *How many students have 12 letters in their names?* (three)

- Reading between the data includes using clusters of information presented in a graph. For example, *How many students have more than 12 letters in their names?* (fifteen), or *How many of the students' name lengths cluster at 6–7 letters?* (fifteen)

- Reading beyond the data involves extending, predicting, or inferring from data to answer questions. For example, *What is the "typical" number of letters in these students' names? If a new student joined the class, how many letters would you predict that student would have in his or her name?* (Student answers will vary.)

These are suggested mid-Problem Summarize questions:

- What does it mean when there is more than one X above a data value? (Several people have names of the same length.)

- How are the frequency tables and line plots related to each other? Does the table help you set up the graph? (Both show the frequency of each name length. The table makes it clear which numbers are needed on the axis of the graph, especially the maximum and minimum data values.)

- Besides making the number line, what other information would someone need to see in order to understand what the graph is about? (Graphs should include a title and label for the data axis.)

- Why do you think that having the same scale for both line plots is advantageous? (You can make comparisons when the line plots have the same scale. A visual comparison will be easier.)

Continue with the rest of the Explore, Questions C and D.

- Do you see any clusters of data for the Chinese class? (Fifteen people (half the students) have name lengths that cluster in the interval of 6–7 letters. There are also several people who have name lengths of 9 letters.)

- Do you see any clusters of data for the U.S. class? (Twenty-one people (more than half the students, or 7 out of 10 of the students) have name lengths in the cluster of 9–13 letters. There are also several people who have name lengths of 15 letters.)

- Is there anything surprising about the data? Where do you see these surprises? (The graphs help you see such things as clusters of data values and gaps in the data; they also highlight the ability to compare shortest and longest name lengths.)

- What comparisons did you make between the two classes? (At this point, students are unlikely to use summary statistics to make comparisons. They may note that the shortest name length in the U.S. class list has the same number of letters as the longest name length in the Chinese class list. Or, the longest name length in the U.S class list has about twice as many letters as the longest name length in the Chinese class list.)

Note: These are the kinds of questions that are often used when considering data distributions; see Guidelines for Describing Distributions in the Mathematics Background **Interpreting Results.**

Students continue working in pairs to complete Questions C and D. For Question D, encourage students to use the graphs to help them describe typical name lengths.

Planning for the Summary

What evidence will you use in the summary to clarify and deepen understanding of the Focus Question?

What will you do if you do not have evidence?

Summarize

Orchestrating the Discussion

In the mid-Problem Summarize, you will want to give time to show and explain the graphs students made. Use Questions A and B to guide your discussion for those sections. For Questions C and D, ask:

Suggested Questions

- Looking at the graph, what surprises you about the data? (Students might say that they are surprised that Chinese names could be as short as 4 letters, that there are U.S. names with 15 letters and 17 letters but none with 16 letters, or that the longest Chinese name is the same as the shortest U.S. name.)

- Looking at the graphs, what do you think is the typical name length of a student in the U.S. class? The Chinese class? Explain your thinking.

If you focus on the distributions separately, the students may answer the question in different ways. Focusing on both distributions together, it helps enormously if both sets of data are displayed using the same scales (and sized with the same interval widths). Discuss with students why this is important. Discuss what is typical and how they can support their ideas about what is typical. Students may suggest that 6 letters is a typical name length for Chinese students. Some students will combine a few name lengths in a cluster and say that 6–7 letters is a typical name length for Chinese students. Likewise, for the U.S class, some students will say 15 letters is the most typical length while others will opt for a cluster of numbers, such as 9–13 letters.

- Why would you say name lengths of 6 or 7 letters is typical for the Chinese class? (When data values with almost the same numbers of observations cluster together, it is hard to make a convincing case that one data value is more typical than another.)

- Do you think it is reasonable to say 6–7 letters instead of just one number for a typical length? (Leave this open. Students will learn various ways to talk about "typical," some of which involve identifying just a single data value, and some that involve identifying clusters of data.)

- Some of you said that 11 letters and 13 letters are the most typical lengths for the U.S. names. Some of you used a span of 11–13 letters. What justification can you give for each of these answers? (Students might say a length of 11 and 13 letters occurred most frequently. Some might say that there are very few names outside of the 11–13 span, except for the names with 15 letters. Again, leave this open.)

Also discuss any other comparisons that were not considered in the mid-Problem Summarize. For example, pose the following:

- Name lengths of 11 and 13 occur with greater frequency than the name lengths with 9 letters for the U.S. students. What does this statement tell you about the way the distribution looks? (There will be more X's above 11 and 13 and fewer X's above 9.)

- Half the Chinese names are either 6 or 7 letters in length. What does this tell you about the total number of names with those name lengths? (There will be 15 X's above the data values 6 or 7.)

Tie this discussion to the Focus Questions.

- Data are the measurements or counts related to an attribute that is the focus of a statistical investigation. In this case, the data values are name lengths. Gender is also an attribute (as listed on the labsheets). You could compare the two classes by using numbers of girls and boys, but the focus of Problem 1.1 is on a different attribute.

- *Observation* is another word for the *data value* relating to the attribute of name length in this situation.

- Two standard representations are highlighted: line plots and frequency tables. Other representations are possible, including bar graphs. Students will learn more representations in this Unit.

- Comparing two distributions can involve looking at the overall shape of each distribution to get a general sense of whether the data values are symmetrical around a central value or if there is something unusual about the shape. Students can describe locations of clusters or gaps in the distributions. Students can also compare what they think are typical name lengths for each class.

Reflecting on Student Learning

Use the following questions to assess student understanding at the end of the lesson.

- What evidence do I have that students understand the Focus Question?
  - Where did my students get stuck?
  - What strategies did they use?
  - What breakthroughs did my students have today?
- How will I use this to plan for tomorrow? For the next time I teach this lesson?
- Where will I have the opportunity to reinforce these ideas as I continue through this Unit? The next Unit?

ACE Assignment Guide

- **Applications:** 1–4
- **Connections:** 15–16
- **Labsheet 1ACE:** Exercises 1–4 is a copy of the Exercises in the Student Edition. Students can use this labsheet to mark up or make notes on the table.

Describing Name Lengths
What Are the Shape, Mode, and Range?

▼ Problem Overview

> *Focus Question* What are measures of central tendency and variability (or spread)? How do you compute and use mode and range?

Problem Description

In Problem 1.2, students analyze name-length data from a class of students from Japan. They are introduced to describing the *shape of data* and to finding one measure of center (mode) and one measure of spread (range).

Problem Implementation

Have students work in pairs on this Problem.

Materials

- **Labsheet 1.2:** Name Lengths Table 2
- **Labsheet 1ACE:** Exercise 17 (accessibility)
- **Half-Inch Grid Paper**

Using Technology

The **Data and Graphs** online tool contains the data of the Japanese class from Problem 1.2. If your students have access to computers, they can use this online tool to help them plot the data as well as find measures of center and spread. For ACE Exercise 27, students can use the **Expression Calculator** to help them determine how much revenue the greeting card store collected.

Vocabulary

- maximum value
- minimum value
- mode
- range

Mathematics Background

- The Process of Statistical Investigation
- Components of Statistical Investigation
- Posing Questions
- Collecting Data
- Analyzing Individual Cases vs. Overall Distributions
- Choosing Representations for Distributions
- Guiding Students to Construct and Read Graphs
- Shapes of Distributions
- Describing Data With Measures of Center
- Describing Data With Measures of Variability
- Interpreting Results

At a Glance and Lesson Plan

- At a Glance: Problem 1.2 Data About Us
- Lesson Plan: Problem 1.2 Data About Us

▼ Launch

Launch Video

In this animation, a student completes a project about the number of texts, on average, that each of his friends sends each day. He shows the report for his project to a friend. The two discuss the dot plot shown in the report. You can show this animation before Presenting the Challenge to model good discussion about data for students. This animation also acts as a visual reminder of how to construct dot plots and which specific values on a dot plot should be given attention. Visit Teacher Place at mathdashboard.com/cmp3 to see the complete video.

Connecting to Prior Knowledge

Students continue with the name length of pen pals context. As in Problem 1.1, Problem 1.2 will give you information about what your students know and are able to do based on earlier experiences in Grades K–5.

Presenting the Challenge

Introduce the context: The U.S. class from Problem 1.1 is given a list of names of pen pals from a class in Japan.

Suggested Questions

- How do you think name lengths for a class of students in Japan will compare to the name lengths of students from a class in the United States? (Students will provide their guesses.)

Introduce the new vocabulary: mode, maximum value, minimum value, and range.

- What is the mode of the U.S. class data? Of the Chinese class data? Does this help you compare the classes? (There are two modes in the U.S. data: 11 and 13 letters. The data are bimodal. The mode for the Chinese data is 6 letters. You can use this idea to compare the classes by saying that the typical U.S. name length is greater than the typical Chinese name length.)

- What is the range of the U.S. data? Of the Chinese data? Does this help you compare the classes? (The range of the U.S. data is $17 - 9 = 8$ letters. The range of the Chinese data is $9 - 4 = 5$ letters. You can say that the Chinese name lengths do not vary as much as the U.S. name lengths.)

Refer students to Name Lengths Table 2. Explain that this is a partial list of the Japanese class (20 names out of 30 students).

- Do you think you can use the ideas of mode and range to compare the Japanese name lengths to the U.S. name lengths? What data will you use for this Problem? (The data are the name lengths of Japanese pen pals. If students point out that there are only 20 names on this list and 30 names on the U.S. list, ask why this is an issue. Comparing ranges or modes of data sets of very different sizes may be misleading. A very small set of data might give an inaccurate picture of what is typical. If this does not come up, you probably do not want to distract from the main issue by bringing it up.)

- How do the name lengths of these Japanese students compare to name lengths of the U.S. students?

Have students work in pairs to complete Questions A–C. **Labsheet 1.2: Name Lengths Table 2** contains a copy of the table in the Student Edition. They can use this labsheet to help them add data values to the incomplete dot plot.

▼ Explore

Providing for Individual Needs

The tasks in Problem 1.2 are fairly straightforward. It is possible that students will already be familiar with mode and range.

Question A, part (2), highlights a few characteristics of a distribution's *shape*. In a distribution, the data lose their individual meanings (e.g., Savannah Russell's name length is 15 letters). The data distribution becomes an object that can be examined to consider what you know about name lengths in general based on what the distribution looks like, i.e., its shape. Specifically, the Problem asks students to look at where data *cluster* and where there may be *gaps*.

Help students see that data displayed using a graph show the overall shape of a distribution. They can examine a distribution to see if there is something unusual about the shape. Paying attention to *clusters* and *gaps* is an initial step in focusing on how the data are distributed. As students learn more about shape, other characteristics are introduced. Some students may find it difficult to shift the focus from reading specific information to observing a more general view.

There are two ways to think about variability (or spread) in data. One of these is accessible to students at this point: paying attention to whether the data values are pretty much the same or are quite spread out. Encourage this. The other way of thinking about variability is to pay attention to how close together or spread out the data values are from a measure of center; this is addressed more in later Investigations.

Suggested Questions

- Are the data values for the Japanese name lengths spread out, or are they clustered together around values that are close together? (Some students will focus on the difference between maximum and minimum values (the range). They may think that this shows the values are spread out. If this happens, you might push further on the idea of a *cluster* of values.)

- What are unusual values? Where are most student name lengths clustered? (Lengths of 7, 8, 9, 11, and 14 letters have only a few names associated with them. Most name lengths are clustered round 10–12 or 10–13 letters.)

Note: It is interesting that there are only a few names with 11 letters. If you look at a cluster of values, however, 11 is in the middle of a cluster. You might ask students why they think this happened. It could be that, if there were a larger sample of names, this anomaly would disappear. This topic appears in a Grade 7 Unit, *Samples and Populations*.

- How did you decide on the mode for the Japanese name lengths? (Look for the most X's above a value.)

- Is 12 letters a more typical name length than 10 letters? (This question highlights a problem with using the mode as a measure of center: There might be more than one mode, or there might be several data values that occur with almost the same frequency as the mode. As a summary, mode does have drawbacks. There is no need to push hard on this idea right now. As the Unit progresses, students will have opportunities to think about the pros and cons of using the mode as a measure of center.)

Planning for the Summary

What evidence will you use in the summary to clarify and deepen understanding of the Focus Question?

What will you do if you do not have evidence?

▼ Summarize

Orchestrating the Discussion

Review students' responses to Questions A–C, then consider the Focus Question.

The mode is a measure of central tendency and the range is a measure of variability or how spread out the data are.

Suggested Questions

- How might one measure help you summarize a set of data values? What does the mode summarize? What does the range summarize? (The mode helps to summarize what is a typical value in a data set. The range helps to summarize how much the data values vary.)

- You know the mode for the Japanese class data (12 letters), the Chinese class data (6 letters), and the U.S. class data (11 and 13 letters). Does this help you make comparisons among the data sets? (You can say that a typical name length in the U.S. class is about the same as a typical name length in the Japanese class; it is longer, however, than a typical name length in the Chinese class.)

- You know the range of the Japanese class data (7 letters), the Chinese class data (5 letters), and the U.S. class data (8 letters). Does this help you compare the data sets? (These statistics are not as different from each other as the modes are. The Chinese name lengths are a little less spread out, or vary a little less, than the other data sets.)

Reflecting on Student Learning

Use the following questions to assess student understanding at the end of the lesson.

- What evidence do I have that students understand the Focus Question?
  - Where did my students get stuck?
  - What strategies did they use?
  - What breakthroughs did my students have today?
- How will I use this to plan for tomorrow? For the next time I teach this lesson?
- Where will I have the opportunity to reinforce these ideas as I continue through this Unit? The next Unit?

ACE Assignment Guide

- **Applications:** 5–8
- **Connections:** 17–18
- **Extensions:** 24–28

Labsheet 1ACE: Exercise 17 is optional. It is an example of a way to provide students with additional support for an ACE Exercise.

Describing Name Lengths
What Is the Median?

▼ Problem Overview

Focus Question How do you identify and use the median? How can you compare two distributions of data using the medians?

Problem Description

Students are introduced to a second measure of center: the median. Initially, the focus is on finding the *position* and the *value* of the median. Using the Japanese class data from Table 2, students fold paper strips to see that the position of the median is between the 10th and 11th data values, dividing the data set in half. The value of the median is determined from the 10th and 11th data values (11 and 12 letters). Students find the range, mode, and median, and then use these statistics to describe and compare distributions from the name-length data sets used in Problem 1.2.

Problem Implementation

Have students work in pairs on this Problem.

Materials

- **Labsheet 1ACE:** Exercise 20 (accessibility)
- **Half-Inch Grid Paper**
- **Check Up 1**

sticky notes

Using Technology

If your students have access to computers, they can use the **Data and Graphs** online tool to help them find the median of the data as they add more and more values to the set of data.

Vocabulary

- median
- summary statistic

Mathematics Background

- The Process of Statistical Investigation
- Components of Statistical Investigation
- Posing Questions
- Collecting Data
- Analyzing Individual Cases vs. Overall Distributions
- Choosing Representations for Distributions
- Shapes of Distributions
- Describing Data With Measures of Center
- Interperting Results

At a Glance and Lesson Plan

- At a Glance: Problem 1.3 Data About Us
- Lesson Plan: Problem 1.3 Data About Us

▼ Launch

Connecting to Prior Knowledge

Students learned that the mode is the most frequently occurring value in a distribution. As students make connections to the median in Problem 1.3 and to the mean in Investigation 2, they should realize the mode is rarely used to describe the central tendency in quantitative data because it may be unstable (i.e., it changes often depending on the data collected).

The median is a more important measure of center given its position at the midpoint of a distribution. Its *position* depends on the order of the data values in a data set, so it is sensitive to *the number of data values*. Its *value* is determined from the actual data value (or average of the two data values) at the midpoint. In later Problems, students will contrast this to the behavior of the mean, which is usually sensitive to a change in a data value.

Presenting the Challenge

You can begin by asking students what the word *median* means to them.

Suggested Questions

- When you hear the word *median*, what do you think of? (Students might say "the strip down the middle of a road.")

Have students refer to the data from Problem 1.2 in their books. You may use the following script to begin the Problem:

> In this Problem, you will find out what the median means in a statistical sense. The median is another way to describe what is typical, because its position is the midpoint of an ordered set of data.

> For the name-length data for 20 students from the class of Japanese pen pals, you need to find the *position* and the *value* of the median. The median separates the *ordered* data set in half, so half of the data values are on either side of the median. To find the median, you must first order the data from least to greatest (or greatest to least).

Refer to the Introduction to Problem 1.3 in the Student Edition.

> Write each name length, in *order of size*, in a grid box on a strip of grid paper.

Have students work in pairs on writing each name length in size order, folding the grid paper strip in half, and finding the position of the median. Discuss the Launch questions in the Student Edition as a large group.

- If you put the ends of the strip together and fold the strip in half, where does the crease fall in the list of numbers? (between the numbers, or data values, 11 and 12)

- How many numbers are to the *left* of the crease? (ten numbers)

- How many numbers are to the *right* of the crease? (ten numbers)

Together, read the explanation about what the median does, noting where the crease falls on the strip.

- What is the value of the median for these data? (It is the midpoint between 11 and 12 letters, or $11\frac{1}{2}$ letters.)

  Students may express concern that $11\frac{1}{2}$ letters is not a possible data value for name length; remind them that the *value* of the median is a number that marks the midpoint of the data values and may not be an actual data value, even though we use the data values to determine the median.

- What can you say about all the numbers to the left of the crease? To the right of the crease? (Since the data were ordered from least to greatest, the numbers to the left are all less than the median value of $11\frac{1}{2}$ letters. The numbers to the right are all greater than $11\frac{1}{2}$.)

  Note: If the data values on the strip used to locate the median had been 11, 11, 11, 11, 12, 12, 12, the value of the median would be 11 letters, and would mark the midpoint of the data values in the ordered list that are either less than or equal to the median or greater than or equal to the median. This point is expanded upon later in the Problem.

- What do you know about these Japanese name lengths when you know the median? (Half the name lengths are less than $11\frac{1}{2}$ letters; half are greater.)

Next, have students write each name length on a sticky note; they will use these sticky notes for Problem 1.3, Question A. They will need some additional blank notes to use during the Explore phase.

Tell your students that they are going learn about how adding more data values to the set may change the location of the median.

▼ Explore

Providing for Individual Needs

Have students work in pairs on Question A. Read the Question together and have the students add the additional sticky notes, order the data, and locate the median.

Some students will find it difficult to believe that the median may not change when additional data values are added. They may need to recount to find the median location.

Suggested Questions

- Why did the position and the value of the median change when you added 3 names but not when you added 2 names? (The two names were added in such a way as to balance the two halves of the data around the same median position. The third name caused the position of the median to shift to the left. In this case, the data value of 11 letters is now the value of the median.)

- Suppose you add one extra name that has a name length greater than 14 letters to the 30 names in the Japanese class. How many students would now be on the list, and what would the position of the median now be? (There would be 31 students, so the position of the median would be the 16th data value, when ordered from least to greatest. The value of the median would be 12 letters. While adding the new name does shift the position of the median, there are multiple name lengths having 12 letters, so the value of the median continues to be 12 letters. The median does mark, however, a midpoint that is a different data value of 12 letters in the list of repeated data values of 12 letters.)

  Note: Unlike the mean (which is discussed in later Investigations), the median shifts its *position* because the number of data values has changed. The median is not, however, sensitive to the *value* of the data observation added.

- Why should you say that half the name lengths are greater than *or equal to* the median of 12, not just greater than 12? (The repetition of the values around the median value means that, in this case, there are 13 name lengths of fewer than 12 letters, 6 name lengths of greater 12 letters, and 11 name lengths with exactly 12 letters. Using "or equal to" lets you adjust the original statement about how the median value relates to the entire distribution.)

For Question B, students need the distributions of name lengths for the U.S. and Chinese classes from Problem 1.1. Students may find that using one number to summarize a data distribution is more meaningful when they want to compare two or more distributions (e.g., each class's name lengths). They can also use the shape of each distribution to make comparisons.

- How can you find the medians for the U.S. class and Chinese class data? Is the table of data or graph helpful? (The line plot is helpful because the data are already ordered. However, using the line plot to make an ordered list first may be preferable to trying to count to the middle position directly on the line plot.)

- How do the medians of the three different data sets help you compare class name lengths? (They can be used to describe what is typical of each class.)

- Would making a line plot of the entire set of data for the Japanese class help you make comparisons with the other classes? (Using two classes of 30 students each (instead of the partial listing of Japanese students) would provide a more accurate comparison. At this point students are probably more comfortable comparing summary statistics, such as median, range, or mode, than comparing shapes of the distributions. The distribution of the Japanese class has little variability with many data values at 12 letters; however, this may change with additional observations.)

For Question C:

- You have said that when there is an even number of name lengths, the position of the median is between the middle two data values. Does this mean the value of the median of an even number of name lengths will always be a fraction, such as $11\frac{1}{2}$? (Not necessarily; for example, in Question A, part (4), when the data set is complete, the position of the median is between 12 letters and 12 letters.)

Planning for the Summary

What evidence will you use in the summary to clarify and deepen understanding of the Focus Question?

What will you do if you do not have evidence?

Summarize

Orchestrating the Discussion

To help students understand the median, you may want to make your own large strips of ordered data values. Make one strip for the original 20 values, and make another for the 23 total values included in Question A, part (2). In each case, draw a dark line to indicate the position of the median. You could use gridded chart paper, which is often available in office supply stores.

Hold up the strip with 20 values and lead the students with the suggested script.

> For the strip of 20 values, the fold does not land on a number. It falls between 11 and 12. In this case, where there is an even number of values, the position of the median is halfway between the two middle data values. For this set of data, the value of the median is $11\frac{1}{2}$ letters.

Now, hold up the strip of 23 values.

> For the strip of 23 values, the fold, which is the position of the median, is on a 12. Half the values are to the left of the fold and half are to the right of the fold. The value of the median for this set of names is 12 letters.

Next, direct students to the graph of the complete set of data for the Japanese class.

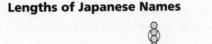

Lengths of Japanese Names

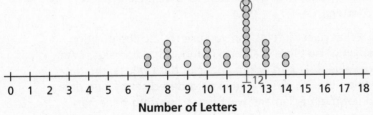

Number of Letters

Suggested Questions

- Look at the complete data set and dot plot. The median name length is 12 letters. Where is this located on the graph? (Its position is shown as a red marker at the "12" on the graph. Notice that there are several data values below the marker. If these are listed in an ordered list, the position of the median is between the two data values circled, or the midpoint of the 15th and 16th data values.)

- What is the value of the median? (The median is 12 letters.)

  Note: You may want to clarify that midway between two of the same number *is* that number.

- Earlier, you found a different measure of center called the mode. How does the median compare with the mode in this data set? (The median (12 letters) is the same as the mode (12 letters) in this particular data set.)

- For this data set, the median has the same value as the mode. Is it possible that the median and mode may not be the same? (Yes. The two sets of data from the U.S. class and the Chinese class each have a mode and a median that are different.)

- If you had several data values, folding a strip of paper to find the position and value of the median or making a set of sticky notes would be inefficient strategies. How else might you find the position and value of the median? (Students may have several valid suggestions. One possibility is to make an ordered list of the name lengths and count in from the ends, pairing one length from the "lesser" end with one length from the "greater" end until you work your way to the middle to find the position.

  Another possibility is to make an ordered list of the name lengths. Then, if there is an even number of data values, divide the number of values in half. The result will be a whole number. Count that many values from one end of the data. The position of the median will be halfway between the number you land on and the next number. If there is an odd number of data values, divide the number of values in half. The result will be a mixed number with the fraction portion being $\frac{1}{2}$. Round the number up to the next whole number, and count that many values from one end of the ordered data. The position of the median is the number you count to. In either case, the value of the median is determined by the data value or values.)

- Look at Question B. What are the median and range of each of the three distributions? (Japanese names: median 12 letters, range 7 letters; Chinese names: median 7 letters, range 5 letters; U.S. names: median 12.5 letters, range 8 letters)

- Look at Question C. What general rules can you use to find the position and value of the median when there is an odd number of data values? An even number of data values? (For an odd number of data values, the data value in the middle (e.g., the 5th data value in an ordered set of nine data values) is the position of the median and will be used to determine its value. The median is this value.

  For an even number of data values, the position of the median is halfway between the two middle data values (e.g, the 5th and 6th data values in an ordered set of ten data values). The value of the median can be determined by finding the value that is halfway between these two data values.)

  Note: Some students will understand that this means adding the two data values and dividing by 2, or finding the mean of the two middle data values.

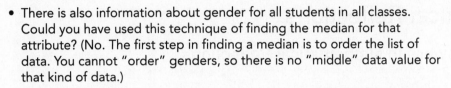

- There is also information about gender for all students in all classes. Could you have used this technique of finding the median for that attribute? (No. The first step in finding a median is to order the list of data. You cannot "order" genders, so there is no "middle" data value for that kind of data.)

  Note: In Investigation 2, students will learn that there are two kinds of data. Some summary statistics cannot be used for certain kinds of data.

Have students summarize their discussion by considering the Focus Question.

Reflecting on Student Learning

Use the following questions to assess student understanding at the end of the lesson.

- What evidence do I have that students understand the Focus Question?
  - Where did my students get stuck?
  - What strategies did they use?
  - What breakthroughs did my students have today?
- How will I use this to plan for tomorrow? For the next time I teach this lesson?
- Where will I have the opportunity to reinforce these ideas as I continue through this Unit? The next Unit?

ACE Assignment Guide

- **Applications:** 9–14
- **Connections:** 19–23
- **Extensions:** 29–30

Labsheet 1ACE: Exercise 20 (accessibility) is optional. It is an example of a way to provide students with additional support for an ACE Exercise.

▼ Mathematical Reflections

Possible Answers to Mathematical Reflections

1. Answers will vary, but will refer to collecting data about name lengths. For example, in Problem 1.1:

   - The question asked us to compare the name lengths of U.S. students and their Chinese pen pals.

   - We counted the letters in the names and listed these in a table of data.

   - We made line plots so we could see which lengths occurred most frequently (the mode). We could also use line plots to find the middle value (the median) or the range.

   - The summary statistics help us compare what name lengths are typical for each class and how much the name lengths vary. The graphs show gaps and clusters of values.

2. A table of data, a line plot, and frequency table are all tools for organizing and visualizing data. All three indicate the possible values of the item being measured (for example, 10 letters or 11 letters). A line plot and a frequency table indicate the number of times each value occurs.

3. **a.** The mode is the value in a data set that occurs most frequently. There may be more than one mode, and a mode may occur at any location in the data. The position of the median divides an ordered set of data in half; half the data values are less than or equal to the value of the median, and half the data values are greater than or equal to the value of the median. The value of the median is not easily affected by the addition of very high or very low values.

    b. The mode and the median for a set of data may or may not be the same. For the data set 1, 2, 3, 3, 4, 5, 6, both the median and the mode are 3. For the data set 1, 1, 1, 3, 5, 6, 6, the mode is 1 and the median is 3.

    c. The range indicates how spread out data are since it is determined by the difference between the maximum and the minimum data values. Combined with a measure of center such as the median, the range helps to give a picture of the data. For example, if you know a data set has a median of 20, you know where the midpoint of the data set is. If, in addition, you know the range is from 18 to 22 (or from 1 to 60), you have a much better idea of what the data may look like.

    d. If we add a new value to a data set, the mode may or may not change. If the new data value has the same value as the mode, then the modal data value increases in frequency and the mode remains unchanged. If the data value has a different value from the mode, then it will change the frequency of another existing data value. It is possible that there are now two data values with equal frequencies, creating a bimodal situation. If we add a new data value to a data set, the median will shift but the actual value of the median may or may not change depending on whether the existing values adjacent to the original median are repeated values of the median value. Even if the value we add is extremely unusual, the median position shifts one data value, and there may be no change in value of the median. If we add a new data value to a data set, the range may or may not change. If the new data value is greater than the original minimum and less than the original maximum, then the range will be unchanged.

4. You can use the mode and median to describe what is typical about a data set. Sometimes a span of values, a cluster, best describes what is typical. The range tells how much the data values vary. These statistics can be used to summarize and compare what is typical about two or more data sets and to compare how spread out the data sets are. Descriptions of distributions can be used to make comparisons. For example, medians can be compared.

Possible Answers to Mathematical Practices Reflections

Students may have demonstrated all of the eight Common Core Standards for Mathematical Practice during this Investigation. During the class discussion, have students provide additional Practices that the Problem cited involved and identify the use of other Mathematical Practices in the Investigation.

One student observation is provided in the Student Edition. Here is another sample student response.

Problem 1.1 asked us to make graphs to display name lengths of the students in the two classes. It didn't tell us what kind of graphs to make. Jim suggested we make a bar graph. Dea tried to remember how to make a graph that used a number line and marked X's above numbers. We decided to try to make the kind of graph that Dea talked about. It sounded pretty easy. We had to decide how to set up the number line and decided the numbers on the line were the number of letters in the names. We went through our data for the U.S. class and marked an X over the number of letters for each student. Jim really wanted us to make a bar graph for the Chinese names. We couldn't remember what to do. Jim said you made bars the heights of the X's on the line plot. So we made another number line and started to make bars to show the number of names of certain lengths. We remembered we needed to add a frequency axis that shows *how many*. With the other kind of graph, we could count the X's.

Note: See the answers to Problem 1.1 for examples of graphs.

MP1: Make sense of problems and persevere in solving them.

What's in a Name?
Organizing, Representing, and Describing Data

People are naturally curious about themselves and others. As you work on this Unit, make notes on how you would describe the "typical" middle-school student. At the end of the Unit, you will use what you have learned to conduct a statistical investigation.

Statistical problem solving involves using data to answer questions. The Problems in each Investigation will help you to think about the steps in a statistical investigation. This involves

- asking a question,
- collecting data,
- analyzing the data,
- interpreting the results and writing a report to answer the question asked.

You have already used bar graphs, line plots, and tables to organize and compare data. In *Data About Us,* you will use other tools and representations.

··

Common Core State Standards

6.SP.A.2 Understand that a set of data collected to answer a statistical question has a distribution that can be described by its center, spread, and overall shape.

6.SP.B.4 Display numerical data in plots on a number line, including dot plots...

6.SP.B.5a Summarize numerical data sets in relation to their context, such as by reporting the number of observations.

Also 6.SP.A.1, 6.SP.A.3, 6.SP.B.5c

8 Data About Us

Notes _____

_____

_____

86   Data About Us   Investigation 1 What's in a Name? Organizing, Representing, and Describing Data

1.1 How Many Letters Are in a Name?

Names are filled with tradition. *Onomatologists* study names to discover clues about family ancestors or where people settled around the world. One characteristic that you might not think about is the *length* of a person's name.

There are times when name length matters. Computers may truncate, or shorten, a long name on a library card or an e-mail address. Likewise, only a limited number of letters may fit on a friendship bracelet.

In Problem 1.1, a middle-school class is studying various countries in Asia, as shown in the map below. The class is pen pals with a class in China.

The table on the next page shows the names of the 30 students in each class. Next to the names are the **data** values or *observations* for name length—the total number of letters in the first and last names of each student.

Notes

Name Lengths Table 1

Chinese Students	Number of Letters	U.S. Students	Number of Letters
Hua Gao	6	Carson Alexander	15
Liu Gao	6	Avery Anderson	13
Xiang Guo	8	Makayla Bell	11
Zhang Guo	8	Hunter Bennett	13
Li Han	5	Jacob Campbell	13
Yu Han	5	Alexandria Clark	15
Miao He	6	Antonio Cook	11
Yu Hu	4	Kaitlyn Cooper	13
Kong Huang	9	Takisha Davis	12
Ping Li	6	Rebecca Diaz	11
Li Liang	7	Sofia Garcia	11
Chen Lin	7	Arlo Gonzales	12
Yanlin Liu	9	Elijah Hall	10
Dan Luo	6	Kaori Hashimoto	14
Lin Ma	5	Dalton Hayes	11
Lin Song	7	Noah Henderson	13
Chi Sun	6	Haley Jenkins	12
Bai Tang	7	Jack Kelly	9
Dewei Wang	9	Bryce Moore	10
Zhou Wu	6	Lillian Richardson	17
Yun Xiao	7	Liam Rogers	10
Hua Xie	6	Savannah Russell	15
Le Xu	4	Kyle Simmons	11
Xiang Xu	7	Adam Smith	9
Chi Yang	7	Marissa Thomas	13
Qiao Zhang	9	Danielle Thompson	16
Zheng Zhao	9	Esperanza Torres	15
Yang Zheng	9	Ethan Ward	9
Chung Zhou	9	Mackenzie Wilson	15
Wu Zhu	5	Nathaniel Young	14

Notes

- An **attribute** is a characteristic or feature about a person or object. What attribute is being investigated here?

- How are the data values for the 60 observations determined?

- What graphs might you make to organize and compare this information?

- Compare the name lengths of the U.S. students to the name lengths of the Chinese students. What do you notice?

In this Problem, you will represent data with tables and graphs in order to examine their **distribution**—the shape of the data set as a whole.

Problem 1.1

A A **frequency table** shows the number of times each value in a data set occurs. It arranges observations in order from least to greatest with their corresponding frequencies.

The frequency table shows some of the data about the Chinese class. The lengths of the first seven names (Hua Gao through Miao He) are recorded using tally marks.

**Lengths of Chinese Names
(From Name Lengths Table 1)**

Number of Letters	Tally	Frequency
1		0
2		0
3		0
4		
5	||	
6	|||	
7		
8	||	
9		

continued on the next page >

Notes _____

_____

_____

Problem **1.1** *continued*

1. a. Some name lengths do not occur, such as a name one letter long. How does the table show this?

b. On a copy of the table, complete the entries for the Chinese class.

2. For the U.S. class data, make a frequency table like the one on the previous page.

3. Compare the two frequency tables of class data.

a. What are the shortest and longest Chinese names?

b. What are the shortest and longest U.S. names?

B A **line plot** is a graph that shows data values on a number line using ✗s or other marks.

1. Make two line plots, one for each class. Use the same *scale* on both line plots.

2. Describe how the frequency tables helped you make the line plots.

C Use the line plots you made in Question B. Look at the shapes of the distributions of the data sets.

1. How would you describe the *shape* of the distribution? Are there any places where the data values **cluster,** or group together? Are there any **gaps,** or places where there are no data values?

2. Write two questions about the Chinese and U.S. classes that you can answer from your graphs.

3. Write three statements to compare the name lengths of the U.S. students and the Chinese students.

4. Describe how the line plots helped you compare the name lengths for the two classes.

D **1.** Identify a typical name length or name lengths for the Chinese class. Explain your reasoning.

2. Identify a typical name length or name lengths for the U.S. class. Explain your reasoning.

A C E Homework starts on page 19.

Notes _____

_____

_____

1.2 Describing Name Lengths
What Are the Shape, Mode, and Range?

Problem 1.1 asked you to describe a typical name length or name lengths for the U.S. class and for the Chinese class. One way to describe what is *typical* is to identify the data value that occurs most frequently. This is the **mode** of the data set. A data set may have more than one mode. Look back at the graphs you made in Problem 1.1.

- What is the mode of the U.S. class data? The Chinese class data?

In any data set, data values vary from a **minimum value** to a **maximum value.** The difference of the maximum data value and the minimum data value is the **range** of the data.

- What is the range of the U.S. class data? The Chinese class data?

Did You Know?

There are almost 7,000 spoken languages in the world today. Languages change as people of different cultures interact with each other. Some languages have identical or similar alphabets, such as English and Spanish. Other languages, such as Arabic and Japanese, use systems of characters that look quite different from the alphabet that we use in the United States.

Notes

The U.S. middle-school class now receives a 20-name list of pen pals from a class in Japan.

Name Lengths Table 2

Japanese Students	Number of Letters
Ai Kiyomizu	10
Daiki Kobayashi	14
Tsubasa Tanaka	13
Eric Katou	9
Kana Hayashi	11
Miyuu Shimizu	12
Ken Satou	8
Manami Ikeda	11
Hina Mori	8
Ryo Takahashi	12
Taka Yamamoto	12
Takumi Itou	10
Haruto Nakamura	14
Tomo Sasaki	10
Youta Kichida	12
Yuki Ine	7
Kiro Suzuki	10
Yumi Matsumoto	13
Yumi Yamasaki	12
Yusuke Yoshida	13

 How do the Japanese name lengths compare to the U.S. name lengths?

14   Data About Us

Notes

_____

_____

_____

In this Problem, you will use *dot plots* to represent the frequency of data. **Dot plots** and line plots are the same types of graphs. Instead of **✗**s, dot plots use filled-in circles, or dots.

Problem **1.2**

Ⓐ The students in the U.S. class start making a dot plot to show the distribution of the Japanese name-length data. They record the data values for the first 12 names in the list on the dot plot below.

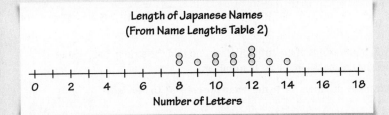

Length of Japanese Names
(From Name Lengths Table 2)

Number of Letters

1. On a copy of the dot plot, insert the data for the last eight names (Haruto Nakamura to Yusuke Yoshida).

2. Look at the shape of the distribution.

   a. Are there *clusters* of data? Explain your reasoning.

   b. Are there gaps in the distribution? Explain.

Ⓑ 1. What is the *mode* of this distribution?

2. Is the mode a good description of the typical name length of the Japanese students? Why or why not?

Ⓒ 1. What is the *range* of the data?

2. Use the range of each data set to compare the lengths of U.S., Chinese, and Japanese names.

ⒶⒸⒺ Homework starts on page 19.

Investigation 1 **What's in a Name? Organizing, Representing, and Describing Data** 15

Notes _____

_____

_____

1.3 Describing Name Lengths
What Is the Median?

Another way to describe what is typical is to mark the midpoint, or the **median**, of a data set. To identify the median, begin by making an *ordered list* of the data values.

Use a strip of 20 squares from a sheet of grid paper to organize the Japanese pen-pal data from Problem 1.2. Write the name lengths in order from least to greatest on the grid paper, as shown below.

7	8	8	9	10	10	10	10	11	11	12	12	12	12	12	13	13	13	14	14

- If you put the ends of the strip together and fold the strip in half, where does the crease fall in the list of numbers?

- How many numbers are to the left of the crease? To the right?

The median is always located at the "half-way" point in a set of ordered data. Since there are 20 data values, the *position* of the median is at the crease that falls between the 10th and 11th data values. The *value* of the median is determined using the actual values of the 10th and 11th data values.

- What is the median of the data set?

A **summary statistic** is one number calculated from all the data values in a distribution. It summarizes something important about the distribution. The median is a summary statistic. The range and the mode are also summary statistics.

- What can you say about the lengths of the Japanese students' names when you know the median?

Notes _____

_____

_____

Problem 1.3

A The sticky notes below display the name-length data for the Japanese students. The red line shows the *position* of the median, the midpoint of the 20 observations. The *value* of the median is $11\frac{1}{2}$ letters, determined by the 10th and 11th data values of "11" and "12" letters.

$11\frac{1}{2}$

| 7 | 8 | 8 | 9 | 10 | 10 | 10 | 10 | 11 | 11 | 12 | 12 | 12 | 12 | 12 | 13 | 13 | 13 | 14 | 14 |

Median

1. The Japanese teacher sent over two more names, Arisa Hasimoto and Yui Inoue. How many observations are there now? What is the *position* of the median? What is the *value* of the median? Explain.

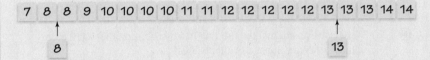

| 7 | 8 | 8 | 9 | 10 | 10 | 10 | 10 | 11 | 11 | 12 | 12 | 12 | 12 | 12 | 13 | 13 | 13 | 14 | 14 |

8   13

2. One more name, Hina Abe, is added. How many observations are there now? What is the *position* of the median? What is the *value* of the median? Explain.

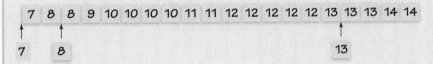

| 7 | 8 | 8 | 9 | 10 | 10 | 10 | 10 | 11 | 11 | 12 | 12 | 12 | 12 | 12 | 13 | 13 | 13 | 14 | 14 |

7   8   13

continued on the next page >

Notes _____

Problem 1.3 *continued*

3. The names Aya Yamaguchi, Ayumi Rin, Eri Matsumoto, Haruka Kimura, Kazu Ohayashi, Kazuki Yamada, and Sayake Saitou are added to the list. There are now 30 names from the Japanese class.

   a. Does the position of the median change from its location in part (2)? Explain.

   b. Does the value of the median change? Explain.

   c. Use the complete set of Japanese names. Half of the data values are *less than or equal to* the value of the median. Half are *greater than or equal to* the value of the median. Explain why.

B Compare the Japanese data to the Chinese and U.S. data from Problem 1.1.

   1. Identify the value of the median and the range for each of the three data sets.

   2. Use these statistics to write at least three statements comparing the three name-length distributions.

C **1.** What is the position of the median in a distribution that has 9 data values? 19 data values? 999 data values?

   2. What is the position of the median in a distribution that has 10 data values? 20 data values? 1,000 data values?

   3. Describe how to locate the position of the median and find the value of the median when

   a. there is an odd number of data values.

   b. there is an even number of data values.

ACE Homework starts on page 19.

Notes _____

_____

_____

Applications

For Exercises 1–4, use the table below.

Name Lengths Table 3

Korean Pen Pals	Number of Letters	Korean Pen Pals	Number of Letters
Kim Ae-Cha	8	Hwang Il	7
Lee Chin-Hae	10	Song Ja	6
Park Chin	8	Ahn Jae-Hwa	9
Choi Chung-Cha	12	You Jung	7
Jung Chung-Hee	12	Hong Kang-Dae	11
Kang Bae	7	Kim Hyo-Sonn	10
Cho Dong-Yul	10	Yi Mai-Chin	9
Yoon Eun-Kyung	12	Pak Mi-Ok	7
Chang Hei-Ran	11	Kim Mun-Hee	9
Lim Hak-Kun	9	Yun Myung	8
Han Hei	6	Sin Myung-Hee	11
Shin Hwan	8	Gwon Myung-Ok	11
Suh Eun-Kyung	11	Hong Sang-Ook	11
Kwon Hyun	8	Jeong Shin	9
Son Hyun-Ae	9	Bak Soo	6

1. Make a frequency table and a dot plot for the Korean class data.

2. What are the shortest and longest Korean names?

3. How would you describe the shape of the distribution of Korean data?

4. Identify a typical name length or name lengths for the Korean class data. Explain your reasoning.

Investigation 1   What's in a Name? Organizing, Representing, and Describing Data   19

Notes

5. Recall the name length tables from Problems 1.1 and 1.2 and the names from Exercises 1–4. Below are four dot plots representing each set of names. There are no titles to show which graph represents which set of data.

a. Write a correct title for each graph, such as *Graph A: Name Lengths From __?__*. Explain your reasoning.

b. Write four statements that compare the name lengths from the different classes.

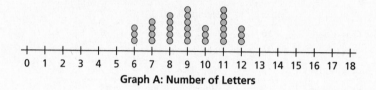
Graph A: Number of Letters

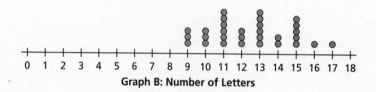
Graph B: Number of Letters

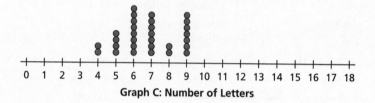
Graph C: Number of Letters

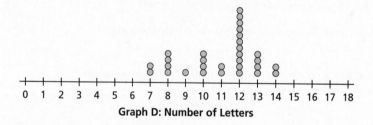
Graph D: Number of Letters

Notes

c. Jasmine says that the graphs show a lot of empty space. She thinks the graphs work better if they look like the dot plots below. How are these graphs different from the dot plots displayed in part (b)? Do you agree with Jasmine? Explain your reasoning.

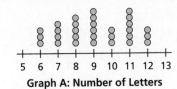

Graph A: Number of Letters

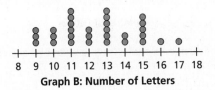

Graph B: Number of Letters

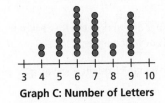

Graph C: Number of Letters

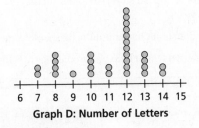

Graph D: Number of Letters

Investigation 1   What's in a Name? Organizing, Representing, and Describing Data   **21**

Notes _____

_____

The U.S. class is also pen pals with a Russian class. For Exercises 6–9, use the bar graph below.

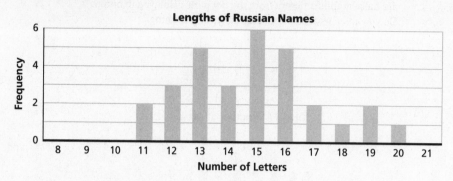

Lengths of Russian Names

6. Which value for name length occurs most frequently? What is this summary statistic called?

7. How many Russian students are in this data set? Explain how you got your answer.

8. What is the range of number of letters in the Russian pen pals' names? Explain how you got your answer.

9. What is the median name length? Explain how you got your answer.

10. Alicia has a pet rat that is 1 year old. She wonders if her rat is old compared to other rats. At the pet store, she finds out that the median lifespan of a rat is 2.5 years.

   a. What does the median tell Alicia about the lifespan of a rat?

   b. What other information would help her predict her rat's lifespan?

Rat Facts
- Rats are gentle and friendly. They bond with their owners and are fun to play with.
- Rats are noctural. They are most active at night.
- Average Lifespan is 2.5 years.
- Rats may be lactose intolerant; be careful in giving them cheese!
- A rat's front teeth could grow up to 5 or 6 inches each year, but they are worn down by gnawing.

Notes

Make a line plot for a set of data that fits each description.

11. 24 names that vary in length from 8 letters to 20 letters

12. 7 names with a median length of 14 letters

13. 13 names with a range of 9 letters and a median length of 13 letters

14. 16 names with a median length of $14\frac{1}{2}$ letters and that vary in length from 11 letters to 20 letters

Connections

15. Below is a bar graph that shows the number and type of pet owned by a class of middle-school students.

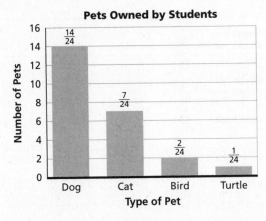

Pets Owned by Students

a. The fraction $\frac{14}{24}$ shows the *relative frequency* of pet dogs. What does the numerator tell you? What does the denominator tell you?

b. Can you use the fractions on the bars to determine the number of students surveyed? Explain why or why not.

Notes

16. Each grid is numbered 1 to 100. Find the rule that describes the
    white numbers.

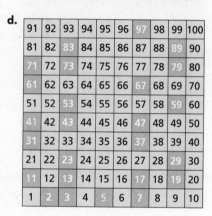

a.

91	92	93	94	95	96	97	98	99	100
81	82	83	84	85	86	87	88	89	90
71	72	73	74	75	76	77	78	79	80
61	62	63	64	65	66	67	68	69	70
51	52	53	54	55	56	57	58	59	60
41	42	43	44	45	46	47	48	49	50
31	32	33	34	35	36	37	38	39	40
21	22	23	24	25	26	27	28	29	30
11	12	13	14	15	16	17	18	19	20
1	2	3	4	5	6	7	8	9	10

b.

91	92	93	94	95	96	97	98	99	100
81	82	83	84	85	86	87	88	89	90
71	72	73	74	75	76	77	78	79	80
61	62	63	64	65	66	67	68	69	70
51	52	53	54	55	56	57	58	59	60
41	42	43	44	45	46	47	48	49	50
31	32	33	34	35	36	37	38	39	40
21	22	23	24	25	26	27	28	29	30
11	12	13	14	15	16	17	18	19	20
1	2	3	4	5	6	7	8	9	10

c.

91	92	93	94	95	96	97	98	99	100
81	82	83	84	85	86	87	88	89	90
71	72	73	74	75	76	77	78	79	80
61	62	63	64	65	66	67	68	69	70
51	52	53	54	55	56	57	58	59	60
41	42	43	44	45	46	47	48	49	50
31	32	33	34	35	36	37	38	39	40
21	22	23	24	25	26	27	28	29	30
11	12	13	14	15	16	17	18	19	20
1	2	3	4	5	6	7	8	9	10

d.

91	92	93	94	95	96	97	98	99	100
81	82	83	84	85	86	87	88	89	90
71	72	73	74	75	76	77	78	79	80
61	62	63	64	65	66	67	68	69	70
51	52	53	54	55	56	57	58	59	60
41	42	43	44	45	46	47	48	49	50
31	32	33	34	35	36	37	38	39	40
21	22	23	24	25	26	27	28	29	30
11	12	13	14	15	16	17	18	19	20
1	2	3	4	5	6	7	8	9	10

Notes

17. Make a coordinate grid like the one below. Along the *x*-axis, write the numbers 1 to 30. Do the same for the *y*-axis. For each number on the *x*-axis, plot its factors above it.

The graph below gives part of the answer, showing the factors for numbers 1 through 6.

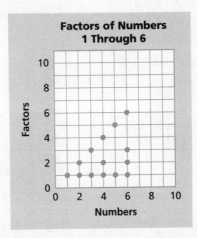

Factors of Numbers 1 Through 6

a. Which numbers have only two factors? What is common about the factors they have?

b. What numbers are even numbers? How can you use their factors to help you answer this question?

c. Make observations about the factors of a number.

   i. What is the greatest factor of any number?

   ii. What is the least factor of any number?

   iii. What is the second-greatest factor of any number? How do these factors relate to the greatest factor of any number?

   iv. Make your own observations about the factors of a number.

Notes _____

_____

_____

18. Each graph in parts (a)–(c) is misleading. For each, answer the following:

- What information is the graph seeking to provide?

- What is wrong with how the information is displayed?

a.

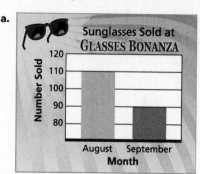

b.

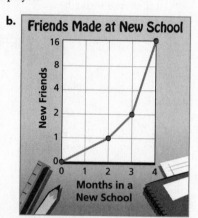

c.

Notes

19. The graph below shows the heights of two brothers, Trevor and Trey, over time.

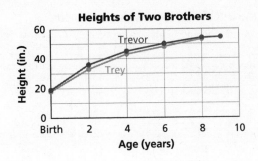

Heights of Two Brothers

a. Write two statements about Trevor's height using the data displayed on the graph.

b. Write two statements about Trey's height using the data displayed on the graph.

c. Write two statements comparing the brothers' heights using the data.

d. Suzanne wrote the statement below. Do you agree with her reasoning? Explain.

> Suzanne:
>
> I know that Trevor is taller than Trey because the line showing his height is above the line showing Trey's height. I also know that Trevor is growing faster than his brother Trey.

Notes

_____

_____

_____

20. The table below shows data collected about some gerbil babies and their growth over time.

Growth in Mass (grams) of Six Gerbils

Name	Age in Days					
	11	13	18	20	25	27
Fuzz Ball	10	11	11	13	16	19
Scooter	12	14	19	28	31	36
Sleepy	11	13	13	22	34	38
Racer	12	13	18	22	32	35
Cuddles	10	12	13	17	25	27
Curious	11	12	12	15	19	22

a. Make a graph showing a line for each gerbil's mass on the same coordinate grid. Think carefully about how you label and scale the y-axis (mass) and the x-axis (age in days). Label each line to indicate which gerbil it represents.

b. Write four statements comparing the growth rates of the six gerbils.

c. Suppose someone asks, "About how much do gerbils grow in the first month after they are born?" How would you answer? Explain.

Notes

For Exercises 21–23, use the bar graphs below. The graphs show
information about a class of middle-school students.

Graph A

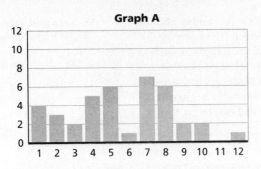

Graph B

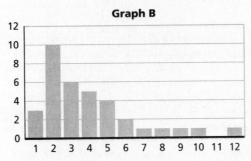

Graph C

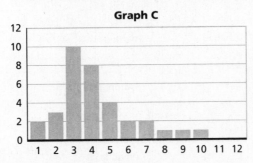

21. Which graph might show the number of children in the students'
families? Explain.

22. Which graph might show the birth months of the students? Explain.

Note: Months are often written using numbers instead of names. For
example, 1 means January, 2 means February, etc.

23. Which graph might show the number of toppings students like on
their pizzas? Explain.

Investigation 1   What's in a Name? Organizing, Representing, and Describing Data   29

Extensions

A greeting card store sells stickers and street signs with first names on them. The store ordered 12 stickers and 12 street signs for each name. The table and the four bar graphs that follow show the numbers of stickers and street signs remaining for the names that begin with the letter A. Use the table and graphs for Exercises 24–30.

24. Use Graph A. How many Alex stickers are left? How many Alex stickers have been sold? Explain.

25. Use Graph B. How many Alex street signs are left? How many Alex street signs have been sold? Explain.

Stickers and Street Signs Remaining

Name	Stickers	Street Signs
Aaron	1	9
Adam	2	7
Alex	7	4
Allison	2	3
Amanda	0	11
Amber	2	3
Amy	3	3
Andrea	2	4
Andrew	8	6
Andy	3	5
Angel	8	4
Ava	10	7

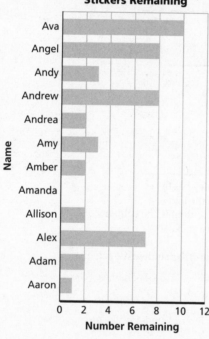

Graph A: Stickers Remaining

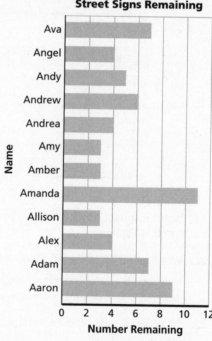

Graph B: Street Signs Remaining

Notes _____

_____

_____

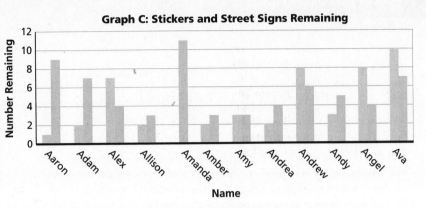

Graph C: Stickers and Street Signs Remaining

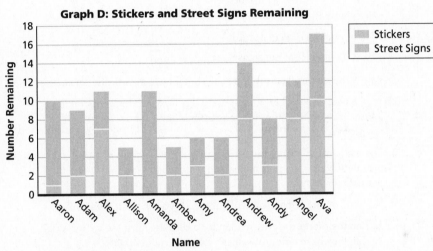

Graph D: Stickers and Street Signs Remaining

26. For names beginning with A, which are more popular, the stickers or the street signs? Explain your answer.

27. If each sticker costs $1.50, how much money has the store collected from selling name stickers that begin with the letter A?

28. For which name has the store sold the most stickers? The least?

29. Graph C is a *double bar graph*. Use this graph to determine the name(s) for which the number of street signs sold and the number of sticker packages sold are the same.

30. Graph D is a *stacked bar graph*. Use this graph to determine whether some names are more popular than others. Justify your answer.

Notes _____

_____

_____

Mathematical Reflections 1

In this Investigation, you learned some ways to organize, represent, and describe a set of data. The following questions will help you summarize what you have learned.

Think about these questions. Discuss your ideas with other students and your teacher. Then write a summary of your findings in your notebook.

1. The process of carrying out a statistical investigation involves asking a question, gathering and analyzing data, and interpreting the results to answer the question. Choose a data set from this Investigation. Use the data set to answer each question below.

   • **What** was the question asked?

   • **How** were the data collected?

   • **How** were the data analyzed and represented?

   • **How** did the results from the analysis help you answer the question?

2. You can represent a set of data using displays such as a data table, a frequency table, and a dot or line plot. **Explain** how these displays are related.

3. The median and mode are two measures of the center of a data distribution. The range is a measure of variability, or how spread out the data are.

   a. **What** does each measure of center tell you about a data set?

   b. Can the mode and the median for a data set have the same value? Can they have different values? **Explain** your answers.

   c. **How** does the range tell you how much the data vary?

   d. Suppose we add a new data value to a set of data. Does this new value affect the mode? The median? The range? **Explain**.

4. **What** strategies can you use to make comparisons among data sets?

Unit Project

....

Think about the survey you will be developing.

 How might you collect and display the data you gather?

Notes _____

_____

_____

Common Core Mathematical Practices

As you worked on the Problems in this Investigation, you used prior knowledge to make sense of them. You also applied Mathematical Practices to solve the Problems. Think back over your work, the ways you thought about the Problems, and how you used Mathematical Practices.

Nick described his thoughts in the following way:

> In Problem 1.1, we used tables and dot plots to show the different sets of data about name lengths. We talked about why we would call each of these data sets a "distribution."
>
> Seeing how the data were distributed across the name lengths, and then noticing things like clusters, gaps, and shape in general, gave us an idea about typical name lengths for each group of students.
>
> When we used the graphs, we made sure to have the same scale on each graph. That made it easier to compare the name lengths of the students from the different countries.
>
> ....
>
> **Common Core Standards for Mathematical Practice**
> **MP4** Model with mathematics

 • What other Mathematical Practices can you identify in Nick's reasoning?

• Describe a Mathematical Practice that you and your classmates used to solve a different Problem in this Investigation.

Notes

Who's in Your Household?
Using the Mean

▼ Investigation Overview

Investigation Description

This Investigation focuses on developing the concept of *mean*. The average number of people in students' households provides the setting. The notion of "evening out" the distribution at a point (the mean) located on the horizontal axis is modeled by using cubes, ordered-value bar graphs, and line plots. The models support development of an algorithm for finding the mean: adding up all of the numbers and dividing by the total number of numbers. Students distinguish between categorical data and numerical data. They also make connections between data types and choice of measures of center and variability (or spread).

Investigation Vocabulary

- categorical data
- mean
- numerical data
- ordered-value bar graph
- skewed distribution
- symmetric distribution

Mathematics Background

- The Process of Statistical Investigation
- Components of Statistical Investigation
- Posing Questions
- Collecting Data
- Analyzing Individual Cases vs. Overall Distributions
- Choosing Representations for Distributions
- Guiding Students to Construct and Read Graphs
- Shapes of Distributions
- Describing Data With Measures of Center
- Choosing an Appropriate Summary Statistic
- Interpreting Results

Planning Chart

Content	ACE	Pacing	Materials	Resources
Problem 2.1	1–3, 17–19	1 day	**Labsheet 2.1** Household Size 1 • Blank Grid and Number Line • Half-Inch Grid Paper 2-cm colored wooden cubes	**Teaching Aid 2.1A** Distribution of Household Size Table 1 **Teaching Aid 2.1B** Mean Distribution of Household Size 1
Problem 2.2	4–7, 20–25, 33–34	1½ days	**Labsheet 2ACE:** Exercises 4–7 (accessibility) • Half-Inch Grid Paper • Blank Grid and Number Line 2-cm colored wooden cubes (optional)	**Teaching Aid 2.2** Mean Distributions of Household Sizes
Problem 2.3	8–9, 26–27	1 day	**Labsheet 2.3A** Skateboard Prices **Labsheet 2.3B** Dot Plots of Skateboard Prices **Labsheet 2ACE:** Exercise 27 (accessibility) calculators	**Teaching Aid 2.3** Symmetric and Skewed Distributions • Data and Graphs
Problem 2.4	10–16, 28–32, 35–37	1 day		• Data and Graphs
Mathematical Reflections		½ day		
Assessment: Partner Quiz		½ day		• Partner Quiz

▼ Goals and Standards

Goals

Statistical Process Understand and use the process of statistical investigation

- Ask questions, collect and analyze data, and interpret data to answer questions

- Describe data with respect to its shape, center, and variability or spread

- Construct and use simple surveys as a method of collecting data

Attributes of Data Distinguish data and data types

- Recognize that data consist of counts or measurements of a variable, or an attribute; these observations comprise a distribution of data values

- Distinguish between categorical data and numerical data, and identify which graphs and statistics can be used to represent each kind of data

Multiple Representations for Displaying Data Display data with multiple representations

- Organize and represent data using tables, dot plots, line plots, ordered-value bar graphs, frequency bar graphs, histograms, and box-and-whisker plots

- Make informed decisions about which graphs or tables can be used to display a particular set of data

- Recognize that a graph shows the overall shape of a distribution, whether the data values are symmetrical around a central value, and whether the graph contains any unusual characteristics such as gaps, clusters, or outliers

Measures of Central Tendency and Variability Recognize that a single number may be used to characterize the center of a distribution of data and the degree of variability (or spread)

- Distinguish between and compute measures of central tendency (mean, median, and mode) and measures of spread (range, interquartile range (IQR), and mean absolute deviation (MAD))

- Identify how the median and mean respond to changes in the data values of a distribution

- Relate the choice of measures of central tendency and variability to the shape of the distribution and the context

- Describe the amount of variability in a distribution by noting whether the data values cluster in one or more areas or are fairly spread out

- Use measures of center and spread to compare data distributions

Mathematical Reflections

Look for evidence of student understanding of the goals for this Investigation in their responses to the questions in *Mathematical Reflections*. The goals addressed by each question are indicated below.

1. Describe a method for calculating the mean of a set of data. Explain why your method works.

Goals

- Ask questions, collect and analyze data, and interpret data to answer questions
- Describe data with respect to its shape, center, and variability or spread
- Distinguish between and compute measures of central tendency (mean, median, and mode) and measures of spread (range, interquartile range (IQR), and mean absolute deviation (MAD))

2. You have used three measures of center—mode, median, and mean—to describe distributions.

   a. Why do you suppose they are called "measures of center"?

   b. What does each tell you about a set of data?

   c. How do you decide which measure of center to use when describing a distribution?

   d. Why might you want to include both the range and a measure of center when reporting a statistical summary?

Goals

- Ask questions, collect and analyze data, and interpret data to answer questions
- Describe data with respect to its shape, center, and variability or spread
- Recognize that a graph shows the overall shape of a distribution, whether the data values are symmetrical around a central value, and whether the graph contains any unusual characteristics such as gaps, clusters, or outliers
- Relate the choice of measures of central tendency and variability to the shape of the distribution and the context
- Distinguish between and compute measures of central tendency (mean, median, and mode) and measures of spread (range, interquartile range (IQR), and mean absolute deviation (MAD))
- Identify how the median and mean respond to changes in the data values of a distribution

3. **a.** One student says you can only use the mode to describe categorical data, but you can use the mode, median, and mean to describe numerical data. Is the student correct? Explain.

   b. Can you find the range for categorical data? Explain.

Goals

- Ask questions, collect and analyze data, and interpret data to answer questions

- Describe data with respect to its shape, center, and variability or spread

- Distinguish between categorical data and numerical data, and identify which graphs and statistics can be used to represent each kind of data

Standards

Common Core Content Standards

6.SP.A.1 Recognize a statistical question as one that anticipates variability in the data related to the question and accounts for it in the answers. *Problems 1, 2, 3, and 4*

6.SP.A.2 Understand that a set of data collected to answer a statistical question has a distribution, which can be described by its center, spread, and overall shape. *Problems 1, 2, and 3*

6.SP.A.3 Recognize that a measure of center for a numerical data set summarizes all of its values with a single number, while a measure of variation describes how its values vary with a single number. *Problems 1, 2, 3, and 4*

6.SP.B.4 Display numerical data in plots on a number line, including dot plots, histograms, and box plots. *Problems 1, 2, and 3*

6.SP.B.5a Summarize numerical data sets in relation to their context, such as by reporting the number of observations. *Problems 2 and 4*

6.SP.B.5b Summarize numerical data sets in relation to their context, such as by describing the nature of the attribute under investigation, including how it was measured and its units of measurement. *Problems 1 and 4*

6.SP.B.5c Summarize numerical data sets in relation to their context, such as by giving quantitative measures of center (median and/or mean) and variability (interquartile range and/or mean absolute deviation), as well as describing any overall pattern and any striking deviations from the overall pattern with reference to the context in which the data were gathered. *Problems 1, 2, 3, and 4*

6.SP.B.5d Summarize numerical data sets in relation to their context, such as by relating the choice of measures of center and variability to the shape of the data distribution and the context in which the data were gathered. *Problems 2, 3, and 4*

6.NS.C.6 Understand a rational number as a point on the number line. Extend number line diagrams and coordinate axes familiar from previous grades to represent points on the line and in the plane with negative number coordinates. *Problems 2 and 3*

6.NS.C.7 Understand ordering and absolute value of rational numbers. *Problems 1, 2, and 3*

Facilitating the Mathematical Practices

Students in *Connected Mathematics* classrooms display evidence of multiple Common Core Standards for Mathematical Practice every day. Here are just a few examples of when you might observe students demonstrating the Standards for Mathematical Practice during this Investigation.

Practice 1: Make sense of problems and persevere in solving them.

Students are engaged every day in solving problems and, over time, learn to persevere in solving them. To be effective, the problems embody critical concepts and skills and have the potential to engage students in making sense of mathematics. Students build understanding by reflecting, connecting, and communicating. These student-centered problem situations engage students in articulating the "knowns" in a problem situation and determining a logical solution pathway. The student-student and student-teacher dialogues help students not only to make sense of the problems, but also to persevere in finding appropriate strategies to solve them. The suggested questions in the Teacher Guides provide the metacognitive scaffolding to help students monitor and refine their problem-solving strategies.

Practice 3: Construct viable arguments and critique the reasoning of others.

In Investigation 2, students work to identify an algorithm for finding the mean of a set of data. They connect this to different models to explain why their algorithm works. They also compare different data sets with the same mean. They must find a way to explain how these data sets can have the same mean.

Practice 8: Look for and express regularity in repeated reasoning.

In Investigation 2, students learn how to find the mean of a set of data using models such as ordered-value bar graphs and dot plots. They find means of many different sets of data. They use the patterns they notice in Problems 2.1 and 2.2 to identify an algorithm for finding the mean of a set of data at the end of Problem 2.2.

Students identify and record their personal experiences with the Standards for Mathematical Practice during the Mathematical Reflections at the end of the Investigation.

What's a Mean Household Size?

▼ Problem Overview

> *Focus Question* How do you go about finding a number that is a good estimate of typical household size based on the given data?

Problem Description

Students explore different ways to describe the average number of people in six households. The mean is introduced through a visual model using cubes. This model is connected to representing data using horizontal ordered-value bar graphs and dot plots.

Problem Implementation

Have students work in pairs on this Problem. Students can make notes on copies of **Labsheet 2.1: Household Size 1**, which includes images from Question A of the Student Edition.

Note: If you have time, you may want to gather data about students' household sizes from your class. This can be done after Problem 2.1. You can use this framework:

- Using the definition from the United States Census, how many people are in your household?

- Collect household size data from everyone in your class.

- Display the distribution of data in some way.

- What is the mean number of people in your class's households? Describe how you found your answer.

Materials

- **Labsheet 2.1:** Household Size 1
- **Blank Grid and Number Line**
- **Half-Inch Grid Paper**
- **Teaching Aid 2.1A:** Distribution of Household Size Table 1
- **Teaching Aid 2.1B:** Mean Distribution of Household Size 1

2-cm colored wooden cubes

Vocabulary

- mean
- ordered-value bar graph

Mathematics Background

- The Process of Statistical Investigation
- Components of Statistical Investigation
- Posing Questions
- Collecting Data
- Analyzing Individual Cases vs. Overall Distributions
- Choosing Representations for Distributions
- Guiding Students to Construct and Read Graphs
- Shapes of Distributions
- Describing Data With Measures of Center
- Interpreting Results

At a Glance and Lesson Plan

- At a Glance: Problem 2.1 Data About Us
- Lesson Plan: Problem 2.1 Data About Us

▼ Launch

Launch Video

This Launch animation illustrates the context of Problem 2.1. In it, dots representing people move around a neighborhood. They end up in their own homes, with each household containing different numbers of people. Students are asked how many people are in the typical household on the street. Show this animation to your students to help them understand the context of the Problem. You can show this animation during the Presenting the Challenge section after discussing the U.S. Census. Visit Teacher Place at mathdashboard.com/cmp3 to see the complete video.

Connecting to Prior Knowledge

Measures of center (mode, median, and mean) help describe data distributions. Choosing which one to report depends on what story you want to tell about the data. This Problem introduces the mean. Later in the Investigation, students will consider how the mode, median, and mean are related, which requires students to be able to compute and use the mode and the median.

Presenting the Challenge

The U.S. Census is a survey that seeks to count the number of people living in the United States and to describe key characteristics about them, such as household size. The people who planned the survey must define household size so that everyone collecting data counts in the same way. Students use the definition for *household* provided by the U.S. Census throughout Investigation 2.

Suggested Questions

- Does anyone know the purpose of the United States Census? (Historically, the purpose of the Census is to count the number of people living in the United States. One reason why this is done is to compute the number of representatives each state will have in the U.S. House of Representatives.)

The Census Bureau has developed a definition of who to count. The Census focuses on counting the people who live in households rather than asking questions like "How many people are in your family?"

The word *household* refers to all the people who live in a *housing unit*, which may be a house, an apartment, some other group of rooms, or a single room, like a room in a boarding house.

- Why do you think the Census asks "How many people are in your household?" instead of "How many people are in your family?" (By defining the word *household* as it does, the Census seeks to eliminate confusion about who to count. Only the people who live in a location and use it as their permanent address at the time the Census is taken are counted as members of that household. When you try to define the word *family*, you might encounter questions about who to count: "What if I have an older sister who doesn't live with us now?", "Can I count my grandmother?", or "How do I count my stepsister and stepbrother?". Following the definition for *household* helps Census takers to report population data accurately.)

You may want to show the Launch Video at this time. Then, have your students consider the six particular households in Problem 2.1.

Have your students construct the physical model, in small groups, by building a tower of cubes for each student's household. *Each tower should be a single color and different from the colors of the other towers.* This way, you can refer to "Ollie the orange tower," "Ruth the red tower," or "Brenda the blue tower."

Have the groups arrange their cube towers in order from smallest to largest.

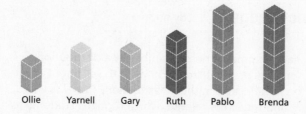

Ollie   Yarnell   Gary   Ruth   Pablo   Brenda

Ask the questions in the introduction to Problem 2.1:

- What is the attribute being investigated? (the number of people in each student's household)

- How can you use the cube stacks to find the *median* of these data ? (Order the cubes from shortest to tallest: 2, 3, 3, 4, 6, 6. The median household size is 3.5 people (the value of the halfway point between the two middle stacks of cubes).)

- How can you use the cube stacks to find the *mode* of these data ? (There are two stacks with a height of 3 and two with a height of 6. These are the modes.)

- How much do the household sizes vary? (The household sizes vary from 2 to 6, a range of 4 people.)

Now turn to the focus on the new concept: *mean*. Ask the students:

- How can you determine the average number of people in a household for these six households? (If students suggest finding the mean by adding up all the numbers and dividing by 6, say that the class will come back to that idea shortly.)

Tell students that they are going to work with another way of finding the mean, or average, of a set of numbers. They will use a method that helps them understand what is meant by the *mean*.

These students decided to find the average by "evening out" the number of cubes in each tower. Try this on your own.

After students have had a few minutes to work with their towers, have a class discussion about what they found. The towers are "evened out" by moving cubes from taller towers to shorter towers. Since each tower was originally a single color, students will be able to see from which towers the "moved data" came.

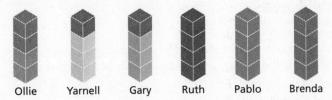

Ollie   Yarnell   Gary   Ruth   Pablo   Brenda

You can say that each household has an average of four people. Another way to say this is that there are, on average, four people per household. Some of the households (Pablo's and Brenda's) actually have more than four people; their extra cubes have been moved to households with fewer than four people (Ollie's, Yarnell's, and Gary's). One household (Ruth's) already had four people, so none of her cubes were moved.

- We call this "evened out" number the mean. How does the mean compare to the median for this set of data? (The mean is 4 and the median is $3\frac{1}{2}$. The two numbers are close in value.)

Note: Using the terminology of "4 people per household" is a way to help students realize that the mean can be used to describe the number of people in each household if each of the six households had the same number of people. They have dealt informally with "per quantities" before in many sharing situations.

You might want to ask about the mean and about other ways to represent the data.

- You found that the mean is 4 by evening out the cube towers. How does this measure of center represent what is *typical* about the number of people in the six households? (Students might say that some households have fewer people and some have more. Four is the number of people that each household would have if every household had the same (typical) number of members.)

- How else might we have represented these data? (Students might say by using a table, a line plot, or a bar graph.)

Tell students that they are going to see a new representation called an *ordered-value bar graph*. This representation lets them show the data as values, as they did using the cube stacks.

You might want to do Problem 2.1, Question A, part (1), as a whole class to ensure that students understand how the ordered-value bar graph relates to the cube stacks and to the dot plot. For Question A, part (2), you can transition to pairs of students working independently to finish the "evening out" activity. You may want to hand out copies of the **Blank Grid and Number Line** or use the **Half-Inch Grid Paper** so that students can make and even out ordered-value bar graphs. When labeling the scales, make sure the numbers on the horizontal axis of the ordered-value bar graph align with those on the horizontal axis of the line/dot plot.

▼ Explore

Providing for Individual Needs

After students understand the cube representation and have discussed the strategy of "evening out," introduce the ordered-value bar graph and the dot plot representations.

You can use **Teaching Aid 2.1A: Distribution of Household Size Table 1** to help students make sense of Question A, part (1).

Suggested Questions

- You made cube stacks and evened, or leveled, them out. What do you call the height of the stacks when they are evened out? (the mean)

- If you make an ordered-value bar graph with horizontal bars on graph paper, how does this graph relate to the cube stacks? (It looks like the cube stacks sideways, displayed horizontally rather than vertically.)

- How might you use the ordered-value bar graph to even out the data values? (You can move individual household members from one bar to another, until the bars are evened out. You would end up with 6 bars, each 4 people in length.)

- How are the ordered-value bar graph and the dot plot related? (The two longest bars represent households of 6 people each. Vertically, below the ends of the bars, you can see "6" on the axis of the graph. On the dot plot, you can see two dots at "6" on the dot plot axis, representing the same two households of 6 people each. You can make these comparisons for each data value.)

- Once you know the mean based on using cube stacks or the ordered-value bar graph, how do you locate the mean on the dot plot? (After the cube stacks or the bars are evened out, you can say you have 6 households with 4 people per household. In the Student Edition, the mean is identified by a blue triangle on the dot plot. On the ordered-value bar graph, you could draw a vertical line at 4 to show the mean.)

- The dot plot keeps the original data about the 6 households. How does the location of the mean on the dot pot relate to the location of the individual dots? (Students might say some dots are to the right (greater than the mean) and some dots are to the left (less than the mean). All the dots on the dot plot would be located at the mean if they were balanced out; that is, they would be stacked above the "4" on the axis. You can show students this different version of the dot plot and ask how it relates to the ordered-value bar graph when the values are evened out by displaying **Teaching Aid 2.1B: Mean Distribution of Household Size 1**. You do not need to push beyond this beginning understanding, however, at this point.)

Note: The small sets of data in this Problem are designed so that the mean will be a whole number. The cubes will all be the same height to indicate the mean. When you use larger and often messier data sets, the mean may be a decimal or a fraction. When this happens, the cube stacks or value bars will be two different heights—one of the tower heights for the data will be greater than the mean, and one of the tower heights for the data will be less than the mean. This will indicate that the mean is not a whole-number value; students can explore how to interpret this when it happens.

- In Question A, part (3), you were asked to think about how you might have predicted that the mean would be 4. Do you have any ideas? (Many students will hold on to the "evening out" idea because it makes sense. They will not be ready to predict yet. Some students might want to reintroduce the "add up and divide" algorithm at this time. If this happens, have them connect these operations to the manipulation of the cubes or bars.)

- You said to add up the numbers and divide by 6. How does adding up and dividing relate to the cube stacks? (There are 24 cubes in all or 24 people in all 6 households.)

- So, how does dividing come into the process? (When you share the cubes, or people, among the stacks, or households, you have to divide the 24 cubes into 6 households.)

- For the two tables, the means are the same but the ranges are different. How is this possible? (There is a smaller minimum value in one data set and the same maximum value, so the ranges are different. When you find the mean by sharing cubes, the smaller minimum value is at the same level as the other cube towers or value bars. You can have different data values and still even out the cube towers to have the same mean.)

Planning for the Summary

What evidence will you use in the summary to clarify and deepen understanding of the Focus Question?

What will you do if you do not have evidence?

▼ Summarize

Orchestrating the Discussion

Ask students how the cube model, the ordered-value bar graph model, and the dot plot/line plot are related.

- How does each model show the data before any evening out is done? (Each has the data values for each student marked in some way.)

- How does each model show the data after the evening-out process is completed? (The cube towers will all be the same height, the value bars will all be the same length, and the dots/X's will all be above 4 on the axis.)

- Does knowing the mean help you answer the question "What is a typical household size?" (Students might say that the mean is in the middle of the data set. They might say some households have more members and some fewer, but no household is far from the mean number of members. Some will say that the median is not a whole number, so they prefer the mean. If this happens, you might ask why the mean is a whole number in this Problem. Some might say they prefer the mode or a range of values, or some might say that they don't like any of these ways of identifying what is a typical household size. Any of these responses is valid. This is the beginning of the discussion about choosing an appropriate measure of center by relating the choice to the shape of the distribution and the context.)

Reflecting on Student Learning

Use the following questions to assess student understanding at the end of the lesson.

- What evidence do I have that students understand the Focus Question?
  - Where did my students get stuck?
  - What strategies did they use?
  - What breakthroughs did my students have today?
- How will I use this to plan for tomorrow? For the next time I teach this lesson?
- Where will I have the opportunity to reinforce these ideas as I continue through this Unit? The next Unit?

ACE Assignment Guide

- **Applications:** 1–3
- **Connections:** 17–19

Comparing Distributions With the Same Mean

▼ Problem Overview

Focus Question How do you interpret, compute, and use the mean?

Problem Description

Students connect ideas from Problem 2.1 and explore the essential understanding that different sets of data may have the same means. They justify the fact that that data sets have specific means using two methods. In one method, students represent the data values with a horizontal ordered-value bar graph and even out data values. Students also use the more standard method of adding up the data values and dividing by the number of data values. Students continue to use line and dot plots interchangeably.

Problem Implementation

Have students work in pairs on this Problem.

Materials

- **Labsheet 2ACE:** Exercises 4–7 (accessibility)
- **Blank Grid and Number Line**
- **Half-Inch Grid Paper**
- **Teaching Aid 2.2:** Mean Distributions of Household Sizes

2-cm colored wooden cubes (optional)

Vocabulary

There are no new glossary terms introduced in this Problem.

Mathematics Background

- The Process of Statistical Investigation
- Components of Statistical Investigation
- Posing Questions
- Collecting Data
- Analyzing Individual Cases vs. Overall Distributions
- Choosing Representations for Distributions
- Guiding Students to Construct and Read Graphs
- Shapes of Distributions
- Describing Data With Measures of Center
- Interpreting Results

At a Glance and Lesson Plan

- At a Glance: Problem 2.2 Data About Us
- Lesson Plan: Problem 2.2 Data About Us

● ▼ Launch

Connecting to Prior Knowledge

The introduction to the Problem and the Launch are intended to connect to the representations and data sets from Problem 2.1.

Refer students to the image of the rulers shown. The rulers represent a "balance" model.

Note: The image of the rulers is meant to be purely a visual. This is not provided to suggest that you replicate this experiment in your class. Because rulers have their own weights, which would affect the balance, any replication of this experiment would most likely not give accurate results.

Suggested Questions

- Study the picture of the rulers. What do you notice? What is meant by a *balance point*? (This is a complex idea, so it is enough just to get opinions on the question at this point. Students might say that the data values/coins are spread on either side of the balance point, or fulcrum. One ruler shows the distribution in balance and the other shows it out of balance.)

- When the distribution is "in balance," what do you notice about the location of the mean? (It is at the fulcrum.)

- Why does the green ruler tip to the left? (Students might say there are more coins on the left. You can point out that there are more data values on the left for the other ruler as well, yet it does not tip to the left. If a student mentions the distance from the coins to the fulcrum, you might continue to probe this idea. If not, then leave this as a puzzle at this point; the ideas of skew and distance from the mean come out of the Problems in this Investigation.)

Discuss the situations about household sizes from Problem 2.1.

- Look at the two different distributions. How are these distributions alike? How are they different? (Possible answer: They have the same mean. The data in Distribution 1 have a greater range.)

- How many households are there in each situation? (six)

- How many total people are there in each situation? (twenty-four)

- How can the means be the same when data values are different? (Students might say that there are the same number of people and households in each set of data; the individual households in each set are just different sizes. When you even out the household sizes, in both cases you have 6 households with 4 members per household.)

Presenting the Challenge

Propose the idea of having additional data sets with the same mean.

Suggested Questions

- Do you think it is possible to have other sets of data with six households and a mean of 4 people that are different from the households in Problem 2.1? (Some students will think this is possible. Some may not agree. Some may not know. Challenge students to work with you to make a new distribution with six households and a mean of 4 people.)

Continue with the Introduction to the challenge.

The data set must have a total of six households. Suppose that the first household has three people. I can show these three people by making a three-cube tower.

Make a tower of three cubes of the same color.

- How many more towers do I need to make to show the remaining households? (five)

Now, suppose another household has eight people. I'll make a tower of eight cubes to represent that household.

Using a different color, make a tower of eight cubes.

- How many people are represented with just these two towers? (eleven)

- What do you think I should do next?

Some students may see that the goal is to have a total of 24 people in the 6 households and that, since 11 people have been accounted for, the remaining 4 households must have 13 people altogether. As you construct each new tower, students will need to count how many more of the 24 people have been accounted for. Be patient with this discussion. Once you have a set of six towers, you can make an ordered-value bar graph and a dot plot. Use the ordered-value bar graph to check for a mean of 4 by evening out the value bars. If the mean is not 4, discuss with students what you need to do to the data set so that the mean will be 4.

Do not work for mastery at this point; have students think about the relationships they need to consider.

Have students begin Problem 2.2.

▼ Explore

Providing for Individual Needs

For Question A, if students are having problems finding a data set with a mean of 4 people per household, encourage them to explore through trial and error.

Suggested Questions

- Let's start with any household size for one household. What would you like to start with? (If a student suggests a large number, such as 12, you might ask, "How many people does this leave for the other 5 households?" Students can make smaller household sizes for the other five households if this is what they want to do. You might make the stack of cubes for the first household (either the 12 proposed or some other number). Then ask, "How many more households do we need? How many people are left for those households?" Continue this line of questioning as you determine all six household sizes.)

If pairs are still having trouble, suggest they work backward, moving from six towers of four cubes to six towers with different numbers of cubes in each but keeping the total number of cubes the same.

- You need to end up with 6 households, each with 4 people. Make cube stacks for this. What do you want to do first to work back to 6 uneven households? (Switch some cubes from one stack to another.)

Be sure that students make an ordered-value bar graph and a line plot to represent their 6 households, as directed in Question A, part (2). They need to connect their work to the other two models/representations.

As you observe the pairs working, do a quick check as you scan their line plots to ensure that the total number of people represented is 24. You may want to keep a class list and note which students have a correct set of data for Question A so that you don't have to check later when students present solutions.

Once students have found a successful strategy for Question A, they can use the same strategy moving forward in Questions B and C.

In Question C, however, students may struggle with the idea of a "half" of a person. Explain to students that the mean of $3\frac{1}{2}$ people does not have to be an actual or possible value in the data set.

- What would be true about the towers of cubes if they were "evened out" to $3\frac{1}{2}$ cubes per tower? (Each household has 3.5 people.)

- How would that look on an ordered-value bar graph? How would that look on the dot plot? (The bars would end at 3.5; the dots would all line up above the 3.5 mark on the scale.)

- You can't really have 3.5 people in a household. Some must have more and some less. How many total people are there in all 6 households? (twenty-one)

- Can you adjust your six dots above the 3.5 mark so that they have "whole" numbers of people but still have a total of 21? (Students might see this as balancing around 3.5; make some households have more and some have fewer.)

Question D pushes on the idea of balance.

- Which representation helped you find the median? (an ordered list)

- Which representation helps you find the mode and range? (either an ordered list or the dot plot)

- Can you estimate the mean just by looking at the dot plot? (Students may not be able to do this, so some will say the mean is 4 people because 4 people is the median and the mode. The dissonance caused by discovering that the mean is *not* 4 people is an important step in understanding what the mean responds to.)

- After evening out cube stacks, you found out the mean is 5 people, not 4 people. Does this surprise you? Why is the mean greater than the median or mode? (This gives your class an opportunity to tie together the add-up-and-divide algorithm and the evening-out process. The larger households of 8 and 10 people have to be included in the evening-out process; they have to be added into the total. There are 40 people to be placed in 5 households; the extra people in the larger households have to be moved to the smaller households, so the mean will be greater. The idea of the dot plot being in balance is a complex one; students can refer to the image in the Problem's introduction in the Student Edition, or you can show them the balances on **Teaching Aid 2.2: Mean Distributions of Household Sizes**. Students will have other opportunities to think about this.)

Question E summarizes the work students did in Problems 2.1 and 2.2. You can expect that most students have moved to considering the total number of people in all the households and the number of households represented. Have students prepare a statement about how to find a mean of a set of data values.

Going Further

1. A set of seven numbers has a mean of 11.

   a. What is the sum of those numbers? (77)

   Students may arrive at this answer by finding an example of a set of seven numbers with a mean of 11. Or, they may realize that one set with a mean of 11 is 11, 11, 11, 11, 11, 11, 11; that is, that any set of seven numbers with a mean of 11 can be "evened out" to make seven data values of 11.

   b. If you replace each of the original numbers with 11, what is the sum? (77)

2. A set of six numbers has a mean of $8\frac{2}{3}$.

   a. What is the sum of those numbers? (52)

   b. Find a set of cube towers to show these data. (You can have four cube towers with nine cubes each and two cube towers with eight cubes each.)

Planning for the Summary

What evidence will you use in the summary to clarify and deepen understanding of the Focus Question?

What will you do if you do not have evidence?

▼ Summarize

Orchestrating the Discussion

In the Summarize, you will want help students understand that:

1. For each of the Questions A–C, there can be different distributions with the same mean.

2. Students can approach Questions A–C, in which they go about making distributions with specific means, in a similar way.

3. Another strategy for finding the mean is to add up all the data values and divide by the number of data values. This algorithm stems from the exploratory work they did so far with cubes, ordered-value bar graphs, and line/dot plots.

Suggested Questions

For Question A, ask the following.

- How many households are represented? (six)

- How many people are there in all the households? (twenty-four)

- What is the mean? (four people)

Once you have determined that the students' distributions are correct, ask the following questions.

- Are any of the distributions identical?

- How many different distributions are shown?

- Is it possible to have different distributions with the same mean? (Answers will depend on students' displays. Yes, it is possible to have different distributions with the same mean.)

Discuss Questions B–D as thoroughly as you do Question A. Have students show their distributions and ask the same questions about the number of households, the total number of people, and the mean as a way to do quick checks for correctness.

You will want to help students synthesize what they know about making distributions with different means. Ask questions that help them focus their observations on identifying common strategies.

- What are some quick ways to come up with different sets of data with six households and a mean of 4 people?

- What are some quick ways to come up with different sets of data with seven households and a mean of 3 people?

- What are some quick ways to make different sets of data with six households and a mean of $3\frac{1}{2}$ people?

Ideally, students will see that if they know the number of households and the mean number of people in the households, they can determine the total number of people in the households. Using this total, they can work backward to identify a data set showing the people distributed among the households.

- How can you use what you know about the total number of people in the households and the number of households to find the mean number of people?

Students have been working with facts about numbers of households and the mean number of people in those households. This question asks them to think about the situation in a slightly different way.

Students have used the number of households and the mean number of people in each household to determine the total number of people.

Known: number of households, mean number of people

Unknown: total number of people

Now, they need to use the number of households and the total number of people to find the mean number of people in each household:

Known: number of households, total number of people

Unknown: mean number of people

Pose an example:

- Suppose there are six households with a total of 36 people. What is the mean number of people in each household? (six people)

- How could you determine the mean without using cubes or an ordered-value bar graph? (Divide the total number of people (36) by the number of households (6).)

Give more examples:

- There are 12 students with a total of 60 people in their households. How could you go about finding the mean number of people in each household? What is the mean number of people in each household? (5 people; Since there are 60 people total, you need to divide the total number of people by the number of households ($60 \div 12 = 5$).)

- Why does your strategy work? (To find the mean, you need to sum all the data values and then divide by the number of data values. In the question above, the data values have already been summed for you.)

Return to the idea of a mean that is not a whole number.

- Why is the mean household size sometimes a fraction and not a whole number? Can you give an example? (The mean is not a whole number when the evening-out, or dividing, process does not result in stacks of cubes of the same size. You can make up an example by starting with a total number of people, say 30, and choosing a number of households that is not a factor of 30, say 8.)

Discuss Question E as a class.

Reflecting on Student Learning

Use the following questions to assess student understanding at the end of the lesson.

- What evidence do I have that students understand the Focus Question?
  - Where did my students get stuck?
  - What strategies did they use?
  - What breakthroughs did my students have today?
- How will I use this to plan for tomorrow? For the next time I teach this lesson?
- Where will I have the opportunity to reinforce these ideas as I continue through this Unit? The next Unit?

ACE Assignment Guide

- **Applications:** 4–7
- **Connections:** 20–25
- **Extensions:** 33–34
- **Labsheet 2ACE:** Exercises 4–7 (accessibility) is optional. It is an example of a way to provide students with additional support for an ACE Exercise.

Making Choices
Mean or Median?

▼ Problem Overview

> *Focus Question* How do the median and the mean respond to the data in a distribution? How do you choose which measure of center to use when describing what is typical?

Problem Description

Students explore how changing data values in a distribution affects the mean and the median. They do this using data about prices of skateboards at four different stores. They also further develop ideas about the shape of a distribution.

Problem Implementation

Have students work in pairs on this Problem.

Materials

- **Labsheet 2.3A:** Skateboard Prices
- **Labsheet 2.3B:** Dot Plots of Skateboard Prices
- **Labsheet 2ACE:** Exercise 27 (accessibility)
- **Teaching Aid 2.3:** Symmetric and Skewed Distributions

calculators

Using Technology

If students have access to computers, they can use the **Data and Graphs** tool to help them work through Problem 2.3, Question B and ACE Exercise 27.

Vocabulary

- skewed distribution
- symmetric distribution

Mathematics Background

- The Process of Statistical Investigation
- Components of Statistical Investigation
- Posing Questions
- Collecting Data
- Analyzing Individual Cases vs. Overall Distributions
- Choosing Representations for Distributions
- Guiding Students to Construct and Read Graphs
- Shapes of Distributions
- Describing Data With Measures of Center
- Choosing an Appropriate Summary Statistic
- Interpreting Results

At a Glance and Lesson Plan

- At a Glance: Problem 2.3 Data About Us
- Lesson Plan: Problem 2.3 Data About Us

▼ Launch

Launch Video

In this animation, a miniature golfer keeps track of his scores on each golf hole. He then decides whether he should report his median golf-hole score or his mean golf-hole score. This animation shows an alternative context for comparing medians and means. You can ask students to discuss the benefits and setbacks of reporting each of the two measures of center. You can show students this animation before Presenting the Challenge. Visit Teacher Place at mathdashboard. com/cmp3 to see the complete video.

Connecting to Prior Knowledge

This Problem builds on knowledge developed in Problems 2.1 and 2.2. The mean, unlike the median, is sensitive to the value of each data value. Students find the mean by "evening out" the data or finding the sum of the data values and then dividing by the number of data values. It makes sense that every change in data, be it in actual values of data in the data set or in the addition or removal of data values, will impact the results of this computation.

The position of median is at the midpoint of a distribution and so is influenced by the number of data values. The value of the median is taken from the data value or values at the halfway point. If we change the number of data values, the position of the median shifts to reflect this change. The value of the median is not sensitive to extreme values. In general, with small shifts, the median keeps its value if there are repeated data values. Or, if the data values surrounding the median are close in value, then the median has only a small change.

Beyond finding these two measures of center for a set of data, students need to sort out when to use which measure for reporting results. The goal of Problem 2.3 is to help students do this.

The definition of mean in the Introduction is likely to be a variation of what students came up with in Problem 2.2.

Presenting the Challenge

Read the Introduction to Problem 2.3. Refer to **Labsheet 2.3A: Skateboard Prices**, which includes the tables found in the Student Edition.

Suggested Questions

- Look at the prices for skateboards in each of the four stores. How are the prices alike or different? (Possible answer: Store D has more expensive skateboards. Store C has only one very expensive skateboard. Stores A and B seem to have cheaper skateboards.)

- What are the mean and median for each distribution? (Students compute these measures in the Problem, but the focus is to compare the measures to each other and to relate the measures to the graphs. You can have different groups of students compute the measures of center and check each other in finding the values of the mean or the median for each distribution. Then report and compare the final results.)

▼ Explore

Providing for Individual Needs

Have students work through Questions A–C. Plan on doing a mini-Summarize prior to discussing Question D.

Following this, students can return to Questions D and E. Question E focuses on the location of the median and the mean in relation to the shape of a distribution.

Suggested Questions

For Question A, students can use **Labsheet 2.3B: Dot Plots of Skateboard Prices**, which provides a copy of the dot plots shown in the Student Edition. Ask the following.

- What are the mean and the median for Stores B and C? (Store B: mean $51.94, median $50; Store C: mean $64.61, median $50)

- Why do you suppose the medians are the same but the means are different? (Possible answer: Store C has one extreme value, a $200 skateboard. The distributions of data look very similar overall, but the one extreme value has an impact on the mean.)

For Question B, once students have made the line plot and computed the mean and the median for Store A, have them add each new data value to the graph, one at a time. With each new value, they should recompute the mean and determine the median. Ask them how they can use what they know about the current mean and median to find the new mean and median. Before adding the new stock, the mean of the data is $48.50 and the median is $50.

You might help students look for patterns they can use to find the new mean(s). There are 18 data values in the original data set. Help students to see that the sum of the 18 data values is actually the same as the mean $\times$ 18 since the mean is the evened-out value. They can add the new data value to this sum: $873 + $200 = $1,073. The new mean is this sum divided by 19 (the new number of data values after adding one to the original 18), which is about $56.47. Recall that the sum of the 19 data values is $1,073. Add the next data value to this sum: $1,073 + $180 = $1,253. The new mean is $1,253 ÷ 20 = $62.65, and so on.

The original median is $50. As each data value is added, the median moves its position. Generally, the value of the median remains the same, as there are repeated data values of $50. When the last data value is added, the median's position shifts to between $50 and $60. This will be true no matter what data value is used for the 24th skateboard, so long as it is greater than $60.

Store A's New Stock

New Stock Price	New Mean	New Median
$200	$56.47	$50
$180	$62.65	$50
$180	$68.24	$50
$160	$72.41	$50
$170	$76.65	$50
$140	$79.29	$55
Question B, part (4): $200	$81.79	$55

For Question C, ask the following.

- How might you use the tables of data to help you figure out which stores are shown on each graph? (Possible answer: In the table, the only store with high skateboard prices is Store D. Store D, however, has no skateboards at $120, which is the maximum value on Graph 1. Store C has a maximum value of $200, which does not appear on Graph 1. That leaves Graph 1 data as being from Stores A and B.)

- Which distribution is likely to have a mean of $107.11? (In Graph 1, $107.11 would be at the top end of the distribution, which doesn't make sense for a mean. So it must be Graph 2. The median is $132.50. The mean and the median are almost identical in Graph 1.)

- Look at Graph 1. Why do you think the median and the mean are almost identical? How is the distribution different from the one in Graph 2? (Possible answer: Graph 2 has two distinct sets of data that make up its distribution, one with lower values and one with higher values. In Graph 1, the data are combined from two similar distributions, so the data cluster around $50.)

- Look at Graph 2. Can you explain why the median would be located at $132.50? Why do you think the mean is so different from the median? (There are 36 data values in this distribution, which is really the combination of data sets. The midpoint is between the 18th and 19th data values, or $132.50. The mean reflects the lower data values.)

For Question D, ask the following.

- What do you think it means to be "resistant to change"? (Students can connect this idea to what it means to "resist." In this case, they should consider when each measure of center resists a change to its value.)

For Question E, have students work on each distribution separately or with a partner.

Planning for the Summary

What evidence will you use in the summary to clarify and deepen understanding of the Focus Question?

What will you do if you do not have evidence?

▼ Summarize

Orchestrating the Discussion

Review students' work for each of the Questions in Problem 2.3. In particular, make sure they pay attention to how data seem to influence the mean and the median.

Return to some of the questions you may have discussed during the Explore phase. These questions get to the heart of the Problem—the mean is affected by the value of every data value in a data set while the median is not.

- In Question A, why do you suppose the medians are the same but the means are different for Stores B and C? (Store C has a very high value ($200), which brings up the mean.)

- When does the mean change in Question B? (The mean changes with each addition of a new skateboard.)

- When does the median change in Question B? (The median doesn't change until the skateboard that costs $140 is added.)

- Look at Graph 2. Why do you think the mean is so different from the median? (The distribution is skewed to the left.)

Use Questions D and E to summarize how the mean and median differ, and why you might choose one measure over another for particular distributions.

Students should consider when each measure of center resists a change to its value.

- Which measure would you use to describe a typical rating for each of the skateboard rating distributions? (Students will begin to see that the mean overreacts to extreme values. They might still choose to use the mean as a measure of what is typical, perhaps because it does reflect all the data. They should not choose the mean just because it looks more "accurate" given the decimal numbers. Neither should they reject the mean just because it is not a data value in the set. Deciding which measure of center to choose requires some deliberation and sophistication. Let students share their reasons so that they can hear the rationalizations of others.)

In general, the mean misrepresents (either underestimates or overestimates) the center of distributions that are skewed to the left or to the right. Generally, it is better to use the median to describe the location of the center for obviously skewed distributions. For symmetric distributions, the mean and the median should both be fairly close (or even equal) to each other. You can display **Teaching Aid 2.3: Symmetric and Skewed Distributions** as you discuss Question E.

Reflecting on Student Learning

Use the following questions to assess student understanding at the end of the lesson.

- What evidence do I have that students understand the Focus Question?
  - Where did my students get stuck?
  - What strategies did they use?
  - What breakthroughs did my students have today?
- How will I use this to plan for tomorrow? For the next time I teach this lesson?
- Where will I have the opportunity to reinforce these ideas as I continue through this Unit? The next Unit?

ACE Assignment Guide

- **Applications:** 8–9
- **Connections:** 26–27
- **Labsheet 2ACE:** Exercise 27 (accessibility) is optional. It is an example of a way to provide students with additional support for an ACE Exercise.

Who Else Is in Your Household?
Categorical and Numerical Data

▼ Problem Overview

> *Focus Question* How do you distinguish different types of data? What statistics are used with different types of data?

Problem Description

Problem 2.4 introduces the distinction between categorical and numerical data. Students consider a number of different questions related to table and graph representations of data collected in response to two different survey questions. They begin to explore which measures of center and spread can be used with which data types.

Problem Implementation

Have students work in pairs on this Problem.

Materials

• Partner Quiz

Using Technology

If students have access to computers, they can use the online **Data and Graphs** tool to help them answer ACE Exercises 35–37. The tool finds summary statistics of data sets and displays graphs of data sets.

Vocabulary

• categorical data
• numerical data

Mathematics Background

- The Process of Statistical Investigation
- Components of Statistical Investigation
- Posing Questions
- Collecting Data
- Analyzing Individual Cases vs. Overall Distributions
- Choosing Representations for Distributions
- Guiding Students to Construct and Read Graphs
- Shapes of Distributions
- Describing Data With Measures of Center
- Choosing an Appropriate Summary Statistic
- Interpreting Results

At a Glance and Lesson Plan

- At a Glance: Problem 2.4 Data About Us
- Lesson Plan: Problem 2.4 Data About Us

▼ Launch

Connecting to Prior Knowledge

Students do quite a bit of work with categorical data in the early grades, but they may not be familiar with the term "categorical data." In the study of statistics, categorical data is of two types: nominal (naming of categories only) and ordinal (has an order or ranking like ratings given to preferences on a scale). Students will focus on nominal data for which the only measure of center to be used is the mode. With ordinal data, the median may be reported as well.

Presenting the Challenge

Refer students to the introduction in the Student Edition. Have a brief discussion about numerical and categorical data. Then ask students to do the following.

Suggested Questions

- Look over the questions in the introduction and think about how you would respond to each. Which questions have words or categories as answers? Which questions have numbers as answers?

It may be helpful to display their answers on posters in two groups.

Questions With Categorical Data Answers	Questions With Numerical Data Answers
In what month were you born?	How much time do you spend watching television each day?
Who is your favorite author?	How many movies have you watched in the last week?
	What's your highest score in your favorite game?

Note: If you represent birth month with a number, "1" for January, and so on, then the answers to "In what month were you born?" are numbers that represent the months. However, these numbers do not represent numerical values; you would not order January < February, just because of this representation. Some care has to be taken in deciding if an answer to a question is categorical or numerical data.)

You might want to keep the poster with these questions displayed. Students may decide to use these questions for their final *Is Anyone Typical?* Project.

Ask the following question. It will help students summarize the distinction between categorical and numerical data, and it will Launch the next part of the Problem, which involves reading information from graphs.

- What kinds of questions would you ask about pets that would give either categorical or numerical answers? (Possible categorical question: What kind of pet do you own?

  Possible numerical question: How many pets do you have?)

Refer students to the Student Edition, which displays the tables and bar graphs. Work with students to make sure they can read the two tables and understand the data as they are presented. Discuss how to read the graphs, highlighting the information shown on the horizontal axis and the vertical axis for each graph. You may want to ask a few questions to sharpen their table and graph comprehension skills. Students should be allowed to move back and forth between the table and the graph. Make sure, however, that they can locate information using both representations. You can ask questions, such as those below, to help students read the data, read between the data, and read beyond the data.

Suggested Questions

Suggested questions for *reading the data*:

- How many students chose a dog as their favorite pet? (seven)
- How many students have 6 pets? (three)

Suggested questions for *reading between the data*:

- How many total students chose dogs or cats as their favorite pets? (eleven)

- How many people have more than 6 pets? (seven)

Suggested questions for *reading beyond the data*:

- What do you know about the kinds of pets these students chose as their favorites? (Answers will vary. The most popular pet (the mode) is the dog; the second most popular is the cat. The presence of cow, horse, duck, and pig may suggest that some of the students live on farms.)

- What do you know about how many pets each of the students has? (Answers will vary. The range is from 0 to 21 pets. Only two people do not have pets. The mode is 2. The data cluster in the interval of 2–6 pets and then spread out with some unusual values occurring in the interval of 14–21 pets.)

- Do you think our class data would be similar to or different from these students' data? (Answers will vary.)

▼ Explore

Providing for Individual Needs

· ·

Students may not understand that the height of each bar indicates how many students have that number of pets. You can ask these questions to help them.

Suggested Questions

For the Favorite Pet graph:

- How many students chose cat as their favorite pet? (four)

- How would knowing how many students chose each pet help you figure out how many students are in the class? (You could add the number of students who chose each pet to find the total number of students in the class.)

For the Number of Pets graph, students may need help in realizing that 0 number of pets has a frequency of 2, which means 2 students own 0 pets. You can ask the following.

- How many students have 1 pet? (two)

- How many total pets do the bars over "1 pet" represent? (two)

- How did you figure that out? (Multiply the number of pets (1) by the frequency of students who have that number of pets (2), $1 \times 2 = 2$.)

- How many student have 0 pets? (two)

- How many 0's would you have in your list of values? (two)

- How would knowing how many students own a certain number of pets help you figure out how many students are in the class? (You could sum the number of students who own each of the number of pets to find the total number of students in the class.)

Some important ideas appear in Question D.

- Can you compute a mode for categorical data like "favorite kind of pet"? Why or why not? (Yes; dog is the most frequently mentioned kind of pet.)

- Can you compute a median for "favorite kind of pet"? Why or why not? (No; you can't order the pets and then find the middle of the list.)

- Can you compute a mean for the "favorite kind of pet?" Why or why not? (No; you can't add up cats and dogs.)

As students work, make sure they record their explanations. Look for strategies to present in the Summarize. You may want students to record their work. They can present their work to the class during the Summarize.

Have students wait to work on Question F until after the Summarize. They need to think about which measures of center are appropriate to use before writing a report.

Planning for the Summary

What evidence will you use in the summary to clarify and deepen understanding of the Focus Question?
What will you do if you do not have evidence?

▼ Summarize

Orchestrating the Discussion

Have a class discussion in which teams of students explain their responses to the questions. It is important for students to understand what they can and cannot know from a set of data, and which statistics they can apply to categorical data and which to numerical data.

To complete this activity, you may want students to work in pairs for about five minutes to write some questions about these data that can and cannot be answered. For questions that cannot be answered, discuss what information would be needed to answer them. Then have students spend five minutes writing a brief summary report of whichever set they choose.

Reflecting on Student Learning

Use the following questions to assess student understanding at the end of the lesson.

- What evidence do I have that students understand the Focus Question?
  - Where did my students get stuck?
  - What strategies did they use?
  - What breakthroughs did my students have today?
- How will I use this to plan for tomorrow? For the next time I teach this lesson?
- Where will I have the opportunity to reinforce these ideas as I continue through this Unit? The next Unit?

ACE Assignment Guide

- **Applications:** 10–16
- **Connections:** 28–32
- **Extensions:** 35–37

Mathematical Reflections

Possible Answers to Mathematical Reflections

1. Possible answer: Add together all of the values. Divide the sum by the number of values. This works because the sum of the values tells you how much is to be shared or "evened out." The number of values is the number of parts into which the total must be divided. Division gives the number in each part.

2. **a.** They are measures of center because they generally fall where most of the data cluster.

   b. The mode is the data value that occurs most frequently. The median is the middle value that separates an ordered set of data in half. The mean is the "balance point," or the value that each item would have if all the data had the same value.

   c. The median is not affected by extremes—by large or small values—in the data; it is often used with skewed data. The mean is affected by extremes. A single extreme value might affect the mean so much that it no longer illustrates what is typical about a data set. The mean is often reported for symmetrical data. The mode is most appropriate to use when describing categorical data. It is not often reported when working with numerical data.

d. A measure of center illustrates what is typical about a data set. You also want to know how much the data values vary. If the range is very large, then reporting a single statistic for the center might be misleading. Sometimes reporting more than one measure of center indicates whether the data is closely clustered (when the mode, median, and mean are close) or spread far apart (when the mean may be affected by extremes at the edge of the range).

Note: There will be further measures of variability in Investigations 3 and 4.

3. a. The student is correct. The mean and median are measures that can only be used with numerical data. The mode, a count of the most frequently occurring data value within a data set, can be used with both numerical and categorical data.

b. No; a measure of spread depends on being able to identify the smallest and largest values. You cannot order categorical data in a logical way.

Possible Answers to Mathematical Practices Reflections

Students may have demonstrated all of the eight Common Core Standards for Mathematical Practice during this Investigation. During the class discussion, have students provide additional Practices that the Problem cited involved and identify the use of other Mathematical Practices in the Investigation.

One student observation is provided in the Student Edition. Here is another sample student response.

In Problem 2.2, Question E, we found that we needed to describe a general method for computing the mean in any situation. Eden said she really liked to even out value bar graphs, but Sarah said that this was hard to do if you have a lot of data. Sarah said that Question D gave clues for writing a general procedure. Thinking about evening out lets her see why this procedure works. Eden and Sarah decided that since they know the total number of households and the total number of people in all the households, they can divide the *total number of people* by the *total number of households*. It's like sharing the people equally among the households. This will give the mean, or the number of people per household if every household has the same number of people.

MP3: Construct viable arguments and critique the reasoning of others.

Notes

STUDENT PAGE

Who's in Your Household? Using the Mean

The United States Census is carried out every ten years. Among other statistics, the Census provides useful information about household size. The Census uses the term *household* to mean all the people who live in a "housing unit" (such as a house, an apartment, or a mobile home).

When you work with a set of numbers, a single statistic is often calculated to represent the "typical" value to describe the center of a distribution. In Investigation 1, you used median and mode. Another *measure of center* is the **mean.** It is the most commonly used measure of center for numerical data. The mean of a set of data is often called the *average*.

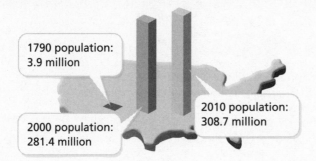

1790 population: 3.9 million

2000 population: 281.4 million

2010 population: 308.7 million

....

Common Core State Standards

6.SP.A.3 Recognize that a measure of center for a numerical data set summarizes all of its values with a single number . . .

6.SP.B.5b Summarize numerical data sets in relation to their context, such as by describing the nature of the attribute under investigation, including how it was measured and its units of measurement.

6.SP.B.5d Summarize numerical data sets in relation to their context, such as by relating the choice of measures of center . . . to the shape of the data distribution and the context in which the data were gathered.

Also **6.NS.C.6, 6.NS.C.7, 6.SP.A.1, 6.SP.A.2, 6.SP.B.4, 6.SP.B.5a, 6.SP.B.5c**

34 Data About Us

Notes _____

_____

_____

148 Data About Us   Investigation 2 Who's in Your Household? Using the Mean

2.1 What's a Mean Household Size?

Six students in a middle-school class use the United States Census guidelines to find the number of people in their households. Each student made a stack of cubes to show the number of people in his or her household. The stacks show that the six households vary in size.

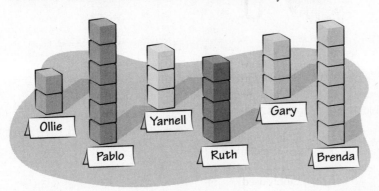

- What is the attribute being investigated?
- How can you use the cube stacks to find the median of the data? The mode?

One way to find the *mean*, or average, household size is to make all the stacks the same height by moving cubes. The evened-out stacks tell you how many people there would be per household if all households were the same size.

- How can you use the cube stacks to find the mean household size for these six students?

Notes

You can also use a table to show the data.

Household Size Table 1

Name	Number of People
Ollie	2
Yarnell	3
Gary	3
Ruth	4
Pablo	6
Brenda	6

- How else might you represent this data set?
- Which representation tells you how many people are in all six households?

In this Problem, you will look at the mean of a data set and how it is calculated.

Problem 2.1

Ⓐ You can use an **ordered-value bar graph** to find the mean of a data set. An ordered-value bar graph and a dot plot are shown below. Both display the number of people in the six households found in Household Size Table 1. You already found the mean, four people, by evening out the cube stacks.

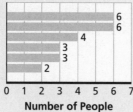

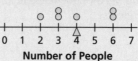

1. Explain how the ordered-value bar graph and dot plot are related.

Notes _____

_____

_____

Problem 2.1 *continued*

2. Brenda used the ordered-value bar graph at the right to identify the mean. Her first steps are shown. On a copy of the graph, complete Brenda's steps.

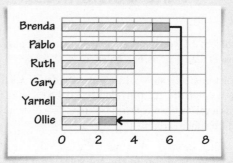

3. Ollie says that, after evening out the bars, the graph looks like six households with four people each. How might you have predicted the mean? Explain.

B Another group of students made the table below for a different set of data.

1. Make an ordered-value bar graph and a dot plot to display the data.

2. Find the mean of the data. Explain how you found it.

3. How does the mean of this data set compare to the mean of the data in Question A?

4. How does identifying the mean on an ordered-value bar graph help you find the mean on a dot plot? Explain.

Household Size Table 2

Name	Number of People
Reggie	6
Tara	4
Brendan	3
Felix	4
Hector	3
Tonisha	4

5. Does knowing the mean help you answer the question, "What is the typical household size?" Explain.

A C E Homework starts on page 48.

Notes

2.2 Comparing Distributions With the Same Mean

In Problem 2.1, you represented data using dot plots. Another way to represent data is by using a balance.

The picture below shows the frequency of the data from Household Size Table 1. When the fulcrum is located at the mean of the distribution, the ruler is level, as the purple ruler shows. The distribution in Household Size Table 1 balances around 4.

Notice that the green ruler tips to the left. When the fulcrum is not located at the mean of the distribution, the ruler is not level.

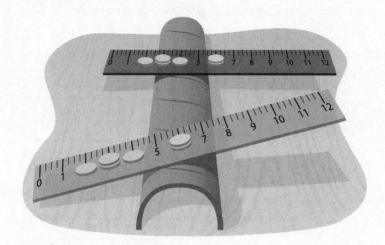

- How does the picture help explain why the mean is often called the *balance point* of a distribution?

- What information do you need to calculate the mean of a data set?

Problem 2.2

A Household Size Table 1 and Household Size Table 2 in Problem 2.1 each show six households with a mean of four people.

1. Make up a different data set of six households that has a mean of four people per household.

2. Make an ordered-value bar graph and a line or dot plot to represent your set of data.

3. Describe how to use your bar graph to verify the mean is four people.

4. Explain how you can find the following on your graphs:

   a. each person's household size

   b. the total number of households

   c. the total number of people in the combined households

   d. How can you use the information in parts (a)–(c) to find the mean?

B A group of seven students has a mean of three people per household.

1. Make up a data set that fits this description.

2. Make an ordered-value bar graph and a line or dot plot to represent your set of data.

3. Describe how to use your bar graph to verify the mean is three people.

4. Suppose you found another data set with seven households and a mean of three people per household, but with a greater range. How would this change the appearance of your line or dot plot?

5. Explain how you can find the following on your graphs:

   a. each person's household size

   b. the total number of households

   c. the total number of people in the combined households

   d. How can you use the information in parts (a)–(c) to find the mean?

continued on the next page >

Notes _____

_____

_____

Problem 2.2 *continued*

C A group of six students has a mean of $3\frac{1}{2}$ people.

   1. Make up a data set that fits this description.

   2. Make an ordered-value bar graph and a line or dot plot to represent your set of data.

   3. How can the mean be $3\frac{1}{2}$ people when "half" a person does not exist?

D The dot plot below shows the household sizes for a group of eight students.

Household Size 3

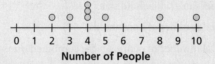

Number of People

   1. Identify the median, mode, and range of the distribution.

   2. Think about viewing the distribution on a balance. Make an estimate or guess about where the mean is located.

   3. Identify the mean of the distribution. How does this compare with your estimate or guess? Explain.

   4. a. Compare the three measures of center—mean, median, and mode. How are they the same or different? Explain.

   b. Is it possible to have the three measures of center of a distribution all be the same? All be different? Explain.

   c. Which measure would you choose to describe the typical household size for the eight households? Explain.

E Look back at the work you did in Questions A–D and in Problem 2.1. Describe a method to compute the mean in any situation.

ACE Homework starts on page 48.

Notes

_____

_____

_____

2.3 Making Choices
Mean or Median?

When you gather data about the typical middle-school student, you may want to inquire about what interests students have. In Problem 2.3, you will use data about skateboard prices to investigate when to use the mean or median to describe what is "typical."

Problem 2.3

The table below shows prices of skateboards at four different stores.

Retail Table 1: Prices of Skateboards (dollars)

Store A	Store B	Store C	Store D
60	13	40	179
40	40	20	160
13	45	60	149
45	60	35	149
20	50	50	149
30	30	30	145
35	15	13	149
60	35	45	100
50	15	40	179
70	70	50	145
50	50	60	149
50	70	70	149
60	50	70	149
50	10	50	149
35	120	90	145
15	90	120	150
70	120	120	149
120		200	149

continued on the next page >

Notes

Problem **2.3** *continued*

A The dot plots below show the data from Stores B and C.

Skateboard Prices

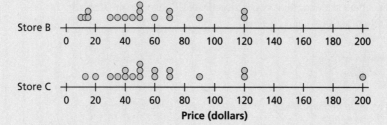

1. Compute the median and mean of the data from the two stores.

2. For each store,

   • Describe how the measures of center and dot plots are related.

   • Describe how the distribution of the data influences the location of the mean and the median.

B Use the information in Retail Table 1.

1. Make a line plot showing the data from Store A.

2. Compute the mean and the median of Store A's prices.

3. Store A decides to stock some higher-priced skateboards. Using a different color, include these data values one at a time on your line plot. After you include each value, find the new mean and the new median of the data. Complete a copy of the table below.

Store A's New Stock

New Stock Price	New Mean	New Median
$200	▩	▩
$180	▩	▩
$180	▩	▩
$160	▩	▩
$170	▩	▩
$140	▩	▩

Notes _____

_____

_____

Problem **2.3** *continued*

4. Suppose the price of the last skateboard were $200, not $140. What would happen to the mean? To the median?

5. When do additional data values influence the mean of the distribution? Influence the median?

6. Which measure of center would you use to answer the question "What is the typical price of skateboards at Store A when all the higher-priced skateboards are included?" Explain your reasoning.

C Each dot plot below shows combined data for two stores from Retail Table 1. For one set of combined data, the mean is $107.11 and the median is $132.50. For the other set of combined data, the mean is $50.17 and the median is $50.00.

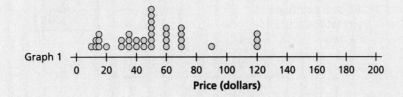

Graph 1

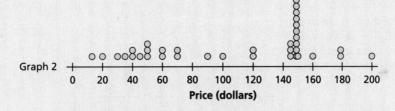

Graph 2

1. Write a complete title for each dot plot by identifying the two sets of data it shows. For example, *Graph 1: Skateboard Prices From Stores _?_ and _?_*. Explain your reasoning.

2. For one graph, the mean and median are almost the same. For the other, the mean and median are different. Explain how the distribution of the data influences the location of the mean or the median.

D In a blog, Dr. Statistics says that "the median is a resistant measure of center, and the mean is *not* a resistant measure of center." Explain the meaning of this statement using your results from Questions A–C.

continued on the next page >

Notes _____

_____

_____

Problem **2.3** *continued*

E A distribution's shape can help you see trends in the data. The shape is **symmetric** if the data are spread out evenly around a center value. The shape is right- or left-**skewed** if the points cluster at one end of the graph.

Three groups of middle-school students were asked: "Using a scale of 1 to 10 (with 10 being the best), how would you rate skateboarding as a sport?" The dot plots below show the responses.

1. Find the mean and median marked on each dot plot. Describe how the measures are influenced, or not, by the shape of the distribution.

2. Describe how the students in each group feel about skateboarding. Which measure of center would you use to answer the question: "What is the students' typical rating?" Explain.

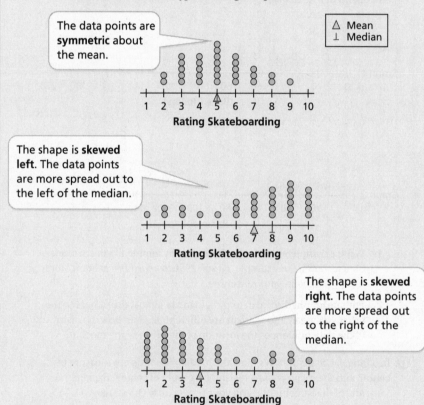

The data points are **symmetric** about the mean.

△ Mean
⊥ Median

Rating Skateboarding

The shape is **skewed left**. The data points are more spread out to the left of the median.

Rating Skateboarding

The shape is **skewed right**. The data points are more spread out to the right of the median.

Rating Skateboarding

A C E Homework starts on page 48.

Notes _____

_____

_____

2.4 Who Else Is in Your Household?
Categorical and Numerical Data

Some statistical questions have answers that are words or categories. For example, "What is your favorite sport?" has answers that are words. Other questions have answers that are numbers. For example, "How many inches tall are you?" has answers that are numbers.

Categorical data can be grouped into categories, such as "favorite sport." They are usually not numbers. Suppose you asked people how they got to school or what kinds of pets they had. Their answers would be categorical data.

Numerical data are counts or measures. Suppose you asked people how tall they were or how many pets they had. Their responses would be numerical data.

- Which questions below have words or categories as answers? Which have numbers as answers?

Notes _____

_____

_____

STUDENT PAGE

One middle-school class gathered data about their pets by tallying students' responses to these questions:

- How many pets do you have?
- What is your favorite kind of pet?

The students made tables to show the tallies, or frequencies. Then they made bar graphs to show the data distributions.

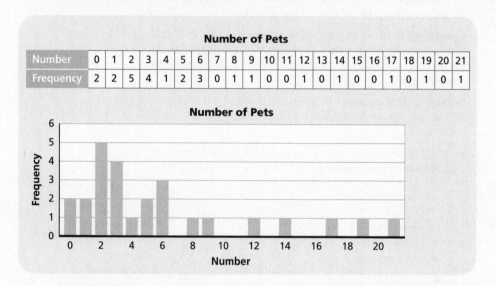

Number of Pets

Number	0	1	2	3	4	5	6	7	8	9	10	11	12	13	14	15	16	17	18	19	20	21
Frequency	2	2	5	4	1	2	3	0	1	1	0	0	1	0	1	0	0	1	0	1	0	1

Number of Pets

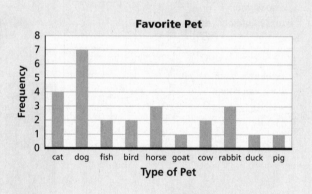

Favorite Pet

Pet	Frequency
cat	4
dog	7
fish	2
bird	2
horse	3
goat	1
cow	2
rabbit	3
duck	1
pig	1

Favorite Pet

Notes _____

_____

_____

Problem 2.4

Decide whether Questions A through E can be answered by using data from the graphs and tables. If so, give the answer and explain how you got it. If not, explain why not.

A Which graph shows categorical data? Numerical data?

B 1. What is the total number of pets the students have?

2. What is the greatest number of pets a student has?

C 1. How many students are in the class?

2. How many students chose a cat as their favorite kind of pet?

3. How many cats do students have as pets?

D 1. What is the mode of the favorite kind of pet? The mean?

2. What is the median number of pets students have? The range?

E 1. Tomas is a student in this class. How many pets does he have?

2. Do the girls in the class have more pets than the boys?

F Using the distribution of the data, how would you describe the number of pets owned by this class? What would you say were the favorite kinds of pets? Use measures of center and other tools to help you describe the results of the survey.

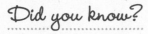 Homework starts on page 48.

Did you know?

Goldfish are trainable. With coaching, goldfish can learn to swim through hoops and tunnels, push a tiny ball into a net, and pull a lever for food.

Notes _____

_____

_____

Applications

For Exercises 1–3, use the line plot below.

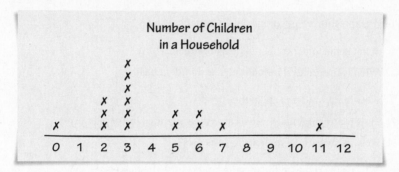

Number of Children in a Household

1. **a.** What is the median number of children in the 16 households? Explain how to find the median. What does the median tell you?

    b. Do any of the 16 households have the median number of children? Explain why this is possible.

2. **a.** What is the mean number of children per household for the 16 households? Explain how to find the mean. What does the mean tell you?

    b. Do any of the 16 households have the mean number of children? Explain why this is possible.

3. Use either the mean or the median to answer this question: "What is the typical household size for the data?" Explain your reasoning.

Notes

For Exercises 4–7, the mean number of people per household in eight households is six people.

4. **Multiple Choice** What is the total number of people in the eight households?

   A. 16   **B.** 64   **C.** 14   **D.** 48

5. Make a line plot showing one possible arrangement of the numbers of people in the eight households.

6. Make a line plot showing a different possible arrangement of the numbers of people in the eight households.

7. Are the medians the same for the two distributions you made? Is it possible to have two distributions that have the same means, but not the same medians? Explain your reasoning.

8. A set of nine households has a mean of $3\frac{1}{3}$ people per household. Make a line plot showing a data set that fits this description.

9. A set of nine households has a mean of five people per household. The largest household in the group has ten people. Make a line plot showing a data set that fits this description.

For Exercises 10–16, tell whether the answers to the question are numerical or categorical data.

10. What is your height in centimeters?

11. What is your favorite musical group?

12. In which month were you born?

13. What would you like to do when you graduate from high school?

14. Use your foot as a unit of measure. How many of your "feet" tall are you?

15. What kind(s) of transportation do you use to get to school?

16. On average, how much time do you spend doing homework each day?

STUDENT PAGE

Notes

Connections

17. During Mr. Wilson's study hall, students spent the following amounts of time on their homework:

$\frac{3}{4}$ hour $\frac{1}{2}$ hour $1\frac{1}{4}$ hours $\frac{3}{4}$ hour $\frac{1}{2}$ hour

a. What is the mean time Mr. Wilson's students spent on homework?

b. **Multiple Choice** What is the median time the students spent on homework?

  F. $\frac{1}{2}$ hour   **G.** $\frac{3}{4}$ hour

  H. 1 hour   **J.** $1\frac{1}{4}$ hours

18. A soccer league wants to find the average amount of water its players drink per game. There are 18 players on a team. During one game, the two teams drank a total of 1,152 ounces of water.

a. How much water did each player drink per game if each player drank the same amount of water?

b. Does this value represent the mean or the median? Explain.

19. Sabrina, Diego, and Marcus entered a Dance-a-thon that ran from 9 A.M. to 7 P.M. The times that each student danced are shown at the right.

a. Write the number of hours each student spent dancing as a mixed number.

b. Look at the data from part (a). Without doing any computations, do you think the mean time spent dancing is the same as, less than, or greater than the median? Explain.

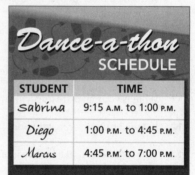

Dance-a-thon SCHEDULE

STUDENT	TIME
Sabrina	9:15 A.M. to 1:00 P.M.
Diego	1:00 P.M. to 4:45 P.M.
Marcus	4:45 P.M. to 7:00 P.M.

Notes

20. Jon has a pet rabbit that is 5 years old. He wonders if his rabbit is old compared to other rabbits. At the pet store, he finds out that the mean life span for a rabbit is 7 years.

    a. What does the mean tell Jon about the life span for a rabbit?

    b. What additional information would help Jon to predict the life span of his rabbit?

21. A store carries nine different brands of granola bars. What are possible prices for each of the nine brands of granola bars if the mean price is $1.33? Explain how you determined values for each of the nine brands. You may use pictures to help you.

For Exercises 22–25, a recent survey of 25 students in a middle-school class yielded the data in the table below.

Mean Time Spent on Leisure Activities by Students in One Class

Activity	Time (minutes per day)
Watching videos	39
Listening to music	44
Using the computer	21

22. Did each student watch videos for 39 minutes per day? Explain.

23. Jill decides to round 39 minutes to 40 minutes. Then she estimates that the students spend about $\frac{2}{3}$ of an hour watching videos. What percent of an hour is $\frac{2}{3}$?

24. Estimate what part of an hour the students spend listening to music. Write your answer as a fraction and as a decimal.

25. The students spend about 20 minutes per day using a computer. How many hours do they spend using a computer in 1 week (7 days)? Write your answer as a fraction and as a decimal.

Notes _____

26. Three candidates are running for the mayor of Slugville. Each has determined the typical income of residents of Slugville, and they use that information for campaign sound bites.

Some of the candidates are confused about "average." Slugville has only 16 residents. Their weekly incomes are $0, $0, $0, $0, $0, $0, $0, $0, $200, $200, $200, $200, $200, $200, $200, and $30,600.

a. Explain what measure of center each of the candidates used as an "average" income for the town. Check their computations.

b. Does anyone in Slugville have the mean income? Explain.

c. Does anyone in Slugville have an income that equals the median? Explain.

d. Does anyone in Slugville have an income that equals the mode? Explain.

e. When you decide to use a measure of center—mode, median, or mean—you must choose which measure best helps you tell the story of the data. What do you consider to be the typical income for a resident of Slugville? Explain your choice of measure.

f. Suppose four more people moved to Slugville. Each has a weekly income of $200. How would the mean, median, and mode change?

27. A recent survey asked 25 middle-school students how many movies they see in one month. The table and line plot below show the data.

Movies Watched in One Month

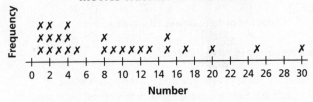

Student	Number	Student	Number	Student	Number
Wes	2	Susan	4	Julian	2
Tomi	15	Gil	3	Alana	4
Ling	13	Enrique	2	Tyrone	1
Su Chin	1	Lonnie	3	Rebecca	4
Michael	9	Ken	10	Anton	11
Mara	30	Kristina	15	Jun	8
Alan	20	Mario	12	Raymond	8
Jo	1	Henry	5	Anjelica	17
Tanisha	25				

Movies Watched in One Month

```
Frequency
X X  X
X X X X        X              X
X X X X X    X X X X X X   X   X      X        X           X
+--+--+--+--+--+--+--+--+--+--+--+--+--+--+--+--+
0  2  4  6  8  10 12 14 16 18 20 22 24 26 28 30
                   Number
```

a. Identify one section of the line plot where about half the data values are grouped and a different section where about one quarter of the data is grouped.

b. What is the range of the data? Explain how you found it.

c. Find the mean number of movies watched by the students. Explain.

d. What do the range and mean tell you about the typical number of movies watched for this group of students?

e. Find the median number of movies watched. Are the mean and the median the same? Why do you think this is so?

Notes _____

For Exercises 28–32, use the graph below. The graph shows the number of juice drinks 100 middle-school students consumed in one day.

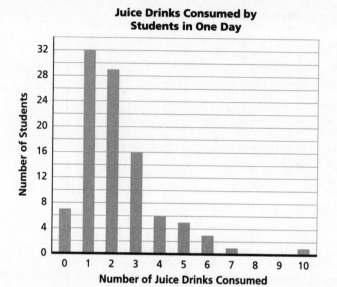

Juice Drinks Consumed by Students in One Day

28. Are the data numerical or categorical? Explain.

29. A student used the graph to estimate that the median number of juice drinks students consume in a day is 5. Is this estimate correct? Explain your answer.

30. Another student estimates that the median number of juice drinks is 1. Is this estimate correct? Explain your answer.

31. What is the total number of juice drinks these 100 students consume in one day? How did you determine your answer?

32. Suppose the survey had asked, "What juice drinks do you like?"

   a. List three possible responses.

   b. Are the data numerical or categorical? Explain.

   c. Describe how to make a bar graph showing the distribution of the data collected in answer to this question. How would you label the horizontal axis? The vertical axis? How would you title the graph? What would each bar on the graph show?

Notes

_____

_____

_____

Extensions

For Exercises 33 and 34, use the newspaper headlines.

33. Do you think that each headline refers to a mean, a median, or something else? Explain.

34. About how many hours per day does the average sixth grader spend watching television or using the Internet if he or she spends 1,170 hours of screen time in a year?

For Exercises 35–37, use the table at the right.

35. Make a bar graph to display the data. Think about how you will set up and label the horizontal and vertical axes with the correct scales.

36. Use the information in your graph to write a paragraph about the pets these students own. How do these results compare to the results from the class data used in Problem 2.4?

37. Estimate how many students were surveyed. Explain your reasoning.

Types of Pets Students Own

Pet	Frequency
bird	61
cat	184
dog	180
fish	303
gerbil	17
guinea pig	12
hamster	32
horse	28
rabbit	2
snake	9
turtle	13
Total	**841**

Notes

Mathematical Reflections 2

In this Investigation, you explored a measure of center called the mean. It is important to understand how the mean, or average, is related to the mode and the median. The following questions will help you summarize what you learned.

Think about these questions. Discuss your ideas with other students and your teacher. Then write a summary of your findings in your notebook.

1. **Describe** a method for calculating the mean of a set of data. Explain why your method works.

2. You have used three measures of center—mode, median, and mean—to describe distributions.

   a. **Why** do you suppose they are called "measures of center"?

   b. **What** does each tell you about a set of data?

   c. **How** do you decide which measure of center to use when describing a distribution?

   d. **Why** might you want to include both the range and a measure of center when reporting a statistical summary?

3. a. One student says you can only use the mode to describe categorical data, but you can use the mode, median, and mean to describe numerical data. Is the student correct? Explain.

   b. Can you find the range for categorical data? Explain.

Unit Project

Think about the survey you will be developing to gather information about middle-school students.

 How might the new ideas you have learned in this Investigation be useful when you are designing a statistical analysis?

Notes

Common Core Mathematical Practices

As you worked on the Problems in this Investigation, you used prior knowledge to make sense of them. You also applied your Mathematical Practices to solve the Problems. Think back over your work, the ways you thought about the Problems, and how you used Mathematical Practices.

Sophie described her thoughts in the following way:

> If a set of seven numbers has a mean of 11, then the sum of the numbers is going to equal 77—no matter what.
>
> For example, the set of numbers 5, 9, 9, 9, 12, 15, and 18 has a mean of 11 and a sum of 77. Another set of numbers, 4, 5, 6, 10, 10, 11, and 31, has a mean of 11. That set of numbers also has a sum of 77.
>
> I can just replace each of the original seven numbers with the number 11, just like evening out the cube stacks. And when I add 11 seven times, the sum is 77.
>
> ....
>
> **Common Core Standards for Mathematical Practice**
> **MP7** Look for and make use of structure

- What other Mathematical Practices can you identify in Sophie's reasoning?
- Describe a Mathematical Practice that you and your classmates used to solve a different Problem in this Investigation.

Notes _____

_____

_____

What's Your Favorite...?
Measuring Variability

▼ Investigation Overview

Investigation Description

Investigation 3 focuses on two measures of variability: interquartile range (IQR) and mean absolute deviation (MAD). Students are introduced to the IQR in the context of deciding how well a group of students estimate cereal portions for two different cereals. Students apply their knowledge of the IQR as a tool to analyze a database of cereals (70) and their sugar content. Finally, students are introduced to the MAD as a way to describe the differences in variation in wait times at an amusement park.

Investigation Vocabulary

- interquartile range (IQR)
- lower quartile
- mean absolute deviation (MAD)
- quartile
- upper quartile
- variability

Mathematics Background

- The Process of Statistical Investigation
- Components of Statistical Investigation
- Posing Questions
- Collecting Data
- Describing Data With Measures of Variability
- Interpreting Results

Planning Chart

Content	ACE	Pacing	Materials	Resources
Problem 3.1	1–3, 12–13	1½ days	**Labsheet 3.1** Serving-Size Estimates empty cereal boxes with different serving sizes (optional)	• Expression Calculator
Problem 3.2	4, 17–20, 26	1½ days	**Labsheet 3.2A** Distribution of Sugar in Cereals **Labsheet 3.2B** Cereal Distributions by Shelf Location **Labsheet 3ACE** Exercise 4 **Labsheet 3ACE:** Exercises 17 and 18 (accessibility) empty cereal boxes with different serving sizes (optional)	• Data and Graphs • Expression Calculator
Problem 3.3	5–11, 14–16, 21–25, 27	1½ days	**Labsheet 3.3A** Wait-Time Distribution for Scenic Trolley Ride **Labsheet 3.3B** Wait-Time Distributions for the Carousel and Bumper Cars **Labsheet 3ACE:** Exercises 14–16 (accessibility)	• Data and Graphs • Expression Calculator
Mathematical Reflections		½ day		
Assessment: Check Up 2		½ day		• Check Up 2

▼ Goals and Standards

Goals

Statistical Process Understand and use the process of statistical investigation

- Ask questions, collect and analyze data, and interpret data to answer questions

- Describe data with respect to its shape, center, and variability or spread

- Construct and use simple surveys as a method of collecting data

Measures of Central Tendency and Variability Recognize that a single number may be used to characterize the center of a distribution of data or the degree of variability (or spread)

- Distinguish between and compute measures of central tendency (mean, median, and mode) and measures of spread (range, interquartile range (IQR), and mean absolute deviation (MAD))

- Identify how the median and mean respond to changes in the data values of a distribution

- Relate the choice of measures of central tendency and variability to the shape of the distribution and the context

- Describe the amount of variability in a distribution by noting whether the data values cluster in one or more areas or are fairly spread out

- Use measures of center and spread to compare data distributions

Mathematical Reflections

Look for evidence of student understanding of the goals for this Investigation in their responses to the questions in *Mathematical Reflections*. The goals addressed by each question are indicated below.

1. Explain and illustrate the following words.

   a. Range

   b. Interquartile range

   c. Mean absolute deviation

   Goals

   - Ask questions, collect and analyze data, and interpret data to answer questions

   - Describe data with respect to its shape, center, and variability or spread

   - Distinguish between and compute measures of central tendency (mean, median, and mode) and measures of spread (range, interquartile range (IQR), and mean absolute deviation (MAD))

2. a. Describe how you can use the range to compare how two data distributions vary.

   b. Describe how you can use the IQR to compare how two data distributions vary.

   c. Describe how you can use the MAD to compare how two data distributions vary.

Goals

- Ask questions, collect and analyze data, and interpret data to answer questions
- Describe data with respect to its shape, center, and variability or spread
- Use measures of spread to compare data distributions
- Describe the amount of variability in a distribution by noting whether the data values cluster in one or more areas or are fairly spread out

Standards

Common Core Content Standards

6.RP.A.3 Use ratio and rate reasoning to solve real-world and mathematical problems, e.g., by reasoning about tables of equivalent ratios, tape diagrams, double number line diagrams, or equations. *Problem 1*

6.RP.A.3a Make tables of equivalent ratios relating quantities with whole-number measurements, find missing values in the tables, and plot the pairs of values on the coordinate plane. Use tables to compare ratios. *Problem 1*

6.SP.A.1 Recognize a statistical question as one that anticipates variability in the data related to the question and accounts for it in the answers. *Problems 1, 2, and 3*

6.SP.A.2 Understand that a set of data collected to answer a statistical question has a distribution which can be described by its center, spread, and overall shape. *Problems 1 and 2*

6.SP.A.3 Recognize that a measure of center for a numerical data set summarizes all of its values with a single number, while a measure of variation describes how its values vary with a single number. *Problems 1, 2, and 3*

6.SP.B.4 Display numerical data in plots on a number line, including dot plots, histograms, and box plots. *Problem 1*

6.SP.B.5c Summarize numerical data sets in relation to their context, such as by giving quantitative measures of center (median and/or mean) and variability (interquartile range and/or mean absolute deviation), as well as describing any overall pattern and any striking deviations from the overall pattern with reference to the context in which the data were gathered. *Problems 1, 2, and 3*

6.SP.B.5d Summarize numerical data sets in relation to their context, such as by relating the choice of measures of center and variability to the shape of the data distribution and the context in which the data were gathered. *Problems 1 and 2*

6.NS.C.6 Understand a rational number as a point on the number line. Extend number line diagrams and coordinate axes familiar from previous grades to represent points on the line and in the plane with negative number coordinates. *Problems 1, 2, and 3*

6.NS.C.7 Understand ordering and absolute value of rational numbers. *Problems 1, 2, and 3*

Facilitating the Mathematical Practices

Students in *Connected Mathematics* classrooms display evidence of multiple Common Core Standards for Mathematical Practice every day. Here are just a few examples of when you might observe students demonstrating the Standards for Mathematical Practice during this Investigation.

Practice 1: Make sense of problems and persevere in solving them.

Students are engaged every day in solving problems and, over time, learn to persevere in solving them. To be effective, the problems embody critical concepts and skills and have the potential to engage students in making sense of mathematics. Students build understanding by reflecting, connecting, and communicating. These student-centered problem situations engage students in articulating the "knowns" in a problem situation and determining a logical solution pathway. The student-student and student-teacher dialogues help students not only to make sense of the problems, but also to persevere in finding appropriate strategies to solve them. The suggested questions in the Teacher Guides provide the metacognitive scaffolding to help students monitor and refine their problem-solving strategies.

Practice 2: Reason abstractly and quantitatively.

Throughout Investigation 3, students find the interquartile ranges and mean absolute deviations of sets of data. They compare these specific values to determine which data sets are more variable than others.

Practice 7: Look for and make use of structure.

Students extend their knowledge about medians that they developed in Investigation 1. They use the structure of finding the median of a set of data to find the median, upper quartile, and lower quartile of new sets of data in Investigation 3.

Students identify and record their personal experiences with the Standards for Mathematical Practice during the Mathematical Reflections at the end of the Investigation.

PROBLEM
3.1

Estimating Cereal Serving Sizes
Determining the IQR

▼ Problem Overview

Focus Question What information does the interquartile range provide about how data vary in a distribution?

Problem Description

Students are introduced to the interquartile range (IQR) as a measure of variability in the context of deciding how well a group of students did in estimating and pouring cereal portions for two different cereals.

Problem Implementation

Have students work in pairs on this Problem.

You may want to complete Question A of the Problem 3.1 as a large group.

Note: For Question E, students may be unfamiliar with the name Seamus and need help in pronouncing it. You can tell them that the name is pronounced SHAY mus.

Materials

• **Labsheet 3.1:** Serving–Size Estimates

empty cereal boxes with different serving sizes (optional)

Using Technology

If students have access to computers, they can use the online **Expression Calculator** tool to help them identify serving-size equivalents of the grams of cereal poured. Students can also use this tool to find possible solutions for ACE Exercise 13.

Vocabulary

• interquartile range (IQR)
• lower quartile
• quartile
• upper quartile
• variability

Mathematics Background

- The Process of Statistical Investigation
- Components of Statistical Investigation
- Posing Questions
- Collecting Data
- Describing Data With Measures of Variability
- Interpreting Results

At a Glance and Lesson Plan

- At a Glance: Problem 3.1 Data About Us
- Lesson Plan: Problem 3.1 Data About Us

▼ Launch

Launch Video

This Launch Video shows characters buying self-serve frozen yogurt. Each character serves himself a different amount of frozen yogurt. The characters wonder if there is a way to determine how much their serving sizes of frozen yogurt vary. You can show your students this video to help them understand the context of the Problem. This context mimics, but is slightly different from, that of Problem 3.1. Show this video to your students before Connecting to Prior Knowledge. Visit Teacher Place at mathdashboard.com/cmp3 to see the complete video.

Connecting to Prior Knowledge

Read the introduction that focuses on survey questions. A sample of an online survey question about choosing a favorite cereal is given along with a graph of the results. The purpose of this sample is to help students think about designing their own surveys for the Unit Project. Discuss how the graph in the introduction of the Student Edition is organized (i.e., how it shows specific choices and a last category of "other" on the horizontal axis) in order to help students analyze the results.

> **What would happen if you just asked: "What is your favorite cereal?"
> Why would you want to give respondents choices?**

Talk with your students about the types of data (i.e., categorical or numerical) that are likely to be collected in response to this kind of question. Most often, it will be categorical data. Student surveys might only involve categorical data if teachers are not careful to emphasize that students should also collect numerical data.

This Investigation continues with three Problems, two of which have a context about cereals but involve collecting numerical data. The third Problem uses the context of amusement-park rides, highlighting different rides and associated wait times.

This Investigation expands the students' ability to think about measures of spread with respect to numerical data. Looking at the degree of variability in a set of data is an essential component of conducting any statistical investigation.

Variability is the essence of statistics. People are different; variability describes just how different people are from each other. Variability, in a statistical sense, is a quantitative measure of how close together, or how spread out, a group of data are. Measures of spread help describe variability.

In Investigation 1, students were introduced to the range as a measure of variability. While the range does provide information about how spread out a distribution is, it is influenced by the presence of outliers. So, it may distort information about the spread of the majority of data values.

In Investigation 3, students look at the interquartile range (IQR) and the mean absolute deviation (MAD) as a way to characterize the variability in a distribution more accurately than the range. Each measure is associated with its respective measure of center.

Presenting the Challenge

To engage students in the context of the Problem and the data set, ask them to brainstorm a list of cereals they are likely to eat. In the Student Edition, the named cereals are not real cereals. If you have some cereal boxes, have students look at the serving sizes. Have students talk about why serving sizes might be different for different kinds of cereals (e.g., nutritional values need to be met, mass or volume of cereals may be different, and so on).

Suggested Questions

- Do you pay attention to serving size when you eat cereal?

- Do you measure your serving size, estimate your serving size, or just fill a bowl?

- How good do you think you are at estimating a serving size?

Note: At this point, you may want to conduct your own experiment. See **Alternative Presentation: Experiment in Estimating Cereal Serving Sizes** at the end of this section.

- In this situation, 12 students collected data on the number of servings of cereal they poured. We need to look at their data and decide how close to one serving they poured. We want to know who poured about the right amount, who poured too much, and who poured too little in their serving-size estimates.

Read Problem 3.1.

- What is the serving size for Wheaty Os? ($\frac{3}{4}$ cup, or 28 grams)

- Look at the table showing the results from each student's pour. What data are in the first row? (grams (mass) of the amount of cereal poured)

- There are 12 data values. What data are in the second row for each student? (The data describe the number of servings the grams poured are; if the serving size is greater than 1, a student overpoured; if it is less than 1, a student underpoured.)

- The data in the second row were not collected. How were the data entries found? (They were computed by dividing the grams poured by 28 grams, which is the serving size for the cereal.)

- There are some missing data in the second row. We need to fill in the missing information. (Have the students calculate the missing data. **Labsheet 3.1: Serving-Size Estimates** contains copies of the tables and dot plots from the Student Edition. Students can use the results of their computations as the data for the Problem.)

- Below the table is a dot plot. What data are plotted? Where on the plot is the data value that you calculated?

Using this graph, ask how well the students in the Problem did in pouring one serving size. Your class may observe that some of the students were inaccurate, while many students seem to be somewhat close to a serving size (e.g., clustered from 0.8 to 1.2 serving sizes).

- How well do students estimate serving size when they pour Wheaty Os? (Collect opinions without comment at this point. Students may estimate the mean or median as a measure of what students typically pour. They might note that there is a lot of variability in the data, from one person who poured 0.71 servings to one who poured 2.11 servings.)

Have the students continue with the Problem. Students should continue to use Labsheet 3.1 so that they can more easily mark an ordered list of data values to identify the IQR.

Alternative Presentation

Experiment in Estimating Cereal Serving Sizes

Materials:

- Boxes of cereal

- Scale that reports mass in grams

- Plastic cereal bowls, all same size and mass

Use three different cereals with different serving sizes.

Each student should complete the following steps:

- Zero out the scale.

- Weigh the bowl and remove it.

- Pour what he or she believes is a serving size into the bowl.

- Zero out the scale. Place the bowl back on.

- Determine the mass of the filled bowl. Subtract the bowl's mass. Record mass in grams.

Repeat for two more cereals (of different types).

Have each student record the data for each type of cereal. The following data should be collected: the name of the cereal, the number of grams poured as an estimate, the number of servings poured as an estimate. Students should not tell their classmates the results.

When all students have finished, collect data on the number of servings students poured for one kind of cereal from all students. Do this for the other two cereals. Have students represent the data in some way.

▼ Explore

Providing for Individual Needs

· ·

Discuss Question A as a large group using **Labsheet 3.1: Serving-Size Estimates**. Students can locate the position of the median first, which divides the set of data in half. The median is also called Quartile 2. They determine the value of the median (Q2) by averaging the middle two data values, 1.04 servings and 1.07 servings. So, Q2 = 1.055 servings. Students then divide the set of data into four equal parts. They locate the position of Quartile 1 (Q1), which marks the midpoint of the data to the left of the median, and the position of Quartile 3 (Q3), which marks the midpoint of the data to the right of the median. To determine the value of Q1, students average 0.86 servings and 0.96 servings, so Q1 = 0.91 servings. They find the value of Q3, by averaging 1.32 servings and 1.54 servings. So, Q3 = 1.43 servings. The interquartile range (IQR), like the range, is the difference between two "end points." For the IQR, the end points are the borders of the middle 50% of data. The IQR is the difference between Q3 and Q1. In this case, Q3 − Q1 = 1.43 − 0.91 = 0.52 servings.

Help students to see that the middle 50% of the data are between Q1 and Q3. They can count all the data values (12) and then the number of data values between Q1 and Q3 (6) to see that half, or 50%, of the data are located here.

Suggested Questions

- Why would the students agree that the middle 50% of the data are pours of cereal that are "about right"? What do you think it means to say the pours are "about right"? (The middle 50% can be considered a cluster of typical pours of cereal for this group. They are clustered around the median. Whether they are "about right" depends on whether they are also close to the goal of 1 serving size, which is the question under investigation.)

- How is the IQR like or unlike the range? (Range tells how spread out all the data are; it is calculated by finding the difference of the minimum and the maximum data values. The IQR also describes the spread of the data. It is centered around the median, however, so it tells how spread out the middle 50% of data are.)

Going Further

- Could the range be large and the IQR be small or vice versa? (For this question, students would have to think of the possible shapes of data that would give rise to these situations. If there is an extreme value at one end or another, the range will be large but the IQR will not be affected. The range will always be greater than or the same as the IQR. Knowing both range and IQR gives an insight into how the data are distributed.)

Students can now complete Questions B–E working in pairs.

- How will you find the IQR for servings of Raisin Flakes? (Start with an ordered list. Divide the list into four groups with each group having the same number of data values. Then find the difference of the first and third quartiles.)

- What does the IQR tell you? (It tells you how variable the middle 50% of the data are. It does not necessarily answer whether or not the pours of cereal are accurate.)

- How might you compare variability for the two sets of data? (If students suggest range, then let them find the range. But suggest that they also compare IQRs.)

- How does IQR show how spread out the data are? (The IQR is the range of the middle 50% of the data.)

- If the IQR were large, would the median be a good measure of center for the data? (This is a subtle point. If this is true, perhaps there is too much variability to rely on the median as a single number to describe what is typical.)

- Are students better at estimating a serving size for Wheaty Os or for Raisin Flakes? (The median pour for Raisin Flakes is close to the goal of one serving (a little less), and the small IQR suggests the data are consistently close to this goal. The median pour for Wheaty Os is also close to the goal (a little greater), but the larger IQR indicates the students are less consistent in estimating these serving sizes.)

Planning for the Summary

What evidence will you use in the summary to clarify and deepen understanding of the Focus Question?

What will you do if you do not have evidence?

▼ Summarize

Orchestrating the Discussion

The purpose of determining the IQR is to be able to decide if one set of data is more variable than another set of data. In this case, you have to consider both the median and the IQR to decide if students consistently estimated a serving size correctly.

It is also helpful to distinguish between range and IQR with students. Some of the questions that you may have discussed with individuals during the Explore phase should be discussed again with the whole class.

Suggested Questions

- What are the medians and IQRs of the two sets of data? (For Wheaty Os, the median is 1.055 servings and the IQR is 0.52 serving. For Raisin Flakes, the median is 0.94 serving and the IQR is 0.375 serving.)

- What does the median tell you? (a typical amount of cereal poured)

- What does the IQR tell you? (the spread of the middle 50% of pours)

- How might you compare the two sets of data? (You can compare the medians to determine whether students typically poured the number of servings for one cereal about the same as another. You can compare the IQRs to see if the servings poured cluster around the middle more for one cereal than for another.)

- Are students better at measuring a serving size for Wheaty Os or Raisin Flakes? (The median pour for Raisin Flakes is close to the goal of one serving (a little less), and the small IQR suggests the data are consistently close to this goal. The median pour for Wheaty Os is also close to the goal (a little greater), but the larger IQR indicates the students are less consistent in estimating these serving sizes.)

Address the Focus Question.

Reflecting on Student Learning

Use the following questions to assess student understanding at the end of the lesson.

- What evidence do I have that students understand the Focus Question?
  - Where did my students get stuck?
  - What strategies did they use?
  - What breakthroughs did my students have today?
- How will I use this to plan for tomorrow? For the next time I teach this lesson?
- Where will I have the opportunity to reinforce these ideas as I continue through this Unit? The next Unit?

ACE Assignment Guide

- **Applications:** 1–3
- **Connections:** 12–13

PROBLEM
3.2

Connecting Cereal Shelf Location and Sugar Content
Describing Variability Using the IQR

▼ Problem Overview

Focus Question How is the interquartile range used to make comparisons among distributions?

Problem Description

Students apply their knowledge of the IQR as a tool to analyze a database of 70 cereals and their sugar contents. They focus on shelf locations of cereals in a supermarket. They analyze these data to see if there are differences in the sugar content of cereals with different shelf locations, looking particularly at which shelf's data seem to vary the most in terms of sugar content per serving.

Problem Implementation

Have students work in pairs on this Problem.

Materials

- **Labsheet 3.2A:** Distribution of Sugar in Cereals
- **Labsheet 3.2B:** Cereal Distributions by Shelf Location
- **Labsheet 3ACE:** Exercise 4
- **Labsheet 3ACE:** Exercises 17 and 18 (accessibility)

empty cereal boxes with different serving sizes (optional)

Using Technology

If students have access to computers, they can use the **Expression Calculator** and the **Data and Graphs** tool to help them answer ACE Exercises 4 and 26.

Vocabulary

There are no new glossary terms introduced in this Problem.

Mathematics Background

- The Process of Statistical Investigation
- Components of Statistical Investigation
- Posing Questions
- Collecting Data
- Describing Data With Measures of Variability
- Interpreting Results

At a Glance and Lesson Plan

- At a Glance: Problem 3.2 Data About Us
- Lesson Plan: Problem 3.2 Data About Us

▼ Launch

Connecting to Prior Knowledge

In this Problem, students determine the IQRs for each of three distributions. They use information about variability to compare the three distributions, rather than focusing only on measures of center and what is typical.

Presenting the Challenge

To engage students in the context of the Problem and the data set, ask them about how cereals are displayed in grocery stores.

Suggested Questions

- What might be some reasons that supermarkets place different kinds of cereals on certain shelves (top, middle, or bottom)? (If you look at the cereal shelves in a supermarket, you will see patterns about where kinds and brands of cereals are located.)

You might bring in some pictures of supermarket shelves, but it is not necessary for students to spend much time speculating now.

Read or summarize the information on sugar content of cereals that is reported at the beginning of Problem 3.2. You can also have students look at empty cereal boxes to see the sugar per serving for those cereals.

The data set of 70 cereals is shown only in graph form. It is duplicated on
Labsheet 3.2A: Distribution of Sugar in Cereals. Have students look at
the graph.

- Is there anything that surprises you about the data and their distribution?
  (Students might mention there are several cereals with 3 or 6 grams of
  sugar. There is a gap at 4 grams.)

- What questions do you have as you look at the distribution? (Students
  might wonder what the individual cereals are, where their favorite cereal
  is on the graph, what cereals are close to the median, or what cereals are
  at the extremes.)

Students do not know the individual cereal names. In Question A, however, there
is a sample of data about specific cereals. Ask students to locate the individual
cereals as possible dots on the dot plot. Give students copies of Labsheet 3.2A
so that they can mark the graph. Work as a class to respond to Question A. When
you work on Question A, highlight that each particular cereal is a case or example
of the category being studied (cereals), and the information in the columns
are attributes of a case. Highlight the attribute—grams of sugar. Attributes are
variables; grams of sugar vary from one case to another, as would grams of sodium
or calories. Look at the attribute—shelf location. Discuss what the values of this
attribute—bottom, middle, and top—mean.

Have the students continue with the Problem. Students can use copies of
Labsheet 3.2B: Cereal Distributions by Shelf Location, which is a copy of the
three dot plots (cereals organized by shelf location) found in the Student Edition.

▼ Explore

Providing for Individual Needs

Students will need to think about ways to compare the three sets of data that
represent cereals on three different shelves.

If students do not see a way to compare the graphs, remind them of the statistics
that summarize distributions.

Suggested Questions

- What would you say is a typical amount of sugar for cereals on each shelf?
  What measure are you using? (The median would be a good measure of
  center here, but students can also use the mean.)

- Are there any other characteristics that appear in one distribution and not
  in another? (There are big gaps in the top-shelf data. Apparently the top-
  shelf cereals fall into two or three groups with respect to how much sugar
  they have.)

- How else might you compare these data sets? (Students might suggest
  range or IQR. IQR is asked for in Question B, part (2).)

- What would this measure tell us? (how variable or spread out the data are)

- What happens when gaps are included in the IQR? (The gaps will make the spread appear greater than if there were no gaps in the IQR. For example, most of the data for the top-shelf cereals are at either end of the distribution of sugar content. This results in a large IQR.)

You might want to wait until after the Summarize to have your students write a report for Question B, part (3).

Planning for the Summary

What evidence will you use in the summary to clarify and deepen understanding of the Focus Question?

What will you do if you do not have evidence?

▼ Summarize

Orchestrating the Discussion

Return to some of the questions you may have discussed with individual students during the Explore phase. Be sure to highlight how measures of center and spread can be used to help compare distributions. Have students consider what each kind of measure contributes to understanding a distribution.

Suggested Questions

- How might you compare these data sets? (You could use the median and IQR.)

- Using the median and IQR, how would you describe the distribution of grams of sugar for the cereals on the top shelf? (The median is 3 grams, and the IQR is 6.5 grams. You could say that a cereal on the top shelf typically has 3 grams of sugar and that the middle 50% of the distribution has between 1.5 and 8 grams of sugar.)

- Is there any other characteristic of the top-shelf distribution that you would like to note? (There are three clusters and two gaps.)

- What is the effect of the gaps on the summary statistics? (It makes the IQR large.)

Students need to compare these groups of cereals to each other, with respect to the attribute grams of sugar. If students have prepared reports, have them share and critique their reports for the other two shelves of cereals, making sure that students go beyond calculating statistics to using the statistics to make comparisons.

If students have not already done so, have them write a report using the measures they found. Have them address the points requested in Question B, part (3).

Reflecting on Student Learning

Use the following questions to assess student understanding at the end of the lesson.

- What evidence do I have that students understand the Focus Question?
  - Where did my students get stuck?
  - What strategies did they use?
  - What breakthroughs did my students have today?
- How will I use this to plan for tomorrow? For the next time I teach this lesson?
- Where will I have the opportunity to reinforce these ideas as I continue through this Unit? The next Unit?

ACE Assignment Guide

- **Applications:** 4
- **Connections:** 17–20
- **Extensions:** 26

Labsheet 3ACE: Exercise 4 contains copies of the dot plots in the Student Edition for Exercise 4. You can give this labsheet to students who may benefit from writing or drawing on the dot plots as they work.

Labsheet 3ACE: Exercises 17 and 18 (accessibility) is optional. It is an example of a way to provide students with additional support for an ACE Exercise.

PROBLEM

3.3

Is It Worth the Wait?
Determining and Describing Variability Using the MAD

▼ Problem Overview

Focus Question What information does the mean absolute deviation provide about how data vary in a distribution?

Problem Description

Students consider wait times for their favorite rides at an amusement park. The mean wait time is known for each of some of the more popular rides. Sally waited longer than the posted average wait time for the Scenic Trolley. Sally wonders how much wait times vary from the posted mean.

Students are introduced to the mean absolute deviation (MAD) as a way to measure the variation of wait times for a ride. They compare the differences in variability of wait times for various popular rides. They learn to compute the MAD and decide how to use average wait time and the MAD to make choices about rides.

Note: In calculating the MAD, students find the distance from each data value to the mean value. Distances are always positive, so they are working with positive numbers only. The *absolute deviation* of 10 from the mean of 25 is $|10 - 25|$, which is $|-15|$, or 15.

Since subtracting integers is not addressed in Grade 6, students will find the *distance* from 10 to 25. They will thus be able to avoid the unnecessary complication of subtracting integers and using absolute values. *Absolute deviation* and *distance* are synonymous.

Problem Implementation

Have students work in pairs on this Problem.

Materials

- **Labsheet 3.3A:** Wait-Time Distribution for Scenic Trolley Ride
- **Labsheet 3.3B:** Wait-Time Distributions for the Carousel and Bumper Cars
- **Labsheet 3ACE:** Exercises 14–16 (accessibility)
- **Check Up 2**

Using Technology

Students can use the **Data and Graphs** tool for Problem 3.3. This tool includes a MAD calculator. They can also use this tool, as well as the **Expression Calculator**, while solving ACE Exercises. Students can use these tools to help them focus on the greater concepts of the Problem rather than focusing on computations.

Vocabulary

• mean absolute deviation (MAD)

Mathematics Background

• The Process of Statistical Investigation
• Components of Statistical Investigation
• Posing Questions
• Collecting Data
• Describing Data With Measures of Variability
• Interpreting Results

At a Glance and Lesson Plan

• At a Glance: Problem 3.3 Data About Us
• Lesson Plan: Problem 3.3 Data About Us

▼ Launch

Launch Video

Two characters wait for two different amusement park rides in this animation. The average wait time for each ride is 25 minutes; however, one character gets to go on one ride many more times than the other does. Students should be able to explain how this is possible. You can show your students this animation to help set context for the Problem before reading the introduction to Problem 3.3 in the Student Edition. Visit Teacher Place at mathdashboard.com/cmp3 to see the complete video.

Connecting to Prior Knowledge

This Problem continues students' exploration of variability. Students look at a statistic that is associated with the mean of a distribution—mean absolute deviation (MAD). The MAD provides information about how all the data values in a distribution differ, on average, from the mean of the distribution. The more data are spread out, the greater the MAD. Like the relationship between the IQR and the median, a small MAD indicates that data are clustered more closely to the mean, and thus, are more like the mean. When the MAD is large, data are less clustered around the mean.

Presenting the Challenge

To engage students in the Problem, begin by talking about how long it takes to wait in lines. Let students relate stories about encountering long, short, and in-between wait times.

Tell students that they can use statistics to decide how variable wait times are. Based on what they know about how wait times vary, they can make decisions about waiting in different situations.

You can show your students the Launch animation at this point. Afterward, you can read the introduction to Problem 3.3 as a class.

Suggested Questions

- You are going to look at different amusement park rides. An amusement park advertises the average wait times for rides. However, people who have waited in line say that they can actually wait much longer (or wait much less time) than the advertised average wait times. What do you think? (It is likely that your students will agree. Talk with them about why they might wait longer or if they ever wonder how much extra, on average, they might have to wait for a ride.)

You can complete Question A as a whole class. Several new representations and a new definition are introduced. A copy of the representations from the Student Edition appear on **Labsheet 3.3A: Wait-Time Distribution for Scenic Trolley Ride**.

- We are going to work through Question A together. Look at the introduction to Question A and the dot plot. Describe the situation. What problem is Sally investigating? (Sally wants to know how to think about how different her wait time is from the mean posted time.)

- Look at Question A, part (1). How can you go about answering that question? (Have students explain how to find the mean wait time (identify the 10 wait times from the graph, add up all the wait times, and divide by 10 to get the mean). Locate where the mean (25 minutes) would be on the line plot. Have them describe what they notice about the actual wait times in relation to the mean wait time.)

PROBLEM
OVERVIEW
▶ LAUNCH
EXPLORE
SUMMARIZE
MATHEMATICAL
REFLECTIONS

- In Question A, part (2), you see two representations: a dot plot and an ordered-value bar graph. They each show the 10 wait times of Scenic Trolley riders. You already know the mean wait time is 25 minutes. How are the distances from each data value to the mean shown on the dot plot? On the ordered-value bar graph? How do these distances help you describe how much, on average, the data values vary from the mean? (Four data values are greater than the mean. The maximum data value is 15 minutes longer than the mean. The next wait time is 10 minutes longer, followed by 6 minutes longer, and then 5 minutes longer. You can do the same thing for the data values that are less than the mean. The minimum wait is 15 minutes shorter, followed by 10 minutes shorter, then 5 minutes shorter, then 3 minutes shorter, then another 3 minutes shorter. The average of these distances is 7.2 minutes. On average, the data values vary by 7.2 minutes from the mean.)

- Write a sentence describing the wait time for the Scenic Trolley that includes the amount of 7.2 minutes. (Push students to express this in their own words. A possible answer might be: Even though the mean wait time is 25 minutes, you can expect to wait 7.2 minutes more or less than this.)

- How can you show direction on the graphs? (Students may offer different ideas about how to show direction on either the dot plot diagram or the ordered-value bar graph. They could use positive and negative numbers, although distances are not negative. They could color-code different directions.)

- In part (2c), Sally looks at the five data values to the left of the mean and the five to the right of the mean. What are the five distances to the left of the mean? To the right? Why are the two sums are the same? (The distances to the left are 15, 10, 5, 3, and 3 minutes. The distances to the right are 15, 10, 6, and 5 minutes. The totals are the same. The sum of distances above the mean balances the sum of distances below the mean since the mean is a balanced, or average, value.

   You don't have to push this, but some students will realize that this is an evening-out situation such as those encountered in Investigation 2. Students may note that the 40-minute wait balances the 10-minute wait, and the 31-minute wait balances the two 22-minute waits.)

- You found the mean distance from the mean wait time was 7.2 minutes. Does this amount appear in the representations? (This does not appear directly on any of the representations.)

- Could Sally have waited more than 25 minutes + 7.2 minutes? (Yes; 7.2 minutes is the average distance from the mean for all the data values. Some will be more than 7.2 minutes from the mean, and some will be less than 7.2 minutes from the mean.)

Have the students continue working on Questions B–D. Be prepared to provide support as needed.

▼ Explore

Providing for Individual Needs

You may want to give students **Labsheet 3.3B: Wait-Time Distributions for the Carousel and Bumper Cars** to use for Questions B and C.

For Question B, students work with a new ride called the Carousel. Help students to see that analyzing the Carousel data is related to what they did with the Scenic Trolley ride.

Suggested Questions

- Look at the data on the graph. How does the variability of the wait times for the Carousel compare to the variability of the wait times for the Scenic Trolley? (Students need to notice that the wait times for the Carousel are clustered closely around the mean of 25 minutes; with the Scenic Trolley, the data are more spread out.)

- How many data values are there for the Carousel data set? (ten)

- How can you find the distances of the wait times from the mean wait time of 25 minutes for the Carousel? (You can list the data values by reading them from the dot plot: 22, 23, 23, 24, 24, 25, 26, 27, 28, 28. You can make an ordered-value bar graph to see the distances visually. You can then make a distance diagram showing distances and directions of distances on either the ordered-value bar graph or the dot plot.)

- How do you find the sum of the distances? (Add up all the distances. The sum is 18 minutes (9 + 9).)

  Note: Some students may write negatives on the distance diagram. Be sure to remind them that distances are always positive.

- How do you find the MAD for the wait times for the Carousel? (Find the average distance from the mean by dividing the sum of the distances by 10 (the number of data values); the MAD is 1.8 minutes.)

- What does the MAD tell you about the wait time for the Carousel ride? (As before, push students to state this in their own words. Possible answers: Typical wait times are 1.8 minutes more or less than the mean. Or, typically a rider waits 25 minutes, give or take 1.8 minutes.)

For Question C, use similar questions as those above. The rides have a different mean wait time; the mean for Bumper Cars is 10 minutes. What is important here is to have students compare two sets of data in terms of variability instead of in terms of a measure of center. The MAD for Scenic Trolley is 7.2 minutes; the MAD for Bumper Cars is 3.6 minutes. The mean wait time for Bumper Cars is 10 minutes while the mean wait time for the Scenic Trolley is 25 minutes. Using the means and the MADs, you would ride the Bumper Cars if you wanted a shorter wait time.

Planning for the Summary

What evidence will you use in the summary to clarify and deepen understanding of the Focus Question?

What will you do if you do not have evidence?

▼ Summarize

Orchestrating the Discussion

Help students summarize what they did to complete Questions B and C. Have them share the sentences they made using the mean and MAD for each ride. They should be able to complete these three sentences:

A person waiting in line at Scenic Trolley will wait a mean time of 25 minutes; however, the wait time could vary, on average, _____ minutes more or less. ($7.2 \approx 7$ minutes)

A person waiting in line at Carousel will wait a mean time of 25 minutes; however, the wait time could vary, on average, _____ minutes more or less. ($1.8 \approx 2$ minutes)

A person waiting in line at Bumper Cars will wait a mean time of 10 minutes; however, the wait time could vary, on average, _____ minutes more or less. ($3.6 \approx 4$ minutes)

Suggested Questions

- Which ride has greater variability in wait times from the mean? How does the MAD help you know this? (The mean wait time for both Scenic Trolley and for Carousel is 25 minutes, but Carousel has a MAD of about 2 minutes, whereas Scenic Trolley has a MAD of about 7 minutes. So, Scenic Trolley has greater variability in wait time. Bumper Cars has a MAD that is between the Carousel MAD and the Scenic Trolley MAD, but Bumper Cars has an average wait time of only 10 minutes, 15 minutes less that the average wait time for Scenic Trolley.)

- For the Carousel distribution, add the distances from each data value on the left side of the mean to the mean. Add the distances from each data value on the right side of the mean to the mean. What do you notice? (The sums of the distances on either side of the mean are equal. The sum of the distances from each data value on the left side of the mean to the mean is 9; the sum of the distances from each data value on the right side of the mean to the mean is also 9.)

- For Question D, which ride would you choose if you only had 30 minutes? (Question D attempts to make the knowledge of average wait time and MAD practical. You know that the ride with the smaller MAD is likely to be the ride whose wait time will be closest to its posted mean. The MAD is an average, however, so it is possible that there could be an unusual wait time even for the ride with the smaller MAD. Choosing the ride with the greater MAD includes an element of risk; if a student really must leave in 30 minutes, then it is possible to stand in line for the Alpine Slide for 30 minutes and not be able to take this ride.)

Reflecting on Student Learning

Use the following questions to assess student understanding at the end of the lesson.

- What evidence do I have that students understand the Focus Question?
  - Where did my students get stuck?
  - What strategies did they use?
  - What breakthroughs did my students have today?
- How will I use this to plan for tomorrow? For the next time I teach this lesson?
- Where will I have the opportunity to reinforce these ideas as I continue through this Unit? The next Unit?

ACE Assignment Guide

- **Applications:** 5–11
- **Connections:** 14–16, 21–25
- **Extensions:** 27

Labsheet 3ACE: Exercises 14–16 (accessibility) is optional. It is an example of a way to provide students with additional support for an ACE Exercise.

▼ Mathematical Reflections

Possible Answers to Mathematical Reflections

1. a. The range is the difference between the minimum and maximum data values in a set of data.

   b. The IQR is the difference between Quartile 1 and Quartile 3 and indicates the spread of the middle 50% of the data in a distribution.

   c. The MAD is a number that describes how all the data values in a distribution differ, on average, from the mean of the distribution. If the MAD is small, then the data are likely to be clustered closely around the mean. As the MAD increases, the data are more likely to be more spread out around the mean. A smaller MAD can indicate that the mean of the distribution is a good estimate of the typical value for those data.

1. a. You can compare the two ranges by comparing their sizes; if one is greater than the other, this suggests that the data distribution is more spread out. You should also examine a graph of each distribution; it could be that there are a few unusual values that influence the range, but when the actual distribution is considered, their spreads are similar.

   b. When you compare IQRs, you are looking at how spread out the middle 50% of the data are. If one IQR is greater than the other, then we can say that the middle 50% of the data in that distribution are more spread out than the other distribution. This means that the data have greater variation (are not as close to the median).

   c. When you compare MADs, you are comparing how data values in two distributions differ, on average, from the means of the respective distributions. The greater the MAD, the greater the data variation from the mean.

Possible Answers to Mathematical Practices Reflections

Students may have demonstrated all of the eight Common Core Standards for Mathematical Practice during this Investigation. During the class discussion, have students provide additional Practices that the Problem cited involved and identify the use of other Mathematical Practices in the Investigation.

One student observation is provided in the Student Edition. Here is another sample student response.

In Problem 3.2, we had to determine IQRs for each of the distributions of grams of sugar in cereals. Robert noticed that for the top shelf, the IQR is 6.5 grams of sugar, but for the other two shelves, it is either 4 or 5 grams. Jenny said that means the cereals on that shelf have more variability in how many grams of sugar are in a serving than those on the other two shelves. Robert looked at the distribution and reasoned about why this might be so. The top shelf is the only shelf that has cereal with less than 3 grams of sugar per serving and a whole lot of cereals that have 3 grams of sugar per serving. There are some gaps as well. For the other two shelves, this is not the case.

MP2: Reason abstractly and quantitatively.

Notes

Investigation 3

What's Your Favorite…? Measuring Variability

 A statistical investigation begins by asking a question. Decisions about what data to collect are based on the question.

When people collect answers to a question, the data may be similar, such as the number of raisins found in each of 30 different half-ounce boxes of raisins. More often, however, the data vary, such as the pulse rates of 30 different people after each person rides a roller coaster.

When you are interested in learning about a person, you may ask a question that begins "What is your favorite . . .?" For example, you might ask "What is your favorite cereal?"

serving size
$\frac{3}{4}$ cup or 28 grams

serving size
1 cup or 30 grams

serving size
$1\frac{1}{4}$ cups or 33 grams

serving size
$\frac{3}{4}$ cup or 30 grams

....

Common Core State Standards

6.SP.A.1 Recognize a statistical question as one that anticipates variability in the data related to the question and accounts for it in the answers.

6.SP.A.3 Recognize that a measure of center for a numerical data set summarizes all of its values with a single number, while a measure of variation describes how its values vary with a single number.

Also 6.RP.A.3, 6.RP.A.3a, 6.NS.C.6, 6.NS.C.7, 6.SP.A.2, 6.SP.B.4, 6.SP.B.5c, 6.SP.B.5d

Notes _____

_____

_____

The graph below shows the results of an online survey of 4,500 people. Each person took the survey once.

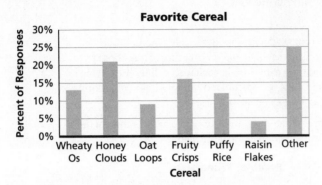

Favorite Cereal

- What do you know about cereal choices from this survey?

You can investigate other information related to cereal. For example, a recent report claims that children "overpour" their cereal, meaning they pour portions that are larger than a single serving size. This is a problem because many cereals have high sugar contents.

- Do you think that children overpour by the same amount for all cereals? Explain.

Understanding and explaining variability in data is the essence of statistical problem solving. **Variability** in numerical data indicates how spread out a distribution of data is. One way to compare data distributions is to describe which data set is *more variable* (spread out) or *less variable* (clustered together). In this Investigation, you will learn some other ways to describe how data vary.

Notes _____

_____

3.1 Estimating Cereal Serving Sizes
Determining the IQR

Twelve middle-school students decided to investigate whether they could pour cereal portions to match actual serving sizes. They chose two different cereals to use in their experiment, each with a different serving size. The students poured all of their estimated servings before checking to see how close they were to the listed serving sizes.

Each student poured an estimated serving size ($\frac{3}{4}$ cup or 28 grams) of the cereal Wheaty Os. Copy and complete the table below.

Pours of Wheaty Os

Grams Poured	52	29	32	59	43	24	28	23	20	30	37	27
Serving Size	1.86	1.04	1.14	▦	▦	0.86	▦	0.82	0.71	1.07	▦	0.96

- How could you compute the data values in the serving-size row?

The dot plot below shows the distribution of the serving-size data. The data values you calculated to complete the table are already included.

Number of Servings of Wheaty Os

- Which measure of center—mean, median, or mode—might you use to describe a typical serving size poured by the students?

- How well do you think students estimated the serving size when they poured Wheaty Os?

You have already learned how to find the median of a data set. In Problem 3.1, you will work with values called **quartiles**—the three points that divide an ordered set of data into four equal groups, with each group containing one-fourth of the data values.

Problem 3.1

A The students agreed that being "about right" means pouring a serving size that is in the middle 50% of the data distribution. The students arranged the twelve Wheaty Os data values in order from least to greatest on sticky notes.

| 0.71 | 0.82 | 0.86 | 0.96 | 1.00 | 1.04 | 1.07 | 1.14 | 1.32 | 1.54 | 1.86 | 2.11 |

1. What is the median?

2. Identify the **lower quartile** (Q1). Its *position* is located midway between the serving sizes 0.86 and 0.96. Find the *value* of the lower quartile.

3. Identify the **upper quartile** (Q3). Its *position* is located midway between the serving sizes 1.32 and 1.54. Find the *value* of the upper quartile.

4. How are the positions of Q1 and Q3 related to the position of the median (sometimes called Q2)?

5. The serving size estimates between Q1 and Q3 are in the middle 50% of the data. Do you agree that serving size estimates in the middle 50% are "about right"? Explain.

6. The **interquartile range (IQR)** is the difference Q3 – Q1. The IQR measures the *spread* of the middle 50% of the data. What is the IQR for the Wheaty Os data?

continued on the next page >

Investigation 3   What's Your Favorite…? Measuring Variability   61

Notes

Problem 3.1 continued

B The students also poured estimated servings ($1\frac{1}{4}$ cup or 33 grams) of Raisin Flakes.

1. On a copy of the table below, write the serving sizes of the data they gathered.

Pours of Raisin Flakes

Grams Poured	44	33	31	24	42	31	28	24	15	36	30	41
Serving Size	1.33	1.00	■	■	■	0.94	■	■	■	1.09	■	■

2. Make a line plot or a dot plot to show the frequency of the distribution of data values. Use the same number-line labels as the Wheaty Os dot plot at the beginning of Investigation 3.

3. Arrange the data in order from least to greatest. What is the median?

4. Find Q1 and Q3. Use these to identify the middle 50% of the data.

5. Describe the estimated servings that are in the middle 50% of the distribution. Do you agree that the estimated servings in the middle 50% are "about right"? Explain.

6. Calculate the IQR of the estimated servings of Raisin Flakes. Explain how you found this number.

C Use the interquartile ranges of the Wheaty Os and Raisin Flakes data.

1. For which cereal are the data more spread out? Explain.

2. Is IQR a good measure of whether students consistently underpour or overpour cereal servings? Explain.

3. How would you describe a typical serving of Wheaty Os as poured by the students? Of Raisin Flakes?

Notes _____

_____

_____

Problem 3.1 continued

D Recall that the range of a data set is a measure of variability (or spread).

   1. Compute the range of the Wheaty Os data. Compute the range of the Raisin Flakes data.

   2. What do the ranges tell you about how the poured servings vary? Explain.

   3. Compare the ranges and the IQRs of each data set. How are they alike? How are they different?

E Each student wrote a report comparing the two data sets. Two students, Seamus and Deanna, gave the answers below. Do you agree with Seamus or with Deanna? Explain your reasoning.

Seamus

For servings of Raisin Flakes, both the range (0.88 g) and the IQR (0.375 g) are less than the range (1.4 g) and IQR (0.52 g) of Wheaty Os.

About one third of the students overpoured the servings of Raisin Flakes (33 g), but almost two thirds of the students overpoured the servings of Wheaty Os (38 g). Students seem more accurate at estimating servings of Raisin Flakes.

Deanna

The median serving size poured for the Raisin Flakes data is 0.94 of a serving. The median serving size poured for the Wheaty Os data is 1.055 of a serving. Students seem to overpour Wheaty Os and underpour Raisin Flakes.

 Homework starts on page 72.

STUDENT PAGE

Notes

3.2

Connecting Cereal Shelf Location and Sugar Content

Describing Variability Using the IQR

Cereal boxes have nutritional information on the side panel. Sugar content is reported in grams per serving.

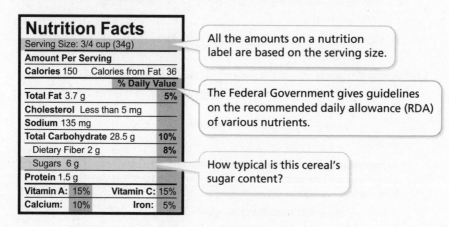

Nutrition Facts

Serving Size: 3/4 cup (34g)

Amount Per Serving

Calories 150   Calories from Fat 36

	% Daily Value
Total Fat 3.7 g	5%
Cholesterol Less than 5 mg	
Sodium 135 mg	
Total Carbohydrate 28.5 g	10%
Dietary Fiber 2 g	8%
Sugars 6 g	
Protein 1.5 g	

Vitamin A:	15%	Vitamin C:	15%
Calcium:	10%	**Iron:**	5%

All the amounts on a nutrition label are based on the serving size.

The Federal Government gives guidelines on the recommended daily allowance (RDA) of various nutrients.

How typical is this cereal's sugar content?

The dot plot below shows the distribution of grams of sugar per serving for 70 cereals. The median is 7.5 grams of sugar, or about 2 teaspoons of sugar, per serving. The red marker (⊥) indicates the median.

Distribution of Sugar in 70 Cereals

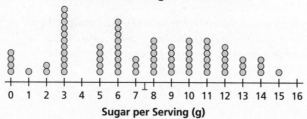

Sugar per Serving (g)

- What surprises you about the data set or its distribution? Explain.

- What questions do you have as you look at the distribution?

Notes _____

You have used two measures of variability: range and interquartile range (IQR). In Problem 3.2, you will use the IQR to describe variability in grams of sugar for different groups of cereals.

Problem 3.2

Ⓐ Use the dot plot on the previous page showing the distribution of sugar in cereals.

1. Are there intervals where the data cluster? What does this tell you about the data?

2. The table below shows some of the data. On a copy of the dot plot from the previous page, locate each data point.

Distribution of Sugar in Several Cereals

Cereals From Data Set	Sugar (grams)	Shelf Location
Bran-ful	5	Bottom
Crispy Bran	6	Top
Wheaty Os	1	Top
Fruity Crisps	13	Middle
Sugary Flakes	11	Top
Frosted Bites	7	Middle
Healthy Nuggets	3	Bottom
Honey Oats	6	Middle
Honey Wheaty Os	10	Top
Raisin Flakes	14	Middle

continued on the next page >

STUDENT PAGE

Notes _____

_____

_____

Problem 3.2 *continued*

B The dot plots below show data for the 70 cereals organized by supermarket shelf location.

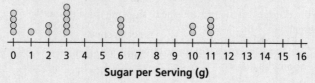

Sugar in Top-Shelf Cereals

Sugar per Serving (g)

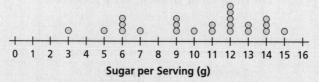

Sugar in Middle-Shelf Cereals

Sugar per Serving (g)

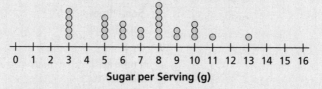

Sugar in Bottom-Shelf Cereals

Sugar per Serving (g)

1. Is there any pattern to how sugary a cereal is and its shelf location? Find ways to describe and compare the three distributions of data.

2. a. Find the IQR for each distribution.

  b. Which of the three distributions has the greatest variability in grams of sugar per serving? The least variability?

Notes _____

_____

_____

continued

3. Write a report comparing the cereals located on each of the shelves. Your report should

- use a measure of center to describe the typical number of grams of sugar in the cereals on each shelf.

- use a measure of spread to describe the variability in the number of grams of sugar in the cereals on each shelf.

- compare the distributions of grams of sugar in the cereals on each of the three shelves by using the measures of center and spread above.

- point out anything unusual or interesting.

A C E Homework starts on page 72.

3.3 Is It Worth the Wait?
Determining and Describing Variability Using the MAD

In your lifetime, you spend a lot of time waiting. Sometimes it feels like you could stand in line forever. For example, you may wait a long time for your favorite ride at an amusement park.

During the summer, one estimate of average wait time at an amusement park is 60 minutes. The most popular rides can accommodate 1,500 people per hour. Lines form when more people arrive than the rides can fit. Amusement parks are designed to minimize wait times, but variability in the number of people who choose a particular ride can result in lines.

Notes _____

_____

_____

Sally and her family spent the day at an amusement park. At the end of the day, Sally noticed the sign below.

- Which ride has the shortest average wait time? The longest?

- Sally waited in line longer than 25 minutes for the Scenic Trolley ride. How could this have happened?

In Investigation 2, you learned that it is possible for a data set to include values that are quite different from the mean. In Problem 3.3, you will find a way to describe *how much* data values vary from an average.

 Problem 3.3

Ⓐ Since Sally waited in line longer than the average wait time, she wondered how much wait times vary.

The dot plot below shows a distribution of ten wait times for the Scenic Trolley ride.

Scenic Trolley Wait Times

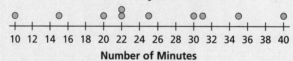

Number of Minutes

1. Sally says that the mean wait time is 25 minutes, just like the sign claimed. Do you agree? Explain.

Notes

Problem **3.3** *continued*

2. Sally wonders how typical a wait time of 25 minutes is. She says "I can find how much, on average, the data values vary from the mean time of 25 minutes." She uses the graph below to find the distance each data value is from the mean.

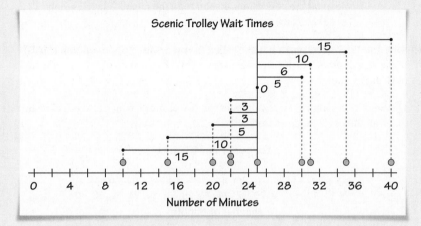

Fred says "That's a good idea, but I used an ordered-value bar graph to show the same idea."

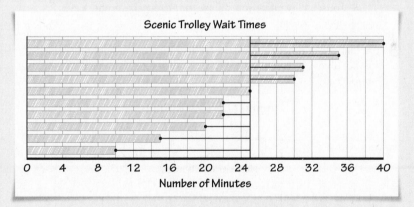

a. Describe how you can use each graph to find how much, on average, the data values vary from the mean time of 25 minutes.

continued on the next page >

Notes _____

_____

_____

STUDENT PAGE

Problem 3.3 *continued*

  b. What does this information tell you about how long you might have
  to wait in line to ride the Scenic Trolley?

  c. Sally noticed that the sum of the distances to the mean for the data
  values less than the mean equaled the sum of the distances to the
  mean for the data values greater than the mean. Does this make
  sense? Explain.

Sally and Fred calculated a statistic called the **mean absolute deviation (MAD)**
of the distribution. It is the average distance (or mean distance) from the mean
of all data values.

B Below is a sample of ten wait times for the Carousel, which also has a mean
  wait time of 25 minutes (indicated by △).

Carousel Wait Times

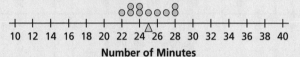

Number of Minutes

  1. Find the mean absolute deviation (MAD) for this distribution.

  2. Compare the MAD for the Scenic Trolley with the MAD for the
  Carousel. Why might you choose the Carousel over the Scenic
  Trolley? Explain.

C The Bumper Cars have a mean wait time of 10 minutes. Like other rides,
  the wait times are variable. Below is a sample of ten wait times for the
  Bumper Cars.

Bumper Cars Wait Times

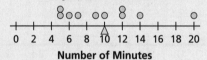

Number of Minutes

  1. What is the MAD for the Bumper Cars data?

  2. Compare the mean wait time of the Scenic Trolley and of the Bumper
  Cars. What do you notice? Then compare the MADs of both rides.
  What do you notice? Explain.

Notes _____

_____

_____

Problem **3.3** *continued*

D Use these two signs for amusement park rides. Suppose you have to leave the park in 30 minutes. You want one last ride. Each ride lasts 3 minutes. Which ride would you choose? Explain.

Average Wait Time: 18 minutes
MAD: 12 minutes

Average Wait Time: 22 minutes
MAD: 2 minutes

ACE Homework starts on page 72.

Notes

Applications

Servers at the Mugwump Diner receive tips for excellent service.

1. **a.** On Monday, four servers earned the tips below. Find the range of the tips.

   b. The four servers shared their tips equally. How much money did each server get? Explain.

   c. Yanna was busy clearing a table when the tips were shared. Yanna also received $16.10 in tips. Suppose Yanna's tips were included with the other tips, and the total was shared equally among the five servers. Without doing any computations, will the four servers receive less than, the same as, or more than they did before Yanna's tips were included? Explain.

2. On Tuesday, all five servers shared their tips equally. Each received $16.45. Does this mean someone originally received $16.45 in tips? Explain.

3. **a.** On Wednesday, Yanna received $13.40 in tips. When tips were shared equally among the five servers, each received $15.25. How could this have happened? Explain.

   b. Based on the information in part (a), what can you say about the variability of the tip data on Wednesday? Explain your reasoning.

Notes

4. Recall the name-length data from Investigation 1. You explored name
   lengths from several different countries. The dot plots below show
   four distributions of data. Each dot plot shows the median ($\perp$).

Chinese Pen-Pal Names

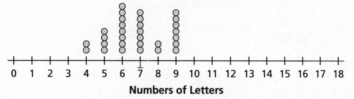

Numbers of Letters

Japanese Pen-Pal Names

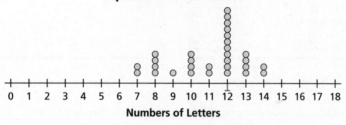

Numbers of Letters

Korean Pen-Pal Names

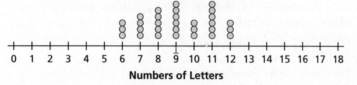

Numbers of Letters

U.S. Student Names

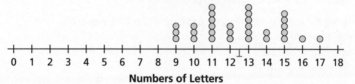

Numbers of Letters

a. What is the interquartile range (IQR) of each distribution? Explain
   how you found each IQR.

b. Using the IQRs, for which distribution is the middle 50% the least
   spread out? The most spread out? Explain.

Notes

5. Below are two ordered-value bar graphs (Sample 1 and Sample 2), each showing nine households with a mean of five people per household.

Sample 1

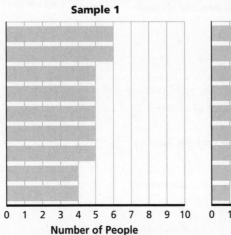

Sample 2

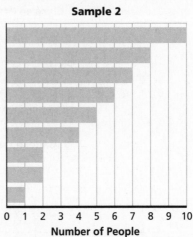

a. For each sample, how many *moves* does it take to even out the bars so that the mean is 5? A "move" is the movement of one person from one household to another household.

b. Draw an ordered-value bar graph showing nine households in which each data value is 5. Use the same scale as the other two graphs and label it Sample 3. How does this show that the mean is five people?

c. The closer a data value is to the mean, the fewer moves it takes to even out the data. In which graph (Sample 1, 2, or 3) are the data closest to the mean (vary the least)? Farthest from the mean (vary the most)? Explain.

d. Using the three ordered-value bar graphs, find the mean absolute deviation (MAD) for each set of data. Based on the MADs, which set of data varies the most from the mean of five people? Varies the least? Explain.

Notes

6. Jeff and Elaine are studying for their final exam. The grading spreadsheet below shows their practice-test scores. Each test has a top score of 100.

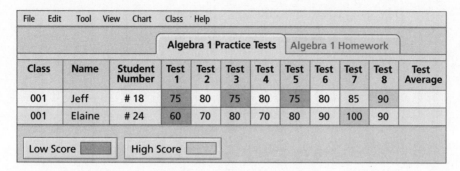

Class	Name	Student Number	Test 1	Test 2	Test 3	Test 4	Test 5	Test 6	Test 7	Test 8	Test Average
001	Jeff	# 18	75	80	75	80	75	80	85	90	
001	Elaine	# 24	60	70	80	70	80	90	100	90	

Low Score [   ]   High Score [   ]

a. Make a line plot of each person's practice tests scores.

b. What are the median and IQR of each distribution?

c. What are the mean and MAD of each distribution?

d. On the day of the exam, who is more likely to receive a score of 80, Jeff or Elaine? Explain your reasoning.

7. The dot plots below show the distributions of ten wait times at two rides.

Amusement Park Ride 1

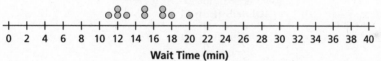

Wait Time (min)

Amusement Park Ride 2

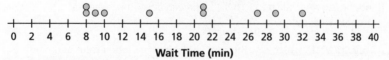

Wait Time (min)

a. Find the mean of each data set.

b. Compute the MAD of each data set.

Notes

c. Compare the MADs. In which distribution do the data vary more from the mean? Explain.

d. i. Make your own data set of ten wait times. Draw a dot plot.

   ii. Compute the MAD.

   iii. Compare the three distributions. In which distribution do the data vary more from the mean? Explain your thinking.

For Exercises 8–10, use the line plots below.

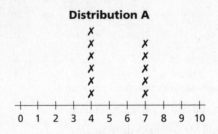

Distribution A

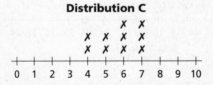

Distribution B

Distribution C

8. Find the interquartile range (IQR) and mean absolute deviation (MAD) of each data set.

9. Using the MAD, which distribution has the least variation from the mean? The most?

10. Using the IQR, which distribution has the greatest spread in the middle 50% of data? The least?

Notes

_____

_____

_____

11. The frequency table below shows the number of pets owned by students in three different sixth-grade classes.

Pet Ownership

Number of Pets	Class 1	Class 2	Class 3
0	5	4	2
1	3	1	2
2	5	5	5
3	2	3	4
4	0	3	1
5	0	1	2
6	1	2	3
7	0	0	0
8	0	0	1
9	0	0	1
10	0	0	0
11	0	1	0
12	0	0	1
13	1	0	0
14	1	0	1
15	0	0	0
16	0	0	0
17	0	0	1
18	0	0	0
19	0	0	1
20	0	0	0
21	0	0	1
22	0	0	0
23	1	0	0
24	1	0	0

a. Draw a line plot or dot plot of each data set. Use the same scale on each graph so you can easily compare the distributions.

b. Compute the median and IQR for each distribution. Write at least three statements to compare the classes using the median and IQR.

c. Below are the means and MADs for each data set. Write at least three statements to compare the classes using the means and MADs.

Pet Ownership Statistics

Number of Pets	Class 1	Class 2	Class 3
Mean	5	2.67	6
MAD	3.6	1.74	4.46

Investigation 3   What's Your Favorite...? Measuring Variability   **77**

Notes

Connections

For Exercises 12 and 13, use the bar graph below.

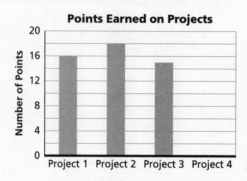

Points Earned on Projects

12. **a.** Malaika's mean score is 17 points. How many points did Malaika receive on Project 4? Explain.

   b. What is the range of Malaika's scores on the four projects? What does this tell you about the variation in her scores?

13. Each project has a maximum score of 20 points.

   a. What would Malaika's mean score be if she had a total of 80 points for the four projects? A total of 60 points?

   b. Give four possible project scores that would result in each mean score in part (a).

   c. What is the range of the scores for each of your sets of four project scores? What does this tell you about how spread out or variable the scores are?

   d. Are these ranges more spread out, or variable, than the range of Malaika's set of scores? Explain.

Notes _____

_____

_____

For Exercises 14–16, use the tables below.

Caffeine Content of Selected Soda Drinks

Name	Caffeine in 8 Ounces (mg)
Soda A	38
Soda B	37
Soda C	27
Soda D	27
Soda E	26
Soda F	24
Soda G	21
Soda H	15
Soda J	23

Caffeine Content of Selected Other Drinks

Name	Caffeine in 8 Ounces (mg)
Energy Drink A	77
Energy Drink B	70
Energy Drink C	25
Energy Drink D	21
Iced Tea A	19
Iced Tea B	10
Coffee Drink	83
Hot Cocoa	2
Juice Drink	33

14. a. Find the mean and median amounts of caffeine in the soda drinks.

   b. Find the mean and median amounts of caffeine in the other drinks.

   c. Using parts (a) and (b), is it possible to say which type of drink—sodas or other drinks—has greater variability in caffeine content? Explain.

   d. Write three statements comparing the amounts of caffeine in sodas and other drinks.

15. Indicate whether each statement is true or false.

   a. Soda B has more caffeine than Soda F or Soda D.

   b. Energy Drink C has about three times as much caffeine per serving as Energy Drink A.

   c. 75% of all the drinks have 25 mg or less of caffeine per serving.

Notes

16. In Exercise 14, you found the means and medians of the sodas and the other drinks. Two MADs and two IQRs are listed below.

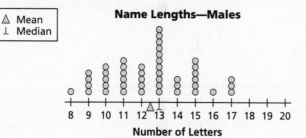

MAD = 5.16 mg
IQR = 10 mg

MAD = 25.93 mg
IQR = 59 mg

a. Which statistics describe the variability of caffeine content in the sodas? Explain your reasoning.

b. Which statistics describe the variability of caffeine content in the other drinks? Explain.

For Exercises 17 and 18, use the dot plots below.

△ Mean
⊥ Median

Name Lengths—Males

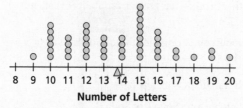

Number of Letters

Name Lengths—Females

Number of Letters

17. Compare the two sets of data. Which group has longer names? Explain.

18. Look at the distribution for females. Suppose that the data for four names with 18 or more letters changed. These students now have name lengths of ten or fewer letters.

a. Draw a dot plot showing this change.

b. Will the change affect the median name length for females? Explain.

c. Will the change affect the mean name length for females? Explain.

Notes _____

_____

_____

19. **Multiple Choice** John's test scores were 100, 84, 88, 96, and 96. His teacher told him that his final grade is 96. Which measure of center did his teacher use to report John's final grade?

    A. Mean   **B.** Median

    C. Mode   **D.** Range

20. **Multiple Choice** Sal's Packages on the Go mails 6 packages with a mean weight of 7.1 pounds. Suppose the mean weight of five of these packages is 6.3 pounds. What is the weight of the sixth package?

    F. 4.26 lb   **G.** 6.7 lb

    H. 10.3 lb   **J.** 11.1 lb

21. **Multiple Choice** Which of the following is true about the IQR?

    A. It describes the variability of the middle 50% of the data values.

    B. It describes, on average, the distance of each data value from the mean.

    C. It uses the minimum and maximum data value in its computation.

    D. It is a statistic that is affected by extremely high values or extremely low values.

22. A gymnast receives the six scores below.

    a. What is her mean score?

    b. What happens to the mean when you multiply each data value by 2? By $\frac{2}{3}$? By 0.2?

    c. Why does the mean change in each situation?

Notes _____

_____

_____

For Exercises 23–25, use the data below.

- Four pop songs have durations of 162, 151, 174, and 149 seconds.

- Four folk songs have durations of 121, 149, 165, and 184 seconds.

23. **Multiple Choice** What is the MAD of the folk songs' durations?

   F. 18 seconds   **G.** 19 seconds   **H.** 18.25 seconds   **J.** 19.75 seconds

24. **Multiple Choice** What is the MAD of the pop songs' durations?

   A. 2 seconds   **B.** 5 seconds   **C.** 6 seconds   **D.** 9 seconds

25. **Multiple Choice** Which of the following statements is true?

   F. The variability in folk songs' durations is about half that of pop songs.

   G. The variability in folk songs' durations is about twice that of pop songs.

   H. The variability in folk songs' durations is about three times that of pop songs.

   J. The variability in folk songs' durations is about four times that of pop songs.

Extensions

26. Mark has an easy way to find his mean test score: "Each math test is worth 100 points. Suppose I get 60 on my first test and 90 on my second. My average would be 75, because half of 60 is 30, half of 90 is 45, and 30 + 45 is 75. Now suppose I had three test scores: 60, 90, and 84. My average would be 78, because one third of 60 is 20, one third of 90 is 30, one third of 84 is 28, and 20 + 30 + 28 = 78."

   Does Mark's method always work? Explain.

27. Use the data set 20, 6, 10, 8, 12, 16, 14, 15, 14, 7.

   a. Find the mean, mode, and median. Then find the IQR and MAD.

   b. Add 3 to each data value in the set. Now determine the mean, mode, median, IQR, and MAD. What happened? Explain.

   c. Multiply each data value in the set by 2. Now determine the mean, mode, median, IQR, and MAD. What happened? Explain.

Notes _____

_____

_____

In this Investigation, you explored how data vary and how summary statistics can be used to describe variability. The following questions will help you summarize what you learned.

Think about your answers to these questions. Discuss your ideas with other students and your teacher. Then, write a summary of your findings in your notebook.

1. **Explain** and illustrate the following words.

   a. Range

   b. Interquartile range

   c. Mean absolute deviation

2. **a. Describe** how you can use the range to compare how two data distributions vary.

   b. Describe how you can use the IQR to compare how two data distributions vary.

   c. Describe how you can use the MAD to compare how two data distributions vary.

Unit Project

Think about the survey you will be developing to gather information about middle-school students.

 Will measures of variability, such as IQR and MAD, help you report observations about your data?

Notes

Common Core Mathematical Practices

As you worked on the Problems in this Investigation, you used prior knowledge to make sense of them. You also applied your Mathematical Practices to solve the Problems. Think back over your work, the ways you thought about the Problems, and how you used Mathematical Practices.

Shawna described her thoughts in the following way:

> I figured out how to compare the IQR and the MAD. The IQR is related to the median. First, I find the median. Then, I find the midpoint of the data that are less than the median and the midpoint of the data that are greater than the median. The IQR is the difference of those two midpoints.
>
> The MAD is related to the mean. First, I find the mean. Then I find the distance each data value is from the mean. To get an average deviation, I add up all the distances and divide the sum by the number of data values.
>
> What this means is that the greater the IQR, the more the data vary from the median. The same goes for the MAD: The greater the MAD, the more the data vary from the mean.

Common Core Standards for Mathematical Practice

MP7 Look for and make use of structure

- What other Mathematical Practices can you identify in Shawna's reasoning?

- Describe a Mathematical Practice that you and your classmates used to solve a different Problem in this Investigation.

Notes

Investigation **4** PLANNING

What Numbers Describe Us?
Using Graphs to Group Data

▼ Investigation Overview

Investigation Description

In Investigation 4, students extend their skills in working with data by comparing data sets using measures of center and spread. Students compare two or more distributions by looking at **outliers** (a new concept), how data vary, and which measures of center are appropriate to use as comparisons.

Students begin to notice that representations such as line plots and bar graphs are not suitable for displaying some data sets; larger patterns within the data sets can only be seen when the data are grouped. Additionally, it is time consuming to graph individual cases of data sets when the sets are so large.

Students learn to construct and analyze histograms and box-and-whisker plots in this Investigation. Box-and-whisker plots and histograms are representational tools that permit grouping data in intervals. They are more efficient and allow for more patterns to be seen when working with large data sets. In box-and-whisker plots, the data are grouped into four quartiles, each of which includes one fourth of the data values. In histograms, students can choose which interval size to use; the interval size remains constant throughout the graph.

Investigation Vocabulary

- box-and-whisker plot (box plot)
- histogram
- interval
- outlier

Mathematics Background

- Posing Questions
- Collecting Data
- Analyzing Individual Cases vs. Overall Distributions
- Choosing Representations for Distributions
- Guiding Students to Construct and Read Graphs
- Shapes of Distributions
- Describing Data With Measures of Variability
- Choosing an Appropriate Summary Statistic
- Interpreting Results

Planning Chart

Content	ACE	Pacing	Materials	Resources
Problem 4.1	1–9, 27, 31	1½ days	**Labsheet 4.1** Students' Travel Times to School **Labsheet 4ACE** Exercise 31 • Graph Paper • Quarter-Inch Grid Paper calculators	**Teaching Aid 4.1** Student Travel Times—Dot Plots and Histograms • Data and Graphs
Problem 4.2	10–16, 28–29	1½ days	**Labsheet 4.2A** Jumping-Rope Contest Data **Labsheet 4.2B:** Mrs. R's Class Data (accessibility) **Labsheet 4.2C** Mr. K's Class Data **Labsheet 4ACE:** Exercises 10–12 (accessibility) calculators	**Teaching Aid 4.2A** Making a Box-and-Whisker Plot **Teaching Aid 4.2B** Mrs. R's Class Data—A Box-and-Whisker Plot • Data and Graphs • Expression Calculator
Problem 4.3	17–26, 30, 32	1½ days	**Labsheet 4.3** 2nd- and 6th-Grade Heights **Labsheet 4ACE** Exercises 17–19 calculators	• Data and Graphs
Mathematical Reflections		½ day		
Assessment: Unit Project		Optional –1 day		• Sample Student Work 1 • Sample Student Work 2
Assessment: Self-Assessment		Take Home		• Self-Assessment • Notebook Checklist • Spanish Self-Assessment
Assessment: Unit Test		1 day		• Unit Test

Goals and Standards

Goals

Statistical Process Understand and use the process of statistical investigation

- Ask questions, collect and analyze data, and interpret data to answer questions

- Describe data with respect to its shape, center, and variability or spread

- Construct and use simple surveys as a method of collecting data

Multiple Representations for Displaying Data Display data with multiple representations

- Organize and represent data using tables, dot plots, line plots, ordered-value bar graphs, frequency bar graphs, histograms, and box-and-whisker plots

- Make informed decisions about which graphs or tables can be used to display a particular set of data

- Recognize that a graph shows the overall shape of a distribution, whether the data values are symmetrical around a central value, and whether the graph contains any unusual characteristics such as gaps, clusters, or outliers)

Measures of Central Tendency and Variability Recognize that a single number may be used to characterize the center of a distribution of data or the degree of variability (or spread)

- Distinguish between and compute measures of central tendency (mean, median, and mode) and measures of spread (range, interquartile range (IQR), and mean absolute deviation (MAD))

- Identify how the median and mean respond to changes in the data values of a distribution

- Relate the choice of measures of central tendency and variability to the shape of the distribution and the context

- Describe the amount of variability in a distribution by noting whether the data values cluster in one or more areas or are fairly spread out

- Use measures of center and spread to compare data distributions

Mathematical Reflections

Look for evidence of student understanding of the goals for this Investigation in their responses to the questions in *Mathematical Reflections*. The goals addressed by each question are indicated below.

1. Describe how you can display data using a histogram.

Goals

- Ask questions, collect and analyze data, and interpret data to answer questions

- Organize and represent data using tables, dot plots, line plots, ordered-value bar graphs, frequency bar graphs, histograms, and box-and-whisker plots

- Distinguish between and compute measures of central tendency (mean, median, and mode) and measures of spread (range, interquartile range (IQR), and mean absolute deviation (MAD))

2. Describe how you can display data using a box plot.

Goals

- Ask questions, collect and analyze data, and interpret data to answer questions

- Organize and represent data using tables, dot plots, line plots, ordered-value bar graphs, frequency bar graphs, histograms, and box-and-whisker plots

- Distinguish between and compute measures of central tendency (mean, median, and mode) and measures of spread (range, interquartile range (IQR), and mean absolute deviation (MAD))

3. a. How can you use histograms to compare two data sets?

 b. How can you use box plots to compare two data sets?

Goals

- Describe data with respect to its shape, center, and variability or spread

- Make informed decisions about which graphs or tables can be used to display a particular set of data

- Recognize that a graph shows the overall shape of a distribution, whether the data values are symmetrical around a central value, and whether the graph contains any unusual characteristics such as gaps, clusters, or outliers.

- Relate the choice of measures of central tendency and variability to the shape of the distribution and the context

- Use measures of center and spread to compare data distributions

- Identify how the median and mean respond to changes in the data values of a distribution

- Describe the amount of variability in a distribution by noting whether the data values cluster in one or more areas or are fairly spread out

4. Numerical data can be displayed using more than one type of graph. How do you decide when to use a dot plot, line plot, bar graph, histogram, or box plot?

Goals

- Ask questions, collect and analyze data, and interpret data to answer questions

- Organize and represent data using tables, dot plots, line plots, ordered-value bar graphs, frequency bar graphs, histograms, and box-and-whisker plots

- Make informed decisions about which graphs or tables can be used to display a particular set of data

Standards

Common Core Content Standards

6.SP.A.1 Recognize a statistical question as one that anticipates variability in the data related to the question and accounts for it in the answers. *Problems 1, 2, and 3*

6.SP.A.2 Understand that a set of data collected to answer a statistical question has a distribution which can be described by its center, spread, and overall shape. *Problem 1, 2, and 3*

6.SP.A.3 Recognize that a measure of center for a numerical data set summarizes all of its values with a single number, while a measure of variation describes how its values vary with a single number. *Problems 1, 2, and 3*

6.SP.B.4 Display numerical data in plots on a number line, including dot plots, histograms, and box plots. *Problems 1 and 2*

6.SP.B.5a Summarize numerical data sets in relation to their context, such as by reporting the number of observations. *Problem 3*

6.SP.B.5c Summarize numerical data sets in relation to their context, such as by giving quantitative measures of center (median and/or mean) and variability (interquartile range and/or mean absolute deviation), as well as describing any overall pattern and any striking deviations from the overall pattern with reference to the context in which the data were gathered. *Problems 1, 2, and 3*

6.SP.B.5d Summarize numerical data sets in relation to their context, such as by relating the choice of measures of center and variability to the shape of the data distribution and the context in which the data were gathered. *Problems 1 and 3*

6.NS.C.6 Understand a rational number as a point on the number line. Extend number line diagrams and coordinate axes familiar from previous grades to represent points on the line and in the plane with negative number coordinates. *Problems 1, 2, and 3*

6.NS.C.7 Understand ordering and absolute value of rational numbers. *Problems 2 and 3*

Facilitating the Mathematical Practices

Students in *Connected Mathematics* classrooms display evidence of multiple Common Core Standards for Mathematical Practice every day. Here are just a few examples of when you might observe students demonstrating the Standards for Mathematical Practice during this Investigation.

Practice 1: **Make sense of problems and persevere in solving them.**

Students are engaged every day in solving problems and, over time, learn to persevere in solving them. To be effective, the problems embody critical concepts and skills and have the potential to engage students in making sense of mathematics. Students build understanding by reflecting, connecting, and communicating. These student-centered problem situations engage students in articulating the "knowns" in a problem situation and determining a logical solution pathway. The student-student and student-teacher dialogues help students not only to make sense of the problems, but also to persevere in finding appropriate strategies to solve them. The suggested questions in the Teacher Guides provide the metacognitive scaffolding to help students monitor and refine their problem-solving strategies.

Practice 2: **Reason abstractly and quantitatively.**

For each Problem in Investigation 4, students compare two data sets. They find the answer to a broad question by linking that question with quantitative data. They find measures of center and spread to find statistical answers to questions.

Practice 4: **Model with mathematics.**

In Investigation 4, students represent data by constructing dot plots, histograms, and box-and-whisker plots. They use these representations to answer questions about data sets.

Practice 5: **Use appropriate tools strategically.**

Students learn to construct histograms and box-and-whisker plots in Investigation 4. To help them make these displays, they might use number lines and grid paper. These tools help them to accurately represent data values in a data set.

Practice 6: **Attend to precision.**

As students calculate mean, median, IQR, and MAD in Investigation 4, they pay attention to making exact calculations. Because these measures of center and spread are used to represent sets of data, it is important for students to be precise.

Students identify and record their personal experiences with the Standards for Mathematical Practice during the Mathematical Reflections at the end of the Investigation.

Traveling to School
Histograms

▼ Problem Overview

> *Focus Question* How can you use a histogram to help you interpret data?

Problem Description

In previous Investigations, students worked with dot plots, line plots, frequency tables, bar graphs, and ordered-value bar graphs. These representations indicate how frequently each data value occurs in a set of numerical data. Such representations may display data that do not vary a great deal. They may also display data that are discrete rather than continuous (where values are counted rather than measured on a continuous scale). For these types of data, the tables, plots, and graphs explored in previous Investigations are appropriate.

When data vary greatly or are measured on a continuous scale, however, it is useful to display the distribution in a histogram. In Problem 4.1, students examine a data set containing information on the morning routines of a group of middle schoolers. The data show how these middle schoolers travel to school, how long it takes them to get to school, and what means of transportation they use. In this Problem, students construct histograms to help them analyze data.

Problem Implementation

Have students work in pairs on this Problem.

You can give students copies of **Labsheet 4.1: Students' Travel Times to School** if you think they would benefit from marking up the table of data values from the Student Edition as they make the histograms. Students may also find it helpful to use **Graph Paper** or **Quarter-Inch Grid Paper** when they construct their histograms.

Materials

- **Labsheet 4.1:** Students' Travel Times to School
- **Labsheet 4ACE:** Exercise 31
- **Graph Paper**
- **Quarter-Inch Grid Paper**
- **Teaching Aid 4.1:** Student Travel Times—Dot Plots and Histograms
calculators

Using Technology

The online **Data and Graphs** tool contains the data on student travel times. If students have access to computers, they can use this tool to work with the data.

Vocabulary

- histogram
- interval

Mathematics Background

- Collecting Data
- Analyzing Individual Cases vs. Overall Distributions
- Choosing Representations for Distributions
- Guiding Students to Construct and Read Graphs
- Interpreting Results

At a Glance and Lesson Plan

- At a Glance: Problem 4.1 Data About Us
- Lesson Plan: Problem 4.1 Data About Us

▼ Launch

Connecting to Prior Knowledge

Read through the introduction to the Investigation in the Student Edition. Discussing the situations mentioned in the introduction will prepare students to answer the Problems in Investigation 4.

To engage students in the Problem situation, read through the introduction of Problem 4.1. Refer your students to the table of data, Students' Travel Times to School. Ask the following questions. Have your students work to answer the questions for a few minutes before pausing to have a whole-class discussion.

Suggested Questions

- Look at the table of data. What three questions did the students ask in order to collect these data? (How long does it take you to travel to school? How far is your home from school? By what means of travel do you get to school ?)

- How might the class have collected the data? (Possible answer: questionnaire)

Make sure your students understand how the distance data are recorded. If students see that the distances are multiples of a quarter mile expressed in decimal form, they will feel more comfortable with the data.

Presenting the Challenge

Have students consider what type of graph might best represent the data.

Suggested Questions

- Would a line plot or a dot plot display the travel-time data well? How would you start to make a line plot? (This is a good opportunity for students to think about what the line plot or dot plot displaying these data would look like. You would have to set up an axis marked from 1 to 60 so that individual points could be plotted. Or, if you mark the axis for every 5 minutes, then you have to approximate where to draw the dots between the tick marks.)

Refer your students to the dot plot in the text. It shows how the points are crowded between the tick marks. As students begin to realize that dot plots or line plots are less effective for spread-out data, tell them that it is often helpful to find ways to group data into intervals. This might be true when the data are quite spread out or when there are few repeated data values. This will help them to see the big picture. Students will be able to see where the data cluster, what clusters of values are typical, what values are unusual, and where there are large gaps in the data.

It is important to work carefully with students to build the idea of counting data values that occur within a given interval. Rushing this process would affect students' abilities to construct accurate histograms.

The Student Edition outlines the steps of constructing histograms starting with a dot plot. Starting with a frequency table is more common, but the dot plot is shown here so that students can notice similarities and differences.

You may want to build the model histogram as a class rather than having students read through the steps in the Student Edition. Students may find the Questions in Problem 4.1 easier to access if they practice building the histogram in the Student Edition together as a group. You can use **Teaching Aid 4.1: Student Travel Times— Dot Plots and Histograms** to help you discuss this process with your students.

- Let's work together to build a histogram. Look at the data. What is the greatest data value? What is the least data value? (The greatest data value is 60 minutes; the least data value is 5 minutes.)

- You can graph this information using an interval size of 10 minutes. Look at the data values. Locate the data values that are in the first interval from 0 to 10, but not including 10. (Students should identify 5 minutes, 6 minutes, and 8 minutes as data values that fit within this first interval. Explain that the data values from 0 minutes to 9.9999999… minutes belong in this interval, but the 10-minute data values belong in the next interval, 10 minutes–20 minutes.)

- What is the frequency, or number of observations, within the interval 0 minutes–10 minutes? (Six travel times that fit in this interval.)

Instruct students to make a bar for the first interval that is 6 units high.

- What data values fit in the next interval, 10 minutes–20 minutes? (10, 11, 15, 17, and 19)

- How many data values are in that interval? (17 data values)

- How can you show this on your histogram? (Draw a bar that spans the interval 10 minutes–20 minutes that is 17 units high.)

- How might you make a frequency table for this information? How might this frequency table help you construct the histogram? (The frequency table can help organize the data. Once you fill out the column on the number of data values within the interval, you know how high each bar in the histogram has to be.)

Note: You may want to show your students how to organize the data into a frequency table such as the one started below. This may help them keep track of their counts.

Interval	Data in the Interval	Number of Data Values in the Interval
0–10	5, 5, 5, 6, 8, 8	6
10–20	10, 10, 10, 10, 11, 15, 15, 15, 15, 15, 15, 15, 15, 17, 17, 19	17
20–30		
30–40		
40–50		
50–60		
60–70		

- In Problem 4.1, you will use the same data to construct a histogram with an interval size of 5 minutes. What might your first step be? (You can make a frequency table for intervals of 5 minutes. Or, you can mark up the frequency table for intervals of 10 minutes since the organization is already partially done.)

If students use a frequency table, make sure that they fill in the table accurately. Make sure that they notice that the intervals from 40–45 minutes and from 45–50 minutes contain no data values.

- How many data values would be in the first interval? (none)

- How is a histogram like a bar graph? (Possible answer: The height of the bar tells the count of a value or set of values.)

- How is a histogram different from a bar graph? (Possible answer: The bars of a histogram touch, whereas the bars of a bar graph do not touch. Each bar of a histogram represents a continuous set of data whereas each bar of a bar graph marks the frequency of a single data value.)

Explore

Providing for Individual Needs

During the Explore phase, students spend time constructing a histogram on their own and looking at how data are organized in a histogram. Ask the following questions to ensure that students understand the process of making histograms. Pay close attention to values on the border of the bars of the histogram.

Suggested Questions

- If the interval size is 5 minutes, what values belong in the first interval? (0 minutes–4.9999… minutes)

- The next interval? (5 minutes–9.9999… minutes)

- Can you use the histogram with an interval size of 10 minutes to help you make the histogram with an interval size of 5 minutes? (No; you have to go back to the table or dot plot. You cannot see the individual values from the histogram with the interval size of 10. In order to see where each data value belongs, you need to know the individual data values.)

- Does this histogram give you any additional information about clusters or gaps? (By making the histogram with the smaller interval size, you notice that the high bar between 10 and 20 minutes on the first histogram is high mainly because of the many data values between 15 and 20 minutes. There are not as many data values between 10 and 15 minutes. So, the second histogram shows more detail than the first.)

Questions B and C ask students to make inferences from the graphs. You may want to ask your students, however, if looking at the table of data might be useful to answer these questions.

- Where can you find exactly which students have to get up earliest and which get to sleep latest? (You need to look back at the table for this level of specificity.)

- Why can't you find this on the histogram? (Individual data are hidden within intervals on the histograms. The data are grouped together so that you can see the big picture.)

- What information did you use to find the median? How did you find the median? (You need an ordered list to find the median, so you need to look at the table. You cannot get this information directly from the histogram. To find the median, find the midpoint of the ordered list of data.)

- Can you make an estimate of where the median will be from the histogram? (There are 40 pieces of data, so you know to look for the 20th and 21st data values. These seem to occur in the largest cluster, 10–20 minutes (for the histogram with interval size 10) or 15–20 minutes (for the histogram with interval size 5). You cannot, however, tell the exact median from either graph.)

- What information did you use to find the range? What's the first step in finding the range? (Locate the maximum and minimum values. You can find these in the table. The graph only provides data as grouped in intervals, so you cannot find the exact range from a histogram. You can estimate the range from a histogram.)

- What information did you use to find the mean? How do you find the mean? (You have to add all the values and divide by 40 (the number of data values). You can only get these data values from the table.)

- Are there any data values that are much greater than the others? Will the median be affected by these values? The mean? (Yes; 50 and 60 are data values that are much greater than the other data values. These will affect the mean because these large data values are added into the total. The median will not be affected by these values being unusually high. The 20th and 21st pieces of data are in the same location, regardless of the sizes of the 39th and 40th data values.)

Going Further

- Will the mean be the same as, greater than, or less than the median? Can you tell without calculating the mean and the median? (Not every student will be able to think this through. Because the mean responds to the two unusually long travel times, it is likely to be greater than the median. You may want to provide another small set of data to have students either predict the answer to this type of question, or to actually calculate the answers. This may help them notice how skew affects measures of center.)

If your students would benefit from an additional challenge, they can use the same table of data and plot a histogram for distances traveled. A histogram of this data is below.

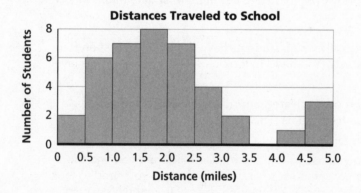

Planning for the Summary

....

What evidence will you use in the summary to clarify and deepen understanding of the Focus Question?

What will you do if you do not have evidence?

▼ Summarize

Orchestrating the Discussion

During the Summarize, the class should discuss the structure of a histogram. Students should understand how are data organized once an interval width is chosen and into which interval a "border" data point (one that touches two intervals) is placed.

Suggested Questions

- Why is it useful to display the data in a histogram? (It helps you to see general patterns in the data.)

- Why might you need to reference the table instead of the graph? (The table allows you to identify individual data values or statistics.)

- Why is a histogram a good choice for this data set? (Dot plots usually show an axis marked for every data value in the table. This would mean either marking the axis for every 1 minute, or trying to place dots above unmarked places on the axis, which is sometimes confusing. Grouping the data into intervals and using a histogram avoids these complications. Histograms display the data in intervals.)

- Which statistic would you use to illustrate a typical travel time for these students? (Students may argue about this. Statisticians usually say that it depends on the question, on what the data look like, and so on. In this case, the histograms show that the data are skewed to the right. The greater travel times, therefore, impact the mean but not the median. This might encourage a statistician to use the median as a representation of the data set. In this case, the measures of center are similar in value, so either could be used to represent the data.)

- How can you use a histogram to interpret data? (A histogram provides a visual representation so that you can see where most of the measurements are located and how spread out they are.)

When students use histograms to analyze data, the histograms might lead them to make one of the following analytical statements:

1. Most of the data are grouped together around the mean or median with very little variation.

2. Although some data are grouped around the mean or median, many other data values are further away from the mean or median.

3. Even when most of the data are close together, they are located a significant distance away from the mean or median.

4. The data are not obviously located around the mean or median and are widely dispersed.

The above can be true for distributions represented using a variety of different graphs. The information in a histogram helps you notice how consistent the data are. It also permits you to sort out the impact of variability. When data are more dispersed, it is more difficult to interpret what might be typical with a single number, such as the mean or the median.

Reflecting on Student Learning

Use the following questions to assess student understanding at the end of the lesson.

- What evidence do I have that students understand the Focus Question?
  - Where did my students get stuck?
  - What strategies did they use?
  - What breakthroughs did my students have today?
- How will I use this to plan for tomorrow? For the next time I teach this lesson?
- Where will I have the opportunity to reinforce these ideas as I continue through this Unit? The next Unit?

ACE Assignment Guide

- **Applications:** 1–9
- **Connections:** 27
- **Extensions:** 31
- **Labsheet 4ACE:** Exercise 31 (accessibility)

This labsheet provides students with a copy of the histogram in ACE Exercise 13. They can use this labsheet to mark up or draw on the histogram in order to help them answer the questions.

PROBLEM

4.2

Jumping Rope
Box-and-Whisker Plots

▼ Problem Overview

Focus Question   How can you interpret data using a box-and-whisker plot?

Problem Description

Students learn to construct box-and-whisker plots (or box plots) in Problem 4.2. They use box plots as tools for comparing two sets of data; the sets contain information on how many consecutive times students jumped during a jumping-rope contest. They connect the questions of this Problem to the IQR. They see how the IQR is represented in a box plot, and they use the IQR to determine which values in a data set are outliers.

Problem Implementation

Have students work in pairs on this Problem.

Materials

- **Labsheet 4.2A:** Jumping-Rope Contest Data
- **Labsheet 4.2B:** Mrs. R's Class Data (accessibility)
- **Labsheet 4.2C:** Mr. K's Class Data
- **Labsheet 4ACE:** Exercises 10–12 (accessibility)
- **Teaching Aid 4.2A:** Making a Box-and-Whisker Plot
- **Teaching Aid 4.2B:** Mrs. R's Class Data—A Box-and-Whisker Plot

calculators

Using Technology

The **Data and Graphs** tool contains data from the jumping-rope contest in Problem 4.2. Students can use this tool, as well as the **Expression Calculator**, to help them solve Problem 4.2 and a number of ACE Exercises.

Vocabulary

- box-and-whisker plot (box plot)
- outlier

Mathematics Background

- Posing Questions
- Analyzing Individual Cases vs. Overall Distributions
- Choosing Representations for Distributions
- Shapes of Distributions
- Describing Data With Measures of Variability
- Interpreting Results

At a Glance and Lesson Plan

- At a Glance: Problem 4.2 Data About Us
- Lesson Plan: Problem 4.2 Data About Us

▼ Launch

Launch Video

The animation for Problem 4.2 provides students with a dynamic visual of how box-and-whisker plots are constructed. In this animation, two contestants begin their second and final round of a free-throw semi-final contest to see who will advance to the final round. Only the upper quartile of the contestants will move on to the final round. Students watch a dot plot transform into a box-and-whisker plot. Show this animation to your students during Connecting to Prior Knowledge. Visit Teacher Place at mathdashboard.com/cmp3 to see the complete video.

Connecting to Prior Knowledge

Box-and-whisker plots group data into four quartiles: 25% of the data are represented by the first whisker, 25% of the data are represented in the left side of the box, 25% are represented in the right side of the box, and 25% are represented by the right whisker. The IQR can be calculated by finding the difference of the endpoints of the box.

Students explored the IQR in Investigation 3. They learned this concept as a distinct measure of variability before connecting it to the box plot, which they will do during this Problem. This helps students to be sensitive to the size of the box (the IQR). They already know that this indicates the variability of a distribution. They can use this information to compare two or more data sets.

The individual cases of data disappear, in a sense, in this graph. Students can only see ranges of values that correspond to the quartiles. No additional detail is evident.

Students need to develop sensitivity for noticing where the median is marked in the box plot. If the median is not located in the middle, the location of the median gives additional detail as to how spread out the data are. In some cases, the median can appear on Q1 or Q3. Then, the box does not have a line breaking the box into two parts. This indicates special conditions with respect to the data distribution.

The lengths of the whiskers also provide information about spread, symmetry, and possible unusual values. Marking outliers provides even more information about variability in the data.

Presenting the Challenge

To engage students in the context of the Problem, refer them to the table of data in the Student Edition. Ask the following questions and have the students consider these questions before starting a whole-class discussion.

Suggested Questions

- Look at the two tables of data. What was question do you think was asked in order to collect this data? (How many consecutive times can you jump while jumping rope?)

- How you think the students collected the data? (Each student jumped rope and counted the number of times they jumped. There may have been multiple trials, and students took their best scores or their mean scores.)

- Would using two line plots or two dot plots be a good way to show the jump-rope data for the two classes? Why or why not? (Students should consider what they would have to do in order to make a line plot or dot plot to display the data. You may want to go through the process of beginning to make a line plot. Fairly quickly, students will begin to see that the data are not really clustered, and it would be difficult to see any patterns in the data. (Additionally, with such a large set of data, constructing such graphs would be very time consuming). Instead, the students should group the data in order to look for patterns.)

Students might suggest making histograms. If students want to do this initially, help them consider interval sizes. Below is a histogram of Mr. K's class data with an interval size of 20 jumps.

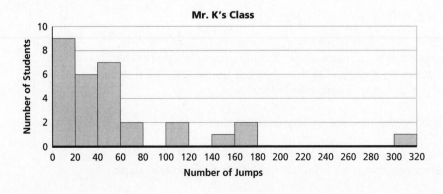

- Mr. K's class claims they did better than Mrs. R's class. What evidence might they be using? (They might compare the best and worst scores for each class or compare the mean or median.)

- Comparing graphs of the two data sets might clarify which class did better. Histograms may be useful, or you could make two box-and-whisker plots.

You may want to construct the box plot of Mr. K's class data together as a class, instead of reading through the Student Edition. Students can use **Labsheet 4.2C: Mr. K's Class Data** to compare the dot plot with the final box plot (and later identify outliers on the same labsheet). This will give them a more active experience in understanding how Mr. K's Class Data can be plotted as a box plot. Alternatively, you can use **Teaching Aid 4.2A: Making a Box-and-Whisker Plot** to model for students how to construct a box plot. Students can consult the Student Edition later for reference. Completing this activity as a class gives students the opportunity to ask questions as they first construct these new plots. First, remind students of their work with the IQR.

- You used the IQR to measure variability in Investigation 3. How do you calculate the IQR? What information does the IQR give you? (First, order the data. Find the quartiles, and then subtract Q1 from Q3. This difference is the IQR. The IQR tells you how spread out the middle 50% of the data are.)

- Let's work together to build a box plot. A box plot is made using the IQR. Look at the tables. How variable do you think these two data sets are? (The data vary widely. The range in Mrs. R's class data is 124 jumps. The range in Mr. K's class data is 299 jumps.)

- Since the table lists the data in order from least to greatest, you can use the table to find and mark the median and the summary statistics for the interquartile range. What are the positions and values of Q1, Q3, and the median for Mr. K's class? (Q1 is 17, the median is 40.5, and Q3 is 65.)

- You need two other numbers to construct a box plot: the minimum data value and the maximum data value. Find these and mark them on the table. (The minimum data value is 1, and the maximum data vale is 300.)

- You can use these five numbers to make a box and the whiskers for the box plot. Look at the box plot for Mr. K's class. It shows where these 5 numbers are located. What percent of the data from Mr. K's class is in the box? (50%)

- What percent is on the lower whisker? (25%)

- What percent is on the upper whisker? (25%)

- The lower whisker and upper whisker both represent 25% of the data. Why is the upper whisker so much longer than the lower whisker? (The data are more spread out above Q3 than they are below Q1. The person who made 300 jumps is partly responsible for this.)

Draw student attention to the new vocabulary word, **outlier**.

- Why is *outlier* a good way to describe the data value of 300 jumps? (It describes a data value that is far from the rest of the data on the graph.)

- Are there any other unusual values for Mr. K's class? (Students may disagree about whether 160 and 151 are also outliers. Leave this open. The exploration in Question C takes care of this dispute.)

- Does the box-and-whisker plot help you see what is typical for the number of consecutive times the students in Mr. K's class can jump? (Students might say 40.5 (the median) jumps is a typical number, or they might sensibly say that any number of jumps between 17 and 65 is typical for this class. Half the data lie in this cluster.)

- What is the first step in making a box plot for Ms. R's class? (Find the five-number summary.)

▼ Explore

Providing for Individual Needs

Hand out copies of **Labsheet 4.2A: Jumping-Rope Contest Data** and **Labsheet 4.2B: Mrs. R's Class Data** (accessibility) to your students. Labsheet 4.2B will help your students walk through the process of making a box plot. Labsheet 4.2A is a copy of the tables of jump-rope data. Students might benefit from marking up the tables.

Students should be able to work though Question A in pairs. They should be able to find the five-number summary for Mrs. R's class, as they have completed these tasks before. Encourage students to identify what they know about each distribution of data.

Suggested Questions

- What are the five numbers you have to look for? (median, Q1, Q3, minimum, and maximum data values)

- There are 30 people in each class. Can you find the midpoint of each data set? (It is between the 15th and 16th data values in the ordered list (31.5 for Mrs. R's class data).)

- Mark the position of the median. How many data values are less than this? Greater than this? (There are 15 data values on either side of the median.)

- How do you find Q1? Q3? (Mark the position Q1 at the midpoint of the lower 15 values. Mark the position of Q3 at the midpoint of the upper 15 values.)

- How can you use the five numbers to describe the distribution of the data from Mrs. R's class? (The median, minimum, maximum, Q1, and Q3 (and the IQR, Q3 − Q1) tell where the data are centered and tell about how spread out the data are.)

  Students may also say, sensibly, that all the data values in the interval between Q3 and Q1 are typical, because this is the middle 50% of the data.

- How does IQR relate to the box on the box plot? (IQR gives the measure of the length of the box plot.)

- How would a high IQR appear on a box plot? What would it mean? (A high IQR would mean the middle of the data is very spread out; an elongated box from Q1 to Q3 shows the same concept.)

Question B gets at the reason for making these types of graphs to display data. Students may want to stick to using summary statistics to compare the classes. Encourage them to examine the graphs also and relate their comparisons to what they see in those box plots.

- You said that the best jumper in Mr. K's class is better than the best jumper in Mrs. R's class. Is it fair to just compare individuals? (You need to compare the whole classes. One very high or low data value may distract from comparing the class data sets.)

- You compared medians and said a typical number of jumps was higher for Mr. K's class. Can you show me where this is on each box plot? (The line in the box that marks the median.)

- Are the IQRs similar? How can you tell this from the graph? (The lengths of the boxes are about the same—and the scales are the same—so the IQRs are the same.)

- If the IQRs are the same, does that mean that the classes' performances in jumping rope are also about the same? (The IQR measures how variable the middle 50% of the data is, but Q1, Q2, and Q3 are all slightly higher for Mr. K's class. So the actual data values within the boxes, the middle 50% of the data, are slightly better for Mr. K's class than for Mrs. R's class.)

Question C introduces students to a more formal way of determining outliers. Generally, the computation for identifying outliers is associated with the box plot and derived from the IQR. After outliers have been identified, you should redraw the box plot, isolating the outliers.

- Where did the "72" come from when checking for outliers in Mr. K's class data? (1.5 × IQR)

- How do you know exactly which data values are outliers? (Check the table for values 72 greater than Q3 or 72 less than Q1.)

- The IQR is the length of the box. How can you check visually whether a data value is an outlier on a graph? (1.5 × length of the box; the upper or lower whiskers would be longer than this length if they contained outliers. You can look at the graph and estimate at what point the data values become outliers.)

Tell the class that they should redraw the box plot to show which data points are outliers. In the case of Mr. K's class, the values 151, 160, 160, and 300 are outliers. The redrawn box plot is shown below.

Consecutive Jumps by Mr. K's Class

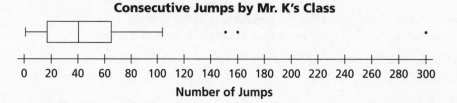

Number of Jumps

Notice that the upper whisker now stops at 104.

- Were there any outliers in Mrs. R's class data? Did you do the 1.5 × IQR calculation, or did you just check the graph? (There are no outliers in this graph. The upper whisker is about the same length as the box. It is not close to 1.5 × length of the box.)

Question D, part (3) asks students to revisit their comparisons made in Question B. Now that outliers are marked, students can see that the distributions for the class data sets without the outliers included look similar. Students may still point out that the middle 50% of Mr. K's class data are slightly greater than the middle 50% of Mrs. R's class data.

Question E is designed to help students develop their sensitivity to how a box plot looks as a way to provide information about the distribution. Students encountered a discussion about shape in Investigation 2. This overview of shape will help them revisit these ideas when looking at box plots rather than dot plots. It is much easier to compare summary statistics like measures of center and spread. Be sure to pick up general points about the shape of the box plots in the Summarize.

Planning for the Summary

What evidence will you use in the summary to clarify and deepen understanding of the Focus Question?

What will you do if you do not have evidence?

▼ Summarize

Orchestrating the Discussion

Ask students to describe the procedure for making a box plot for a set of data: order data from least to greatest, identify the five-number summary, and draw the box and the whiskers in relation to a number line.

Ask students to share what they learned about how the numbers that summarize the data also separate the data into standard percent groupings.

You can check your students' box-and-whisker plots by comparing it to **Teaching Aid 4.2B: Mrs. R's Class Data—A Box-and-Whisker Plot**, which shows Mrs. R's final box plot.

Suggested Questions

- What percent of the data in a box plot fall above the lower quartile? (75%)

- Below the upper quartile? (75%)

- Between the quartiles? (50%)

Continue with these questions:

- You encountered the term *outlier* in the Problem. What is an outlier? How can you establish what numbers are outliers? (An *outlier* is an unexpected data value. To find outliers, multiply the IQR by 1.5. Values that are that amount less than Q1 or that amount greater than Q3 are outliers.)

  You looked at the shape of the data in the Problem. This was also introduced in Investigation 2 using dot plots. Look at the sample box plots in Question E to make sense of what it means to look at shape of the data displayed in a box plot.

- How are the sample box plots similar? (The boxes are all about the same length; that is, the IQRs are about the same. The ranges are about the same. So the variability is similar in each distribution. The medians are all the same as well.)

- How are the sample box plots different? (In the top example, the median is in the middle of the box, and the whiskers are the same length; the data is spread symmetrically about the median. In the second example, the median is squeezed to the lower end of the box, and the upper whisker is longer than the lower whisker; the data are clustered below the median and spread out above the median. In the third example, the data are clustered together above the median and spread out below the median.)

- How does the shape of the box plot give you information about the distribution? (It tells you where the data are clustered and where they are spread out.)

- Can you apply this to the box plots for Mr. K's and Mrs. R's class data? (If you take the outliers out of Mr. K's class data, then the distributions look very similar. Both could be described as roughly symmetric or slightly skewed to the right.)

  Of course, students may justifiably argue that they should not ignore the outliers; they are the expert jumpers, and their scores boost Mr. K's class mean.

If you have time, you may want to have more examples prepared for students to discuss.

- Look back at the travel-time data from Problem 4.1. Here is one of the histograms you made, and below it is the box plot. What can you say about the shape of the data? How is this shown in the histogram? In the box plot? (The two single unexpected values at the right of the histogram are considered outliers in the box plot. The clustered data in the histogram corresponds to the box of the box plot.)

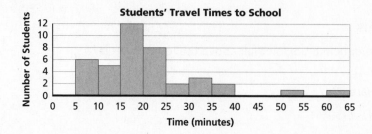

Students' Travel Times to School

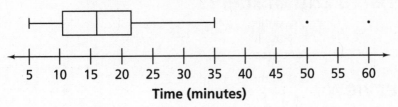

Time (minutes)

Address the Focus Question.

Reflecting on Student Learning

Use the following questions to assess student understanding at the end of the lesson.

- What evidence do I have that students understand the Focus Question?
  - Where did my students get stuck?
  - What strategies did they use?
  - What breakthroughs did my students have today?
- How will I use this to plan for tomorrow? For the next time I teach this lesson?
- Where will I have the opportunity to reinforce these ideas as I continue through this Unit? The next Unit?

ACE Assignment Guide

- **Applications:** 10–16
- **Connections:** 28–29
- **Labsheet 4ACE:** Exercises 10–12 (accessibility)

You can give this labsheet to your students if you think the would benefit from drawing or writing on the data. It may help them keep track of the data they have already accounted for.

How Much Taller Is a 6th Grader Than a 2nd Grader?

Taking Variability Into Consideration

▼ Problem Overview

> *Focus Question* How can you compare and contrast data represented by dot plots, histograms, and box plots?

Problem Description

Students examine dot plots, histograms, and box plots that represent the same data in this Problem. The data are heights of 6th-grade students and 2nd-grade students. Students answer the question *How much taller is a 6th grader than a 2nd grader?* in this Problem. They do this by looking at various representations of the data sets, as well as measures of center and spread.

Problem Implementation

Have students work in pairs on this Problem. You may want to cut **Labsheet 4.3: 2nd- and 6th-Grade Heights** into six cards; each card containing one representation of the sets of data. Give these cards to your students so that they can align the distributions to more easily compare the data.

Materials

- **Labsheet 4.3:** 2nd- and 6th-Grade Heights
- **Labsheet 4ACE:** Exercises 17–19
- Self-Assessment
- Notebook Checklist
- Unit Test

Using Technology

The **Data and Graphs** tool contains the data displayed in Problem 4.3. Students can use this tool to help them understand the information given in Problem 4.3.

Vocabulary

There are no new glossary terms introduced in this Problem.

Mathematics Background

- Posing Questions
- Analyzing Individual Cases vs. Overall Distributions
- Choosing Representations for Distributions
- Choosing an Appropriate Summary Statistic
- Interpreting Results

At a Glance and Lesson Plan

- At a Glance: Problem 4.3 Data About Us
- Lesson Plan: Problem 4.3 Data About Us

▼ Launch

Connecting to Prior Knowledge

This Problem ties together several topics addressed in this Unit. Students consider different graphs of the same data sets and reflect on how each displays data. They also connect measures of center and measures of spread to the graphs and use this information to answer the question posed in the Problem: *How much taller is a 6th grader than a 2nd grader?*

Presenting the Challenge

Students work with two sets of data: heights of 2nd-grade students and heights of 6th-grade students. There are 168 cases or *individuals* (84 in each grade). Students consider two *attributes* for each case: grade level and height. The observations or data values for the attribute of height are measured and reported using inches.

The data distributions for each grade's heights are represented using three different graphs: dot plots, histograms, and box plots. Have students review how each graph is made.

▼ Explore

Providing for Individual Needs

Have students complete the parts of the Problem. You may want to have a mini-summary and class discussion after Questions A and B. The questions being asked are ones that can be used in almost any data situation. When they share their thinking, have them connect their ideas to the particular graph types.

Question C involves relating knowledge of the measures of center (mean or median) to the graphs. Students may want to mark each measure in its approximate location on each graph. When comparing the two grade levels, the question is *How much taller is a 6th grader than a 2nd grader?* not *Are 6th grade students taller than 2nd students?*

Suggested Questions

- What do you notice about the shape of the data? (The 2nd-grade box plot and histogram look roughly symmetric. The 6th-grade box plot and histogram look slightly skewed to the right. The median in both cases is to the left in the box, indicating a tighter cluster of data just before the median. There's more variability, measured by looking at the length of the box/IQR, in the 6th-grade data.)

- How can you answer "How much taller is a 6th grader than a 2nd grader?" (by comparing means or medians)

Question D focuses attention on which distribution is more spread out, or variable. Given the measures, it appears that there is greater variability in the 6th-grade heights.

- How does knowing that there is more variability in the 6th-grade data influence how you will decide how much taller a 6th-grade student is than a 2nd-grade student? (You may want to consider the median rather than the mean, since the mean might be more affected by the variability.)

Planning for the Summary

What evidence will you use in the summary to clarify and deepen understanding of the Focus Question?

What will you do if you do not have evidence?

Summarize

Orchestrating the Discussion

Review each part of the Problem with the students. Questions A and B have a variety of possible responses. It may be helpful to set up a two-column table with one column labeled 6th Grade and the other labeled 2nd Grade. Then, for both, fill in observations. Follow this by filling in comments about shape. Continue with spread, and then compare the categories. Have students talk about this summary table.

Discuss ways in which students thought about and approached the question *How much taller is a 6th grader than a 2nd grader?*

Also address the Focus Question.

Reflecting on Student Learning

Use the following questions to assess student understanding at the end of the lesson.

- What evidence do I have that students understand the Focus Question?
  - Where did my students get stuck?
  - What strategies did they use?
  - What breakthroughs did my students have today?
- How will I use this to plan for tomorrow? For the next time I teach this lesson?
- Where will I have the opportunity to reinforce these ideas as I continue through this Unit? The next Unit?

ACE Assignment Guide

- **Applications:** 17–26
- **Connections:** 30, 32
- **Labsheet 4ACE:** Exercises 17–19 (accessibility)

This labsheet is provided so that students have a hard copy of graphs to compare to the sets involved in this group of ACE Exercises.

▼ Mathematical Reflections

Possible Answers to Mathematical Reflections

1. Organize the data values in order. Determine an interval to use. Make a frequency table and count the frequency of data values in each interval. Use this frequency table to make the histogram. The frequency of each data interval determines the height of each bar of the histogram.

2. Find the five-number summary of the data, which includes the minimum value, the lower quartile, the median, the upper quartile, and the maximum value. The box of the box plot spans from the lower quartile to the upper quartile, and there is a line at the median. The whiskers span from the minimum value to the lower quartile and from the upper quartile to the maximum value. Those five points divide the data distribution into four quartiles, each of which contains 25% of the data.

   Note: Instead of showing individual data values, both histograms and box plots show data that are grouped in intervals. Histograms can have any interval size that you determine; box plots use quartiles, which are set by the data values. With histograms you may be able to see clusters and gaps. With box plots you can see outliers. These types of distributions show variability and spread of data more clearly.

3. **a.** You can use histograms to compare two data sets by comparing the shapes of the histograms. You can identify whether one data set is more skewed than another, or whether one data set contains more clusters of data or gaps in data. You can also use histograms to estimate means and medians. Thus, you can compare the measures of center for the two data sets.

   b. You can use box plots to compare two data sets by looking at the locations of the four quartiles. These quickly show the spread of the data as well as the median. Identify and compare the five-number summary statistics in each data set.

4. In deciding which graph to use, take into account the number of data values. With small data sets, you may want to display data using dot plots or bar graphs. For small data sets, being able to see individual detail may be beneficial. When working with large data sets, using dot plots and bar graphs may not be efficient. You may want to identify overall patterns in the large data sets, so you may want to use a histogram or box-and-whisker plot. Additionally, plotting dot plots for large data sets would take too much time. Measurement data can be displayed using histograms or box plots, since measurement is on a continuous scale. Finally, the context of the problem and the data collected will influence which type of display you choose to use.

Possible Answers to Mathematical Practices Reflections

Students may have demonstrated all of the eight Common Core Standards for Mathematical Practice during this Investigation. During the class discussion, have students provide additional Practices that the Problem cited involved and identify the use of other Mathematical Practices in the Investigation.

One student observation is provided in the Student Edition. Here is another sample student response.

For ACE Exercise 13, we decided to compare the girls' performances in Mrs. R's class to the girls' performances in Mr. K's class.

We drew two box plots:

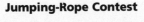

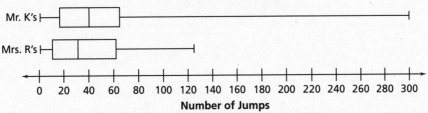

Kashaiah thought that the girls in Mrs. R's class performed better than the girls in Mr. K's class. She said that the median is 80 jumps, and the upper 50% of the data are contained within 80 to about 100 jumps.

Elaine wasn't sure. She said that the median for Mr. K's class is 57 jumps, which is quite a bit less than the median for Mrs. R's class. The upper 50% are between 57 and about 160 jumps, which is a lot more spread out than Mrs. R's class. The top 25% of the girls in Mr. K's class, however, did better than each of the girls in Mrs. R's class.

Then Kashaiah noted that the rest of Mr. K's class did not do as well as Mrs. R's class. Mr. K's class data is to be skewed to the right, and Mrs. R's class data is skewed to the left. So, Kashaiah still thinks that Mrs. R's class did better because the data has a higher median number of jumps. Mr. K's class has some girls who can do a lot of jumping, though!

MP2: Reason abstractly and quantitatively.

Notes

What Numbers Describe Us? Using Graphs to Group Data

People use numbers to describe a variety of attributes, or characteristics, of people, places, and things. These attributes include:

- activities, such as the amount of time it takes a student to get to school
- performances, such as the number of consecutive times a person can jump rope
- physical characteristics, such as a person's height

In this Investigation, you will examine graphs to identify patterns and trends in large sets of data. Grouping data before graphing makes the data easier to analyze. Your analysis can help you draw conclusions about the attribute being studied.

....

Common Core State Standards

6.SP.B.4 Display numerical data in plots on a number line, including dot plots, histograms, and box plots.

6.SP.B.5a Summarize numerical data sets in relation to their context, such as by reporting the number of observations.

6.SP.B.5c Summarize numerical data sets in relation to their context, such as by giving quantitative measures of center (median and/or mean) and variability (interquartile range and/or mean absolute deviation), as well as describing any overall pattern and any striking deviations from the overall pattern with reference to the context in which the data were gathered.

6.SP.B.5d Summarize numerical data sets in relation to their context, such as by relating the choice of measures of center and variability to the shape of the data distribution and the context in which the data were gathered.

Also 6.NS.C.6, 6.NS.C.7, 6.SP.A.1, 6.SP.A.2, 6.SP.A.3

STUDENT PAGE

Notes

4.1 Traveling to School
Histograms

A middle-school class studied the times that students woke up in the morning. They found that two students woke up almost an hour earlier than the others. The class wondered how much time it took each student to travel to school in the morning. The table below shows the data they collected.

- Based on the data, what three questions do you think the class asked?

- How might the class have collected the data?

- What information would a line plot of the data give you? A bar graph?

Students' Travel Times to School

Student	Travel Time (minutes)	Distance (miles)	Mode of Travel	Student	Travel Time (minutes)	Distance (miles)	Mode of Travel
LS	5	0.50	bus	DW	17	2.50	bus
CD	5	0.25	walking	MN	17	4.50	bus
ME	5	0.50	bus	AP	19	2.25	bus
EL	6	1.00	car	MP	20	1.50	bus
KR	8	0.25	walking	AT	20	2.75	bus
NS	8	1.25	car	JW	20	0.50	walking
NW	10	0.50	walking	JB	20	2.50	bus
RC	10	1.25	bus	MB	20	2.00	bus
JO	10	3.00	car	CF	20	1.75	bus
ER	10	1.00	bus	RP	21	1.50	bus
TH	11	1.50	bus	LM	22	2.00	bus
DD	15	2.00	bus	QN	25	1.50	bus
SE	15	0.75	car	AP	25	1.25	bus
AE	15	1.00	bus	CC	30	2.00	bus
CL	15	1.00	bus	BA	30	3.00	bus
HCP	15	1.50	bus	BB	30	4.75	bus
JW	15	1.50	bus	FH	35	2.50	bus
SW	15	2.00	car	KLD	35	0.75	bus
CW	15	2.25	bus	AB	50	4.00	bus
KG	15	1.75	bus	DB	60	4.50	bus

Notes

You can draw a histogram to display the data in the table. A **histogram** is a graph that organizes numerical data into *intervals*.

Step 1: Draw a dot plot or make a frequency table to display the data.

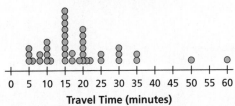

Students' Travel Times to School

Travel Time (minutes)

The data on student travel times vary from 5 minutes to 60 minutes.

- Why is the number line on the dot plot labeled every 5 minutes instead of every minute?

- How can you identify the data values of the dot plot when the number line is labeled every 5 minutes?

Step 2: Determine the frequency of the data values that fall into each interval, or group of consecutive numbers.

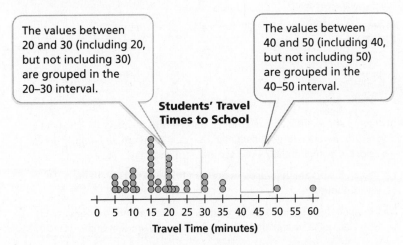

The values between 20 and 30 (including 20, but not including 30) are grouped in the 20–30 interval.

The values between 40 and 50 (including 40, but not including 50) are grouped in the 40–50 interval.

Students' Travel Times to School

Travel Time (minutes)

The height of each bar of the histogram represents the number of data values within a specified **interval,** or group of consecutive numbers.

STUDENT PAGE

Notes

Step 3: Draw the histogram. The histogram below has an interval size of 10 minutes.

Note: In the histogram below, data values of 10 minutes are graphed in the interval 10–20 minutes, data values of 20 minutes are graphed in the interval 20–30 minutes, and so on.

There are 17 observations within the 10–20 interval.

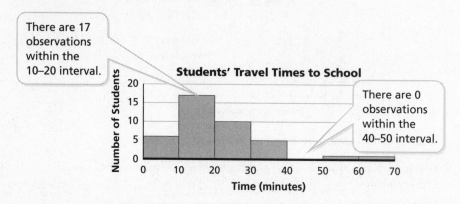

There are 0 observations within the 40–50 interval.

- How is a histogram like a bar graph? How is it different?
- How can you use a dot plot or a frequency table to help you make a histogram?
- What does *interval size* mean?
- Using the same data, what would a histogram with a different interval size look like?

Problem 4.1

In the histogram above, the data are grouped into 10-minute intervals. The data could also be grouped into larger or smaller intervals. Sometimes changing the interval size of the histogram helps you see different patterns in the data.

A 1. Make a histogram that displays the travel-time data. Use an interval size of 5 minutes.

2. Compare the histogram above with the histogram you drew in part (1). How does each histogram help you describe the student travel times?

B Which students most likely wake up the latest in the morning? Explain.

C Which students most likely wake up the earliest? Explain.

Notes _____

_____

_____

Problem 4.1 *continued*

D 1. For the data on travel time, find the mode, the median, the mean, and the range. Explain how you found these statistics.

2. In what interval does the mode fall? The median? The mean?

E Which statistic, the mean or the median, would you choose to report when describing the average time it takes a student to travel to school? Explain.

A C E Homework starts on page 98.

4.2 Jumping Rope
Box-and-Whisker Plots

A **box-and-whisker plot,** or *box plot*, uses five statistical measures: the minimum data value, the lower quartile, the median, the upper quartile, and the maximum data value. These values separate a set of data into four groups with the same number of data values in each group.

The example below shows how these five statistics form a box plot.

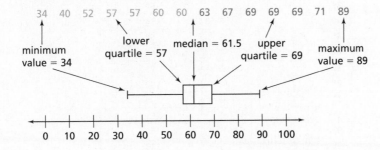

Notes

Two middle-school classes competed in a jumping-rope contest. The tables below show the data from each class.

Number of Consecutive Jumps, Mrs. R's Class	
Gender	Number of Jumps
B	1
B	1
B	5
B	7
B	7
B	7
B	8
B	11
B	11
B	16
B	20
G	20
G	23
B	26
G	30
B	33
B	35
B	36
G	37
B	39
B	40
G	45
B	62
G	80
G	88
G	89
G	91
G	93
G	96
B	125

Number of Consecutive Jumps, Mr. K's Class	
Gender	Number of Jumps
B	1
B	2
B	5
B	7
B	8
B	8
G	14
B	17
B	17
G	27
B	27
B	28
B	30
G	30
B	39
B	42
G	45
B	47
B	50
G	52
G	54
G	57
B	65
G	73
G	102
G	104
G	151
G	160
B	160
G	300

- Mr. K's class claims it is better at jumping rope than Mrs. R's class. What evidence might Mr. K's class be using?

90   Data About Us

Notes _____

_____

_____

The dot plots below show the distributions of the data from the tables.

- How are the dot plots similar? How are they different?

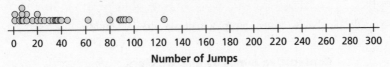

Consecutive Jumps by Mrs. R's Class

Number of Jumps

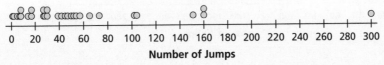

Consecutive Jumps by Mr. K's Class

Number of Jumps

The minimum value (1), the lower quartile (17), the median (40.5), the upper quartile (65), and the maximum value (300) are shown on the dot plot below.

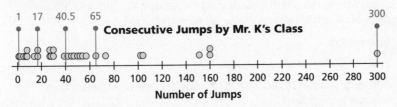

Consecutive Jumps by Mr. K's Class

Number of Jumps

This box plot shows the same distribution of data as the dot plot above.

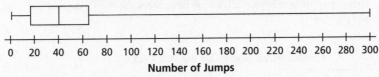

Consecutive Jumps by Mr. K's Class

Number of Jumps

An **outlier** is an unusually high or low data value in a distribution. It could indicate that a value was recorded incorrectly. It could also indicate that the data value is unusual and is important to study.

- What values might be outliers in the data set for Mr. K's class?

- Look at the box-and-whisker plot. What is the typical number of jumps for a student in Mr. K's class? Explain your reasoning.

- Use what you know about box plots. Explain how box plots group a data distribution into quartiles, or four equal parts.

Investigation 4   **What Numbers Describe Us? Using Graphs to Group Data**   91

Notes _____

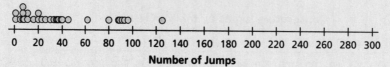

Problem 4.2

In this Problem, you will use box plots to compare data from the two classes.

A Use the dot plot below. Draw a box plot to display the data for Mrs. R's class.

Consecutive Jumps by Mrs. R's Class

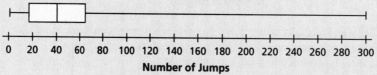

Number of Jumps

B Which class performed better in the jump-rope activity? Use information from the dot plots, box plots, and tables to explain your reasoning.

C Mr. K's class notices unusually high values in its class data. The students in the class want to test whether the data values 102, 104, 151, 160, and 300 are outliers. Mr. K tells his class to do the following test on the data:

- Find the IQR.

- Find the product of $1\frac{1}{2}$ and the IQR.

- Add the product of $1\frac{1}{2}$ and the IQR to Quartile 3. Any value greater than this sum is an outlier.

- Subtract the product of $1\frac{1}{2}$ and the IQR from Quartile 1. Any value less than this sum is an outlier.

1. Locate any outliers from Mr. K's class data. Mark them on a copy of the box plot below.

Consecutive Jumps by Mr. K's Class

Number of Jumps

2. Does Mrs. R's class data include outliers? Explain your reasoning. If Mrs. R's class data contains outliers, redraw your box plot to show which data values are outliers.

Notes

Problem **4.2** *continued*

D **1.** Calculate the mean of Mr. K's class data. Then calculate the mean and the median for Mr. K's class data without the outliers.

2. Do the outliers in Mr. K's class data have more of an effect on the median or on the mean? Explain.

3. Consider what you know about the outliers in the data. Does this change your answer to Question B? Explain.

E In Investigation 2, you used the words *symmetric* and *skewed* to describe the shapes of distributions. These descriptions can also be applied to distributions represented by box plots.

Below are three box plots. They show symmetric and skewed distributions.

The shape is symmetric.

The shape is skewed to the right. Data are more spread out to the right of the median.

The shape is skewed to the left. Data are more spread out to the left of the median.

1. How does the location of the median in a box plot provide information about its shape?

2. How would you describe the shape of Mr. K's class data?

3. How would you describe the shape of Mrs. R's class data?

4. How does the shape of each distribution help you compare the two classes?

ACE Homework starts on page 98.

Investigation 4   **What Numbers Describe Us? Using Graphs to Group Data**   93

Notes _____

_____

_____

4.3 How Much Taller Is a 6th Grader Than a 2nd Grader?

Taking Variability Into Consideration

You can use various physical measures, such as height, to describe people. In this Problem, you will compare the heights of 6th-grade students and the heights of 2nd-grade students.

It is important to identify which graphs are most useful for answering different questions. You have used several types of graphs in this Unit: dot plots, line plots, histograms, and box plots. While answering the questions in this Problem, think about which graphs are most helpful.

- How much taller is a 6th grader than a 2nd grader?

Problem 4.3

A The following dot plot, histogram, and box plot display data on the heights of a group of 6th-grade students. Use these graphs to answer parts (1)–(5).

Heights of 6th Graders

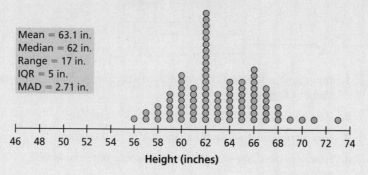

Mean = 63.1 in.
Median = 62 in.
Range = 17 in.
IQR = 5 in.
MAD = 2.71 in.

Height (inches)

Notes

Problem **4.3** *continued*

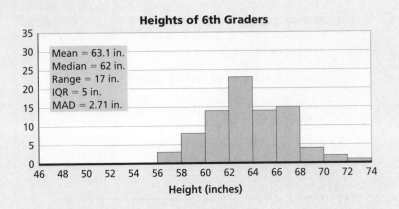

Heights of 6th Graders

Mean = 63.1 in.
Median = 62 in.
Range = 17 in.
IQR = 5 in.
MAD = 2.71 in.

Height (inches)

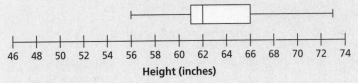

Heights of 6th Graders

Height (inches)

1. Use one or more of the graphs to find the number of students in the group. Explain your reasoning.

2. What do you notice about the data values and their distribution? Explain which graph is most useful when describing the distribution.

3. Describe any clusters or gaps in the distribution. Explain which graph is most useful for identifying clusters or gaps.

4. Describe the spread of the distribution. Which data values occur frequently? Which data values occur infrequently? How close together are the data values? Explain which graph is most useful when describing how the data vary.

5. Describe how the dot plot, histogram, and box plot displaying the data are alike. Describe how they are different.

continued on the next page >

Notes

Problem 4.3 continued

B The dot plot, histogram, and box plot below display data on the heights of a group of 2nd-grade students. Use these displays to answer parts (1)–(5) of Question A for the 2nd-grade data.

Heights of 2nd Graders

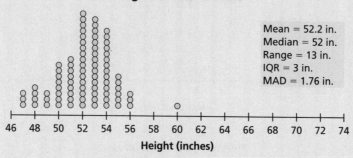

Mean = 52.2 in.
Median = 52 in.
Range = 13 in.
IQR = 3 in.
MAD = 1.76 in.

Height (inches)

Heights of 2nd Graders

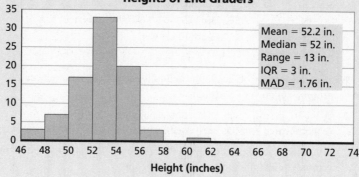

Mean = 52.2 in.
Median = 52 in.
Range = 13 in.
IQR = 3 in.
MAD = 1.76 in.

Height (inches)

Heights of 2nd Graders

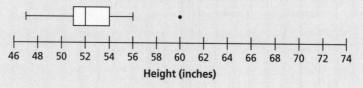

Height (inches)

Notes

Problem 4.3 *continued*

C Compare the graphs of the 6th-grade students to the graphs of the 2nd-grade students. For parts (1)–(4), consider the question below.

How much taller is a 6th-grade student than a 2nd-grade student?

1. Use the dot plots, means, and medians of both sets of data to answer the question. Explain your reasoning.

2. Use the histograms, means, and medians of both sets of data to answer the question. Explain your reasoning.

3. Use the box plots and medians of both sets of data to answer the question. Explain your reasoning.

4. Suppose you were writing a report to answer the question above. Which type of graphs would you choose to display? Explain.

D Use the range, IQR, and MAD for the 6th-grade and the 2nd-grade distributions. Is one distribution more spread out than the other? Explain.

E Suppose you were asked to write a report answering the question below. How would you collect data to answer the question? How would you display the data? What measures would you report?

How much taller is an 8th-grade student than a 6th-grade student?

ACE Homework starts on page 98.

Did You Know?

Growth patterns in humans change over time. While people's heights change significantly through their late teens or early twenties, their heads grow much more slowly after early childhood.

Head and Body Growth Over Time

The length of a **baby's** head is one quarter of its total height.

Age 2   Age 6   Age 12

The length of an **adult's** head is one seventh of its total height.

Notes

Applications

For Exercises 1–4, use the dot plot and histograms below. The graphs show the number of minutes it takes a class of students to travel to school.

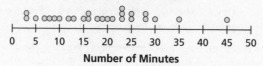

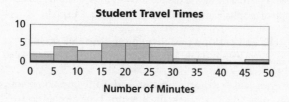

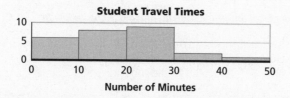

1. How many students spend exactly 10 minutes traveling to school?

2. Which histogram can you use to determine how many students spent at least 15 minutes traveling to school? Explain your reasoning.

3. How many students are in the class? Explain how you can use one of the histograms to find your answer.

4. What is the median time it takes the students to travel to school? Explain your reasoning.

Notes _____

For Exercises 5–9, use the graphs below. The graphs compare the percent of real juice found in different juice drinks.

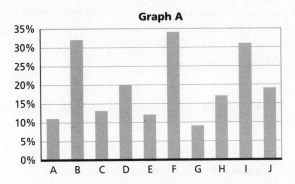

Graph A

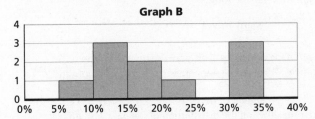

Graph B

5. **a.** Which juice drink(s) has the greatest percent of real juice? The least percent of real juice? Which graph did you use to find your answer? Explain why you chose that graph.

   b. For each juice you named in part (a), what percent of real juice does the drink contain? Which graph did you use? Explain.

6. **a.** Which graph can you use to find the percent of real juice found in a typical juice drink? Explain your reasoning.

   b. What is the typical percent of real juice? Explain your reasoning.

7. What title and axis labels would be appropriate for Graph A? For Graph B?

8. If you were given only Graph A, would you have enough information to draw Graph B? Explain your reasoning.

9. If you were given only Graph B, would you have enough information to draw Graph A? Explain your reasoning.

STUDENT PAGE

Notes

For Exercises 10–12, use the information below.

Jimena likes to hike in the hills. She drives to a new place almost every weekend. The distances Jimena traveled each weekend for the past 30 weekends are listed at the right.

Weekend Travel				
33	10	95	71	4
38	196	85	19	4
209	101	63	10	4
27	128	32	11	213
95	10	77	200	27
62	73	11	100	16

10. **a.** Draw a box-and-whisker plot to display the data.

 b. Why is the left-hand whisker of the box plot (between of the box plot the minimum value and Quartile 1) so short?

 c. Why is the right-hand whisker of the box plot (between Quartile 3 and the maximum value) so long?

 d. What information does the median give about the distances Jimena traveled?

 e. Find the mean of the distances. Compare the mean and the median distances. What does your comparison tell you about the distribution?

11. **a.** Draw a histogram showing the distribution of the data. Use an interval size of 20 miles.

 b. How many weekends did Jimena drive at least 20 miles but less than 40 miles? Explain how you can use the histogram to find your answer.

 c. How many weekends did Jimena drive 100 miles or more? Explain how you can use the histogram to find your answer.

 d. Use the median you found in Exercise 10. In what interval of the histogram does the median fall? How is this possible?

12. Consider the box plot you made in Exercise 10 and the histogram you made in Exercise 11.

 a. Compare the shape of the histogram to the shape of the box plot.

 b. How does the height of the first bar in the histogram relate to the length of the left-hand whisker in the box plot?

 c. How does the histogram help you understand the length of the right-hand whisker in the box plot?

Notes

For Exercises 13 and 14, use the jump-rope data from Problem 4.2.

13. Draw two box plots to compare one gender in Mrs. R's class to the same gender in Mr. K's class. For example, make box plots to compare either the girls from the two classes or the boys from the two classes. Did the girls (or boys) in one class do better than the girls (or boys) in the other class? Explain your reasoning.

14. Make a box plot for all the girls in Mrs. R's class and Mr. K's classes combined. Make a box plot for all the boys in Mrs. R's and Mr. K's classes combined. Compare the box plots. Who did better, the boys or the girls? Explain your reasoning.

15. **Multiple Choice** Which value is NOT needed to construct a box plot?

    A. upper quartile

    B. minimum value

    C. median

    D. mean

16. Tim and Kadisha used the box plots below.

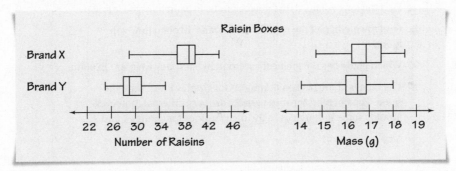

Tim says that Brand X raisins are a better deal than Brand Y raisins because Brand X has more raisins in each box. Kadisha says that since each box has a mass of about 16 or 17 grams, the brands give you the same amount for your money. Do you agree with Tim or with Kadisha? Explain.

Notes

For Exercises 17–19, use the dot plots below. The dot plots show the weights of backpacks for students in Grades 1, 3, 5, and 7.

Grade 1 Backpack Weights

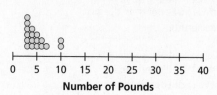

Number of Pounds

Grade 3 Backpack Weights

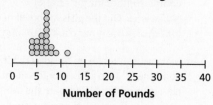

Number of Pounds

Grade 5 Backpack Weights

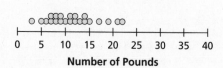

Number of Pounds

Grade 7 Backpack Weights

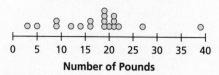

Number of Pounds

17. Use the dot plots above.

   a. Find the range of the data for each grade. Explain how you found it.

   b. Find the median of the data for each grade. Explain how you found it.

   c. Which grade has the greatest variation in backpack weights? Explain.

   d. The ranges of the backpack weights for Grades 1 and 3 are the same. The dot plots for these grades are very different, however. Identify some differences in the distributions for Grades 1 and 3

Notes _____

_____

_____

18. The box plots show the data from the dot plots on the previous page.

A.
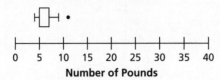

B.
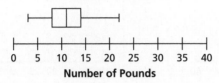

C.
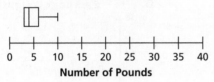

D.
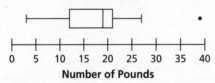

a. Which box plot shows the Grade 1 distribution? Explain.

b. Which box plot shows the Grade 3 distribution? Explain.

c. Which box plot shows the Grade 5 distribution? Explain.

d. Which box plot show the Grade 7 distribution? Explain.

e. Describe the shape of each distribution. Tell whether each is symmetric or skewed. Explain your reasoning.

STUDENT PAGE

Notes

19. The histograms below display the same data sets as the dot plots and box plots on the previous pages.

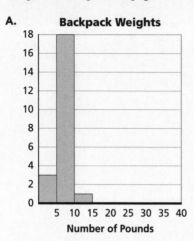

A. Backpack Weights

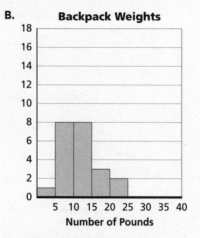

B. Backpack Weights

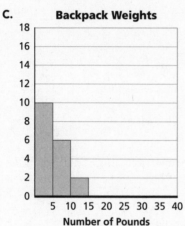

C. Backpack Weights

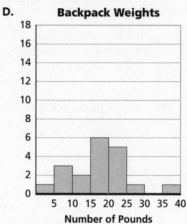

D. Backpack Weights

a. Which histogram shows the Grade 1 distribution? Explain.

b. Which histogram shows the Grade 3 distribution? Explain.

c. Which histogram shows the Grade 5 distribution? Explain.

d. Which histogram show the Grade 7 distribution? Explain.

e. Describe the shape of each distribution. Tell whether each is symmetric or skewed. Explain your reasoning.

Notes _____

_____

_____

For Exercises 20–23, use the box plots below. Each box plot shows the distribution of heights of 30 students at a particular grade level.

Heights of Middle-School Students

8th Grade

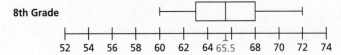

7th Grade

6th Grade

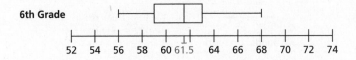

5th Grade

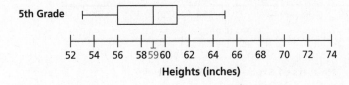

Heights (inches)

20. How much taller is an 8th grader than a 7th grader? Explain your reasoning.

21. On average, how much do students grow from Grade 5 to Grade 8? Explain.

22. Describe the shape of the Grade 6 distribution. Is it symmetric or skewed? Explain.

23. Describe the shape of the Grade 8 distribution. Is it symmetric or skewed? Explain.

Notes

For Exercises 24–26, use the histograms below. Each histogram shows
the heights of 30 students in several grades.

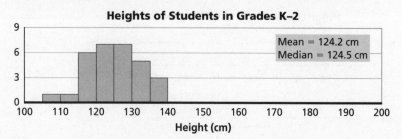

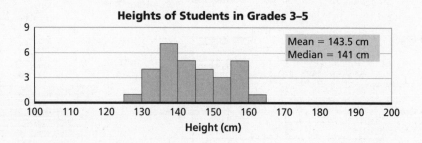

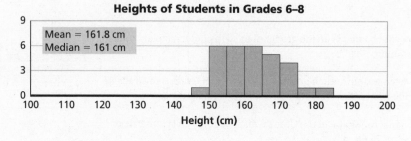

24. On average, how much taller is a student in Grades 6–8 than a
student in Grades K–2? Explain.

25. On average, how much taller is a student in Grades 6–8 than a
student in Grades 3–5? Explain.

26. How is the shape of the histogram for Grades 3–5 different from the
other histograms? Why might this be so?

Notes

Connections

27. Suppose the sum of the values in a data set is 250, and the mean is 25.

   a. Write a data set that fits this description.

   b. Do you think other students in your class wrote the same data set you did? Explain.

   c. What is the median of your data set? Does the median of a data set have to be close in value to the mean? Explain.

28. Each of the students in a seventh-grade class chose a number from 1 to 10 at random. The table below shows the results.

Number Chosen	Percent Who Chose the Number
1	1%
2	5%
3	12%
4	11%
5	10%
6	12%
7	30%
8	9%
9	7%
10	3%

   a. Draw a bar graph of the data.

   b. According to the data, is each number from 1 to 10 equally likely to be chosen?

   c. What is the mode of the data?

   d. Nine students chose the number 5. How many students are in Grade 7? Explain.

STUDENT PAGE

Notes _____

_____

_____

29. Moesha's mean score for six algebra quizzes is 79.5. She has misplaced a quiz. Her scores on the other quizzes are 82, 71, 83, 91, and 78. What is her missing score?

30. The tablet below shows data for the ages and heights of two 2012–2013 professional basketball teams.

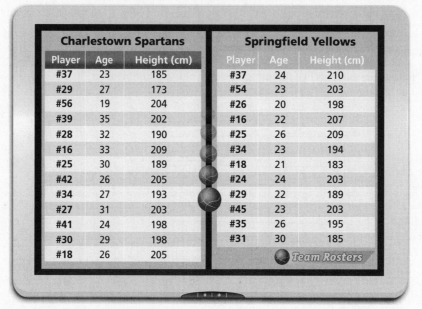

Charlestown Spartans			Springfield Yellows		
Player	Age	Height (cm)	Player	Age	Height (cm)
#37	23	185	#37	24	210
#29	27	173	#54	23	203
#56	19	204	#26	20	198
#39	35	202	#16	22	207
#28	32	190	#25	26	209
#16	33	209	#34	23	194
#25	30	189	#18	21	183
#42	26	205	#24	24	203
#34	27	193	#29	22	189
#27	31	203	#45	23	203
#41	24	198	#35	26	195
#30	29	198	#31	30	185
#18	26	205			

Team Rosters

a. Compare the ages of the two teams. Use statistics and graphs to support your answer.

b. Compare the heights of the two teams. Use statistics and graphs to support your answer.

c. Based on the data for these two teams, what age is a typical professional basketball player? What height is a typical professional basketball player? Do you think your generalizations are accurate? Why or why not?

Notes

Extensions

31. Alejandro and Katya are researching baseball facts. They find out
that the durations of baseball games vary from game to game. The
graph below shows the data Alejandro and Katya collected about the
duration of baseball games.

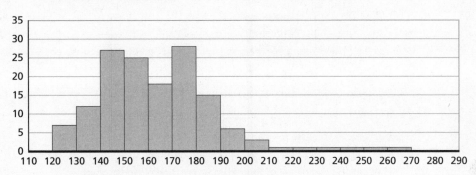

a. What title and axis labels would be appropriate for this graph?

b. Describe the shape of the graph. What does the shape tell you
about the length of a typical baseball game?

c. How many games are represented in the graph?

d. Estimate the lower quartile, the median, and the upper quartile
of the data distribution. What do these statistics tell you about the
length of a typical baseball game?

32. Each box-and-whisker plot below has a median of 4. For each plot,
provide a possible data set that would result in the distribution.

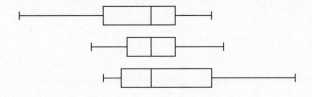

Notes _____

_____

_____

Mathematical Reflections 4

In this Investigation, you drew box plots and histograms to organize data into groups or intervals. You also used histograms and box plots to analyze and compare data distributions. The following questions will help you to summarize what you have learned.

Think about these questions. Discuss your ideas with other students and your teacher. Then write a summary of your findings in your notebook.

1. **Describe** how you can display data using a histogram.

2. **Describe** how you can display data using a box plot.

3. **a. How** can you use histograms to compare two data sets?

   b. How can you use box plots to compare two data sets?

4. Numerical data can be displayed using more than one type of graph. **How** do you decide when to use a dot plot, line plot, bar graph, histogram, or box plot?

Unit Project

Think about the survey you will be developing to gather information about middle school students.

 Which type of graph will best display the data you collect?

Notes

Common Core Mathematical Practices

As you worked on the Problems in this Investigation, you used prior knowledge to make sense of them. You also applied Mathematical Practices to solve the Problems. Think back over your work, the ways you thought about the Problems, and how you used Mathematical Practices.

Ken described his thoughts in the following way:

During Problem 4.3, and the rest of this Investigation, we realized that histograms and box plots group data. You don't see individual data values in those types of graphs. Histograms group data in intervals that you choose. Box plots group data into quartiles. Quartiles group the data into four equal parts.

It is easy to use graphs that show individual data values when the data values are not spread out and there aren't too many. When the values are spread out, or when there are a lot of data values, it's easier to use graphs that group data.

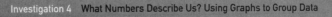

Common Core Standards for Mathematical Practice
MP4 Model with mathematics

- What other Mathematical Practices can you identify in Ken's reasoning?

- Describe a Mathematical Practice that you and your classmates used to solve a different Problem in this Investigation.

Notes

The Problems in this Unit helped you understand the process of statistical investigation. You learned how to:

• Distinguish between categorical data and numerical data

• Organize and represent data with tables, dot plots, line plots, frequency bar graphs, ordered-value bar graphs, histograms, and box-and-whisker plots

• Calculate and interpret measures of center and measures of spread

• Compare two or more distributions of data

Use Your Understanding: Data and Statistics

You can gather and analyze data in statistical investigations to help you make sense of the world around you. Follow these steps when you need to conduct an investigation.

• Pose questions.

• Collect data.

• Analyze data.

• Interpret the results.

For Exercises 1–4, use the information below.

> **Pet Ownership Survey Results**
> • Over 70 million households in the United States own a pet.
> • About 6 out of 10 households in the United States own at least one pet.
> • About two-fifths of pet owners have multiple pets.

1. What questions might have been asked in this survey?

2. Which questions from part (1) collected categorical data? Numerical data? Explain your reasoning.

Notes _____

_____

_____

3. What kinds of people may have responded to the survey?

4. Who might be interested in these results?

Explain Your Reasoning

5. Tyler decided to survey his classmates. He posed two questions:

   What is your favorite kind of pet?

   How many pets do you have?

   Each classmate responded to the questions using student response systems. The answers appeared on the board.

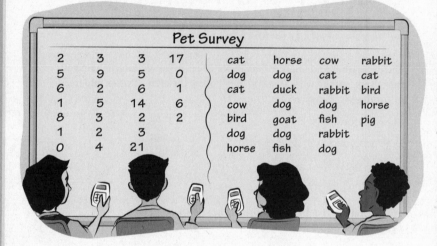

Pet Survey							
2	3	3	17	cat	horse	cow	rabbit
5	9	5	0	dog	dog	cat	cat
6	2	6	1	cat	duck	rabbit	bird
1	5	14	6	cow	dog	dog	horse
8	3	2	2	bird	goat	fish	pig
1	2	3		dog	dog	rabbit	
0	4	21		horse	fish	dog	

   a. Which data set goes with which question? Explain your reasoning.

   b. Which data set includes categorical data?

   c. Which data set includes numerical data?

   d. Make a frequency table for each set of data.

6. Which types of graphs can be used to display categorical data? Explain your reasoning.

7. Which types of graphs can be used to display numerical data? Explain your reasoning.

Notes _____

_____

_____

For Exercises 8–11, use the information below.

A local candle-shop owner wonders which of his products lasts the longest. The owner does an experiment. He records the number of minutes that each candle burns. He completes 15 trials for each type of candle.

Candle-Burning Durations (minutes)

Trial	Brilliant Candle	Firelight Candle	Shimmering Candle
1	60	66	68
2	49	68	65
3	58	56	44
4	57	59	59
5	61	61	51
6	53	64	58
7	57	53	61
8	60	51	63
9	61	60	49
10	62	50	56
11	58	64	59
12	56	60	62
13	61	58	64
14	59	51	57
15	58	49	54

8. For each type of candle, find the median candle-burning time. Find the IQR. Explain how you found the median and IQR.

9. For each type of candle, find the mean candle-burning time. Find the MAD. Explain how you found the mean and MAD.

10. The dot plots, histograms, and box plots below show data on two of the candles. For each graph, identify the candle.

Dot Plot A

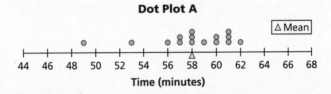

Time (minutes)

Notes

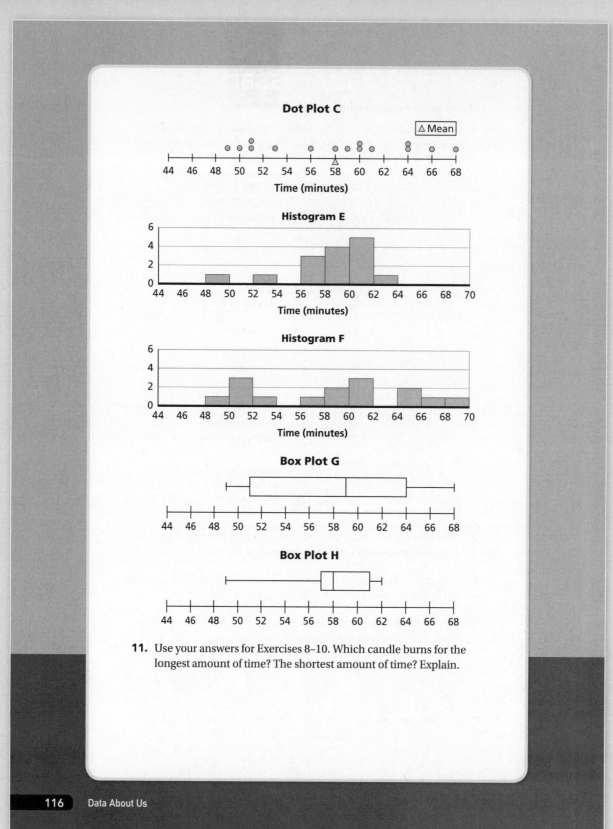

Dot Plot C

△ Mean

Time (minutes)

Histogram E

Time (minutes)

Histogram F

Time (minutes)

Box Plot G

Box Plot H

11. Use your answers for Exercises 8–10. Which candle burns for the longest amount of time? The shortest amount of time? Explain.

Notes

English / Spanish Glossary

A **analyze** Academic Vocabulary
To think about and understand facts and
details about a given set of information.
Analyzing can involve providing a written
summary supported by factual information,
a diagram, chart, table, or a combination of
these.

related terms *examine, evaluate, determine,
observe, investigate*

sample Analyze the following data to find the
mean and the mode.

analizar Vocabulario académico
Pensar para comprender datos y detalles
sobre un conjunto determinado de
información dada. Analizar puede incluir un
resumen escrito apoyado por información
real, un diagrama, una gráfica, una tabla o
una combinación de estos.

términos relacionados *examinar, evaluar,
determinar, observar, investigar*

ejemplo Analiza los siguientes datos para
hallar la media y la moda.

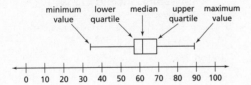

Getting to School

Student	Krista	Mike	Lupe	Kareem
Time (min)	10	15	20	10

Tiempo para ir a la escuela

Estudiante	Krista	Mike	Lupe	Kareem
Tiempo (minutos)	10	15	20	10

attribute An attribute is a characteristic or
feature that is being investigated.

atributo Un atributo es una característica o
cualidad que está siendo investigada.

B **box-and-whisker plot, or box plot** A
display that shows the distribution of values
in a data set separated into four equal-size
groups. A box plot is constructed from a
five-number summary of the data.

**gráfica de caja y bigotes o diagrama de
caja** Una representación que muestra la
distribución de los valores de un conjunto de
datos separados en cuatro grupos de igual
tamaño. Un diagrama de caja se construye
con un resumen de cinco números de
los datos.

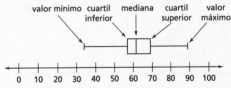

Notes

C **categorical data** Non-numerical data sets are categorical. For example, the responses to "What month were you born?" are categorical data. Frequency counts can be made of the values for a given category. The table below shows examples of categories and their possible values.

datos categóricos Los conjuntos de datos no numéricos son categóricos. Por ejemplo, las respuestas a "¿En qué mes naciste? " son datos categóricos. Los conteos de frecuencia se pueden hacer a partir de los valores de una categoría dada. La siguiente tabla muestra ejemplos de categorías y sus posibles valores.

Category	Possible Values
Month people are born	January, February, March
Favorite color to wear	magenta, blue, yellow
Kinds of pets people have	cats, dogs, fish, horses

Categoría	Valores posibles
Mes de nacimiento de las personas	enero, febrero, marzo
Color preferido para vestir	magenta, azul, amarillo
Tipos de mascotas que tienen las personas	gatos, perros, peces, caballos

cluster A group of numerical data values that are close to one another.

For example, consider the data set 2, 2, 2, 2, 3, 3, 7, 7, 8, 9, 10, 11. There is a *cluster* of data values at 2 (or from 2 to 3) and a *gap* between data values 3 and 7.

grupo Un grupo de valores de datos numéricos que están cercanos unos a otros

Por ejemplo, considera el conjunto de datos 2, 2, 2, 2, 3, 3, 7, 7, 8, 9, 10, 11. Hay un *grupo* de valores de datos en 2 (o de 2 a 3) y una *brecha* entre los valores de datos 3 y 7.

D **data** Values such as counts, ratings, measurements, or opinions that are gathered to answer questions. The table below shows data for mean temperatures in three cities.

datos Valores como los conteos, las calificaciones, las mediciones o las opiniones que se recopilan para responder a las preguntas. Los datos de la siguiente tabla muestran las temperaturas medias en tres ciudades.

Daily Mean Temperatures

City	Mean Temperature (°F)
Mobile, AL	67.5
Boston, MA	51.3
Spokane, WA	47.3

Temperaturas medias diarias

Ciudad	Temperatura media (°F)
Mobile, AL	67.5
Boston, MA	51.3
Spokane, WA	47.3

distribution The entire set of collected data values, organized to show their frequency of occurrence. A distribution can be described using summary statistics and/or by referring to its shape.

distribución Todo el conjunto de valores de datos recopilados, organizados para mostrar su frecuencia de incidencia. Una distribución se puede describir usando la estadística sumaria y/o haciendo referencia a su forma.

Notes _____

_____

_____

E **explain** Academic Vocabulary

To give facts and details that make an idea easier to understand. Explaining can involve a written summary supported by a diagram, chart, table, or a combination of these.

related terms *analyze, clarify, describe, justify, tell*

sample Explain how to determine the mean and the mode of the data set 10, 15, 20, 10.

The mean is $\frac{10+15+20+10}{4}$ = 13.75.

The mode of this data is 10 because 10 is the value that occurs most often.

explicar Vocabulario académico

Proporcionar datos y detalles que hagan que una idea sea más fácil de comprender. Explicar puede incluir un resumen escrito apoyado por un diagrama, una gráfica, una tabla o una combinación de estos.

términos relacionados *analizar, aclarar, describir, justificar, decir*

ejemplo Explica cómo determinar la media y la moda del conjunto de datos 10, 15, 20, 10.

La media es $\frac{10+15+20+10}{4}$ = 13.75.

La moda de estos datos es 10 porque 10 es el valor que ocurre con mayor frecuencia.

F **frequency table** A table that lists all data values, and uses tally marks or some other device to show the number of times each data value occurs.

tabla de frecuencias Una tabla que enumera todos los valores de datos y usa marcas de conteo o algún otro recurso para mostrar el número de veces que se produce cada valor de datos.

Lengths of Chinese Names (From Name Lengths Table 1)		
Number of Letters	Tally	Frequency
1		0
2		0
3		0
4		▪
5	||	▪
6	|||	▪
7		▪
8	||	▪
9		▪

Notes _____

_____

gap A value or several consecutive values, between the minimum and maximum observed data values, where no data value occurred.

For example, consider the data set 2, 2, 2, 2, 3, 3, 7, 7, 8, 9, 10, 11. There is a *cluster* of data values at 2 (or from 2 to 3) and a *gap* between data values 3 and 7.

brecha Un valor o varios valores consecutivos, entre los valores de datos mínimo y máximo observados, donde no se produjo ningún valor de datos.

Por ejemplo, considera el conjunto de datos 2, 2, 2, 2, 3, 3, 7, 7, 8, 9, 10, 11. Hay un *grupo* de valores de datos en 2 (o de 2 a 3) y una *brecha* entre los valores de datos 3 y 7.

H

histogram A display that shows the distribution of numeric data. The range of data values, divided into intervals, is displayed on the horizontal axis. The vertical axis shows frequency in numbers or in percents. The height of the bar over each interval indicates the count or percent of data values in that interval.

The histogram below shows quality ratings for certain brands of peanut butter. The height of the bar over the interval from 20 to 30 is 4. This indicates that four brands of peanut butter have quality ratings greater than or equal to 20 and less than 30.

histograma Una representación que muestra la distribución de datos numéricos. El rango de valores de datos, dividido en intervalos, se representa en el eje horizontal. El eje vertical muestra la frecuencia en números o en porcentajes. La altura de la barra sobre cada intervalo indica el conteo o porcentaje de valores de datos en ese intervalo.

El siguiente histograma representa la calificación de la calidad de ciertas marcas de mantequilla de maní. La altura de la barra sobre el intervalo de 20 a 30 es 4. Esto indica que cuatro marcas de mantequilla de maní tienen una calificación mayor que o igual a 20 y menor que 30.

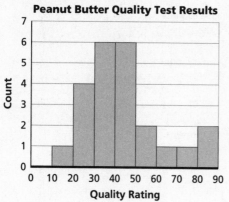

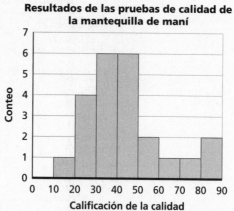

Notes _____

_____

_____

interquartile range (IQR) The difference of the values of the upper quartile (Q3) and the lower quartile (Q1).

In the box-and-whisker plot below, the upper quartile is 69, and the lower quartile is 58. The IQR is the difference 69–58, or 11.

$$IQR = 69 - 58 = 11$$

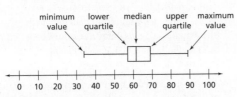

rango entre cuartiles (REC) La diferencia de los valores del cuartil superior (C3) y el cuartil inferior (C1).

En el siguiente diagrama de caja y bigotes, el cuartil superior es 69 y el cuartil inferior es 58. El REC es la diferencia de 69 a 58, u 11.

$$REC = 69 - 58 = 11$$

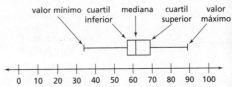

interval A continuous group of numbers. For example, a survey might collect data about people's ages. The responses could be grouped into intervals, such as 5–9, 9–12, and 12–16.

The interval 5–9 would include all ages 5 and older but not quite 9. If your ninth birthday were tomorrow, your data would fall into the interval 5–9.

intervalo Un grupo continuo de números. Por ejemplo, una encuesta puede recopilar datos sobre las edades de las personas. Las respuestas se pueden agrupar en intervalos, como 5 a 9, 9 a 12 y 12 a 16.

El intervalo de 5 a 9 incluiría todas las edades de 5 y mayores de cinco, pero no exactamente 9. Si tu noveno cumpleaños fuera mañana, tus datos se encontrarían en el intervalo de 5 a 9.

line plot A way to organize data along a number line where the ✗s (or other symbols) above a number represent how often each value is mentioned. A line plot made with dots is sometimes referred to as a dot plot.

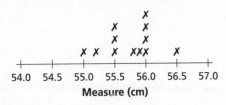

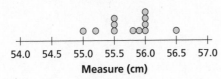

diagrama de puntos Una manera de organizar los datos a lo largo de una recta numérica donde las ✗ (u otros símbolos) colocadas encima de un número representan la frecuencia con que se menciona cada valor. Un diagrama de puntos hecho con puntos algunas veces se conoce como gráfica de puntos.

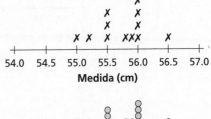

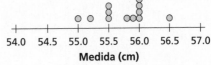

Notes

lower quartile The median of the data to the left of the median (assuming the data are listed from least value to greatest value).

For example, consider a data set with an odd number of items:

1, 2, 5, 6, 7, 8, 8, 10, 12, 15, 20

There are 11 items. The median of the data set is 8. (Six values are at or below 8 and six are at or above 8.) The median of the data to the left of the median (1, 2, 5, 6, 7) is 5. The lower quartile is 5.

Now consider a data set with an even number of items:

2, 3, 4, 5, 6, 6, 8, 8

There are eight items. The median of the data set is 5.5, the average of 5 and 6. The data items to the left of the median are 2, 3, 4, and 5. The median of these values is 3.5. The lower quartile is 3.5.

....

M **maximum value** The data item with the greatest value in a data set. In the data set 2, 2, 2, 2, 3, 3, 7, 7, 8, 9, 10, 11, the maximum value is 11.

cuartil inferior La mediana de los datos a la izquierda de la mediana (asumiendo que los datos indicados van de menor a mayor).

Por ejemplo, considera un conjunto de un número impar de datos:

1, 2, 5, 6, 7, 8, 8, 10, 12, 15, 20

Hay 11 valores de datos. La mediana del conjunto de datos es 8. (Seis valores están en o encima de 8 y seis están en o debajo de 8). La mediana de los datos a la izquierda de la mediana (1, 2, 5, 6, 7) es 5. El cuartil inferior es 5.

Ahora considera un conjunto de un número par de datos:

2, 3, 4, 5, 6, 6, 8, 8

Hay ocho valores de datos. La mediana del conjunto de datos es 5.5, el promedio de 5 y 6. Los valores de datos a la izquierda de la mediana son 2, 3, 4 y 5. La mediana de estos valores es 3.5. El cuartil inferior es 3.5.

valor máximo El dato con el mayor valor en un conjunto de datos. En el conjunto de datos 2, 2, 2, 2, 3, 3, 7, 7, 8, 9, 10, 11, el valor máximo es 11.

Notes _____

_____

_____

mean The value found when all the data are combined and then redistributed evenly. For example, the total number of siblings for the data in the line plot below is 56. If all 19 students had the same number of siblings, they would each have about 3 siblings. Differences from the mean "balance out" so that the sum of differences below and above the mean equal 0. The mean of a set of data is the sum of the values divided by the number of values in the set.

Number of Siblings Students Have

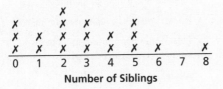

Number of Siblings

media El valor que se halla cuando todos los datos se combinan y luego se redistribuyen de manera uniforme. Por ejemplo, el número total de hermanos y hermanas en los datos del siguiente diagrama es 56. Si los 19 estudiantes tuvieran la misma cantidad de hermanos y hermanas, cada uno tendría aproximadamente 3 hermanos o hermanas. Las diferencias de la media se "equilibran" de manera que la suma de las diferencias por encima y por debajo de la media sea igual a 0. La media de un conjunto de datos es la suma de los valores dividida por el número de valores en el conjunto.

Número de hermanos y hermanas que tienen los estudiantes

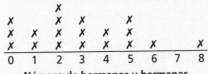

Número de hermanos y hermanas

mean absolute deviation (MAD) The average distance of all of the data values in a data set from the mean of the distribution.

desviación absoluta media (DAM) La distancia media de todos los valores de datos en un conjunto de datos a partir de la media de la distribución.

median The number that marks the midpoint of an ordered set of data. At least half of the values lie at or above the median, and at least half lie at or below the median. For the sibling data (0, 0, 0, 1, 1, 2, 2, 2, 3, 3, 3, 4, 4, 5, 5, 5, 6, 8), the median of the distribution of siblings is 3 because the tenth (middle) value in the ordered set of 19 values is 3.

When a distribution contains an even number of data values, the median is computed by finding the average of the two middle data values in an ordered list of the data values. For example, the median of 1, 3, 7, 8, 25, and 30 is 7.5 because the data values 7 and 8 are third and fourth in the list of six data values.

mediana El número que marca el punto medio de un conjunto ordenado de datos. Por lo menos la mitad de los datos se encuentran en o encima de la mediana y por lo menos la mitad se encuentran en o debajo de la mediana. Para los datos de los hermanos y hermanas (0, 0, 0, 1, 1, 2, 2, 2, 2, 3, 3, 3, 4, 4, 5, 5, 5, 6, 8), la mediana de la distribución de hermanos y hermanas es 3 porque el décimo valor (el del medio) en el conjunto ordenado de 19 valores es 3.

Cuando una distribución contiene un número par de valores de datos, la mediana se calcula hallando el promedio de los dos valores de datos del medio en una lista ordenada de los valores de datos. Por ejemplo, la mediana de 1, 3, 7, 8, 25 y 30 es 7.5, porque los valores de datos 7 y 8 son tercero y cuarto en la lista de seis valores de datos.

English/Spanish Glossary   123

Notes

minimum value The data item with the least value in a data set. In the data set 2, 2, 2, 2, 3, 3, 7, 7, 8, 9, 10, 11, the minimum value is 2.

valor mínimo El dato con el menor valor en un conjunto de datos. En el conjunto de datos 2, 2, 2, 2, 3, 3, 7, 7, 8, 9, 10, 11, el valor mínimo es 2.

mode The value that appears most frequently in a set of data. In the data set 2, 2, 2, 2, 3, 3, 7, 7, 8, 9, 10, 11, the mode is 2.

moda El valor que aparece con mayor frecuencia en un conjunto de datos. En el conjunto de datos 2, 2, 2, 2, 3, 3, 7, 7, 8, 9, 10, 11, la moda es 2.

N numerical data Values that are numbers such as counts, measurements, and ratings. Here are some examples.

- Number of children in families
- Pulse rates (number of heart beats per minute)
- Heights
- Amounts of time people spend reading in one day
- Ratings such as: on a scale of 1 to 5 with 1 as "low interest," how would you rate your interest in participating in the school's field day?

datos numéricos Valores que son números como conteos, mediciones y calificaciones. Los siguientes son algunos ejemplos.

- Número de hijos e hijas en las familias
- Pulsaciones por minuto (número de latidos del corazón por minuto)
- Alturas
- Cantidades de tiempo que las personas pasan leyendo en un día
- Calificaciones como: en una escala de 1 a 5, en la que 1 representa "poco interés", ¿cómo calificarías tu interés por participar en el día de maniobras de tu escuela?

O ordered-value bar graph A bar graph in which the bars are arranged by increasing (or decreasing) order of length.

gráfica de barras de valores ordenados Una gráfica de barras en la que las barras están ordenadas en orden de longitud creciente (o decreciente).

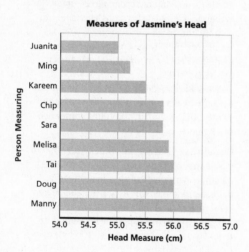

Measures of Jasmine's Head

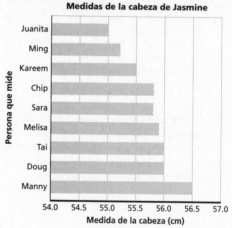

Medidas de la cabeza de Jasmine

Notes

outlier A value that lies far from the "center" of a distribution and is not like other values. *Outlier* is a relative term, but it indicates a data point that is much higher or much lower than the values that could be normally expected for the distribution.

To identify an outlier in a distribution represented by a boxplot, measure the distance between Q3 and any suspected outliers at the top of the range of data values; if this distance is more than $1.5 \times$ IQR, then the data value is an outlier. Likewise, if the distance between any data value at the low end of the range of values and Q1 is more than $1.5 \times$ IQR, then the data value is an outlier.

valor extremo Un valor que se encuentra lejos del "centro" de una distribución y no es como los demás valores. El *valor extremo* es un término relativo, pero indica un dato que es mucho más alto o mucho más bajo que los valores que se podrían esperar normalmente para la distribución.

Para identificar un valor extremo en una distribución representada por un diagrama de caja, se mide la distancia entre C3 y cualquier valor que se sospeche es extremo en la parte superior del rango de los valores de datos; si esta distancia es mayor que $1.5 \times$ REC, entonces el valor de datos es un valor extremo. Del mismo modo, si la distancia entre cualquier valor de datos en la parte inferior del rango de valores y C1 es mayor que $1.5 \times$ REC, entonces el valor de datos es un valor extremo.

P   **predict** Academic Vocabulary
To make an educated guess based on the analysis of real data.

related terms *estimate, survey, analyze, observe*

sample Dan knows that the mean life span of his type of tropical fish is 2 years. What other information could help Dan predict how long his fish will live?

> If Dan also knew the median life span he would have more information to predict how long his fish will live. The mean could be skewed because of one or more outliers.

predecir Vocabulario académico
Hacer una suposición basada en el análisis de datos reales.

términos relacionados *estimar, encuestar, analizar, observar*

ejemplo Dan sabe que la media de vida de su tipo de pez tropical es de 2 años. ¿Qué otra información podría ayudar a Dan a predecir cuánto vivirá su pez?

> Si Dan también supiera la mediana de vida, tendría más información para predecir cuánto vivirá su pez. La media podría estar sesgada debido a uno o más valores extremos.

Q   **quartile** One of three points that divide a data set into four equal groups. The second quartile, Q2, is the median of the data set. The first quartile, Q1, is the median of the lower half of the data set. The third quartile, Q3, is the median of the upper half of the data set.

cuartil Uno de los tres puntos que dividen un conjunto de datos en cuatro grupos iguales. El segundo cuartil, C2, es la mediana del conjunto de datos. El primer cuartil, C1, es la mediana de la mitad inferior del conjunto de datos. El tercer cuartil, C3, es la mediana de la mitad superior del conjunto de datos.

Notes _____

_____

_____

R **range** The difference of the maximum value and the minimum value in a distribution. If you know the range of the data is 12 grams of sugar per serving, you know that the difference between the minimum and maximum values is 12 grams. For example, in the distribution 2, 2, 2, 2, 3, 3, 7, 7, 8, 9, 10, 11, the range of the data set is 9, because $11 - 2 = 9$.

rango La diferencia del valor máximo y el valor mínimo en una distribución. Si se sabe que el rango de los datos es 12 gramos de azúcar por porción, entonces se sabe que la diferencia entre el valor mínimo y el máximo es 12 gramos. Por ejemplo, en la distribución 2, 2, 2, 2, 3, 3, 7, 7, 8, 9, 10, 11, el rango del conjunto de datos es 9, porque $11 - 2 = 9$.

represent Academic Vocabulary
To stand for or take the place of something else. Symbols, equations, charts, and tables are often used to represent particular situations.

representar Vocabulario académico
Significar o tomar el lugar de algo más. Los símbolos, las ecuaciones, las gráficas y las tablas a menudo se usan para representar situaciones particulares.

related terms *symbolize, stand for*

términos relacionados *simbolizar, significar*

sample Jerry surveyed his classmates about the number of pets they have. He recorded his data in a table. Represent the results of Jerry's survey in a bar graph.

ejemplo Jerry hizo una encuesta entre sus compañeros de clase sobre el número de mascotas que tienen. Anotó sus datos en una tabla. Representa los resultados de la encuesta de Jerry en una gráfica de barras.

How Many Pets?

Number of Pets	Number of Students
0 pets	10
1 pet	11
2 or more pets	8

¿Cuántas mascotas?

Número de mascotas	Número de estudiantes
0 mascotas	10
1 mascota	11
2 o más mascotas	8

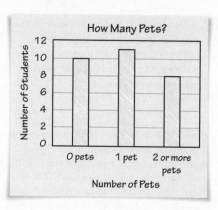

126   Data About Us

Notes _____

scale The size of the units on an axis of a graph or number line. For instance, each mark on the vertical axis might represent 10 units.

escala El tamaño de las unidades en un eje de una gráfica o recta numérica. Por ejemplo, cada marca en el eje vertical puede representar 10 unidades.

shape of a distribution The shape of a distribution can be described by identifying clusters and gaps, and by noting whether the distribution is symmetric or skewed.

forma de una distribución La forma de una distribución se puede describir al identificar grupos y brechas, y al observar si la distribución es simétrica o asimétrica.

skewed distribution Any distribution that is not symmetrical about the mean.

distribución asimétrica Cualquier distribución que no es simétrica alrededor de la media.

summary statistic A single number that conveys basic, but important, information about a distribution. Examples of summary statistics include the mean, median, mode, range, MAD, and IQR.

estadística sumaria Un solo número que transmite información básica, pero importante, sobre una distribución. Los ejemplos de la estadística sumaria incluyen la media, la mediana, la moda, el rango, la DAM y el REC.

symmetric distribution A distribution in which the mean and median are the same or almost the same, and in which the values above and below the mean form an approximate mirror image.

distribución simétrica Una distribución en la que la media y la mediana son iguales o casi iguales y en la que los valores por encima y por debajo de la media forman una imagen reflejada aproximada.

table A tool for organizing information in rows and columns. Tables let you list categories or values and then tally the occurrences.

tabla Una herramienta para organizar información en filas y columnas. Las tablas permiten que se hagan listas de categorías o de valores y luego se cuenten las incidencias.

Favorite Colors

Color	Number of Students
Red	6
White	15
Blue	9

Colores favoritos

Color	Número de estudiantes
Rojo	6
Blanco	15
Azul	9

Notes

upper quartile The median of the data to the right of the median (assuming the data are listed from least value to greatest value).

For example, consider a data set with an odd number of items:

1, 2, 5, 6, 7, 8, 8, 10, 12, 15, 20

There are 11 items. The median of the data set is 8. (Six values are at or below 8 and six are at or above 8.) The median of the data to the right of the median (8, 10, 12, 15, and 20) is 12. The upper quartile is 12.

Now consider a data set with an even number of items:

2, 3, 4, 5, 6, 6, 8, 8

There are eight items. The median of the data set is 5.5, the average of 5 and 6. The data items to the right of the median are 6, 6, 8, and 8. The median of these values is 7, the average of 6 and 8. The upper quartile is 7.

cuartil superior La mediana de los datos a la derecha de la mediana (asumiendo que los datos indicados van de menor a mayor).

Por ejemplo, considera un conjunto de un número impar de datos:

1, 2, 5, 6, 7, 8, 8, 10, 12, 15, 20

Hay 11 valores de datos. La mediana del conjunto de datos es 8. (Seis valores están en o encima de 8 y seis están en o debajo de 8). La mediana de los datos a la derecha de la mediana (8, 10, 12, 15 y 20) es 12. El cuartil superior es 12.

Ahora considera un conjunto de un número par de datos:

2, 3, 4, 5, 6, 6, 8, 8

Hay ocho valores de datos. La mediana del conjunto de datos es 5.5, el promedio de 5 y 6. Los valores de datos a la derecha de la mediana son 6, 6, 8 y 8. La mediana de estos valores es 7, el promedio de 6 y 8. El cuartil superior es 7.

variability An indication of how widely spread or closely clustered the data values are. Range, minimum and maximum values, and clusters in the distribution give some indication of variability. The variability of a distribution can also be measured by its IQR or MAD.

variabilidad Indicación de cuán dispersos o agrupados están los valores de datos. El rango, los valores mínimo y máximo, y los grupos en la distribución dan cierta indicación de variabilidad. La variabilidad de una distribución también se puede medir por su REC o por su DAM.

Notes

Index

Notes

Index

Notes _____

_____

_____

Acknowledgments

Cover Design

Three Communication Design, Chicago

Text

113 American Pet Products Association

Data from "*2011–2012 National Pet Owners Survey*" from the American Pet Products Association (APPA).

Photographs

Photo locators denoted as follows: Top (T), Center (C), Bottom (B), Left (L), Right (R), Background (Bkgd)

002 Solent News/Splash News/Newscom; **003** WaterFrame/Alamy; **013** (CL) Plusphoto/AmanaimagesRF/Getty Images, (CR) iStockPhoto/Thinkstock, (BC) Jeayesy/Fotolia, **022** Lculig/Shutterstock; **047** Solent News/Splash News/Newscom.

Notes _____

_____

_____

At a Glance   Problem 1.1   Pacing 1½ Days

1.1 How Many Letters Are in a Name?

Focus Question What are "data"? How do you represent data using a frequency table or a line plot? How can you compare two distributions of data?

Launch

Use Problem 1.1 to assess students' abilities with respect to statistics.

Suggested Questions

- *What attribute is being investigated in Problem 1.1? How do you determine the data values? How might you represent them?*
- *How can you compare the name lengths for these two classes?*

Explore

Some students may need support in making and interpreting line plots. You may wish to do a mid-Problem Summarize after Questions A and B.

Suggested Questions

- *How do you locate the shortest and longest data values?*
- *How can you use the shortest and longest name lengths to set up number lines for making the line plots?*

Students should use the same scale for the two distributions.

- *How are the frequency tables and line plots related to each other? Does the table help you set up the graph?*
- *Do you see any clusters of data for the Chinese class? The U.S. class?*

Summarize

Have students show and explain the graphs they made.

Suggested Questions

- *What is the typical name length in the U.S. class? The Chinese class?*
- *Some of you said that 11 letters and 13 letters are the most typical lengths for the U.S. names. Some of you used a span of 11–13 letters. What justification can you give for each of these answers?*

Key Vocabulary

- attribute
- cluster
- data
- distribution
- frequency table
- gap
- line plot
- scale
- shape of a distribution
- table

Materials

Labsheets
- 1.1A: Name Lengths Table 1
- 1.1B: Frequency Table: Lengths of Chinese Names
- 1ACE: Exercises 1–4
- Half-Inch Grid Paper

Accessibility Labsheet
- 1.1C: Frequency Table: Lengths of U.S. Names
- Data and Graphs Tool

ACE
Assignment Guide for Problem 1.1

Applications: 1–4 | Connections: 15–16

Answers to Problem 1.1

A. 1. a. There are no tally marks next to the name lengths of 1, 2, and 3.

b. **Lengths of Chinese Names**

Number of Letters	Frequency
0	0
1	0
2	0
3	0
4	2
5	4
6	8
7	7
8	2
9	7

2. **Lengths of U.S. Names**

Number of Letters	Frequency
0	0
1	0
2	0
3	0
4	0
5	0
6	0
7	0
8	0
9	3
10	3
11	6
12	3
13	6
14	2
15	5
16	1
17	1

3. a. shortest name length is 4 letters; longest name length is 9 letters

b. shortest name length is 9 letters; longest name length is 17 letters

B. 1. **Lengths of Chinese Names**

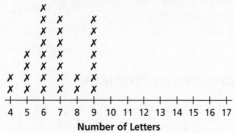

Lengths of U.S. Names

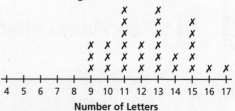

2. From the frequency tables, use the shortest name length and the longest name length to set up a number line. Look at the Frequency column to see how many *X*s to put above each tick mark.

C. 1. Answers will vary. Chinese names are shorter than U.S. names. The longest Chinese name length (9 letters) is the shortest U.S. name length. There aren't as many different name lengths for Chinese names as there are for U.S. names. U.S. name lengths seem to cluster around 11–13 letters. Chinese name lengths seem to cluster around 6–7 letters. There aren't any clear gaps in either distribution.

2. Answers will vary. Possible answer: Are there some names lengths that occur more often than others? For each graph, what is the difference between the longest number of letters and the shortest number of letters?

3. Answers will vary. Students might use either of the statements in part (1). Also, the shortest name length for the Chinese class (4 letters) is 5 letters less than the shortest name length for the U.S. class. The shortest name length for the U.S. class (9 letters) is the same as the longest Chinese name length.

4. Answers will vary. Line plots help you locate clusters and gaps and also let you see the overall shape. In this situation, the Chinese class data are less than the U.S. class data in terms of name length; the only shared name length is 9 letters.

D. 1. Answers will vary. Name lengths seem to cluster around 6–7 letters, with another frequent name length being 9 letters.

2. Answers will vary: There are three different name lengths that occur more often than others: 11, 13, and 15 letters.

At a Glance   Problem 1.2   Pacing $\frac{1}{2}$ Day

1.2 Describing Name Lengths: What are the Shape, Mode, and Range?

> **Focus Question** What are measures of central tendency and variability (or spread)? How do you compute and use mode and range?

Launch

Introduce the context: the U.S. class from Problem 1.1 is given a list of pen pals from a class in Japan.

Suggested Questions

- *How do you think name lengths for a class of students in Japan will compare to the name lengths of students from a class in the United States?*

Introduce the new vocabulary: mode, maximum value, minimum value, and range.

- *What is the mode for the U.S. class data? For the Chinese class data? Does this help you compare the classes?*

- *What is the range for the U.S. data? For the Chinese data? Does this help you compare the classes?*

- *Do you think you can use the ideas of mode and range to compare the Japanese name lengths to the U.S. name lengths? What data will you use for this Problem?*

Explore

In a distribution, the data lose their individual meanings (e.g., Savannah Russell's name length is 15 letters). The data distribution becomes an object that can be examined to consider what you know about name lengths in general based on what the distribution looks like, i.e., its shape. Specifically, the Problem asks students to look at where data *cluster* and where there may be *gaps*. Help students see that data displayed using a graph show the overall shape of a distribution.

Suggested Questions

- *Are the data values for the Japanese name lengths spread out, or are they clustered together around values that are close together?*

Some students will focus on the difference between maximum and minimum values (the range). They may think that this shows the values are spread out. If this happens, you might push further on the idea of a *cluster* of values.

- *What are unusual values? Where are most student name lengths clustered?*

- *How did you decide on the mode for the Japanese name lengths?*

- *Is 12 letters a more typical name length than 10 letters?*

Key Vocabulary

- maximum value
- minimum value
- mode
- range

Materials

Labsheets
- 1.2: Name Lengths Table 2
- Half-Inch Grid Paper

Accessibility Labsheet
- 1ACE: Exercise 17

- Data and Graphs Tool
- Expression Calculator Tool

This question highlights a problem with using the mode as a measure of center: there might be more than one mode, and there might be several data values that occur with the almost the same frequency as the mode. As a summary, mode does have drawbacks. As the Unit progresses, students will have opportunities to think about the pros and cons of using the mode as a measure of center.

Summarize

Suggested Questions

- *How might one measure help you summarize a set of data values? What does the mode summarize? What does the range summarize?*

- *You know the mode for the Japanese class data (12 letters), the Chinese class data (6 letters), and the U.S. class data (11 and 13 letters). Does this help you make comparisons among the data sets?*

- *You know the range of the Japanese class data (7 letters), the Chinese class data (5 letters), and the U.S. class data (8 letters). Does this help you compare the data sets?*

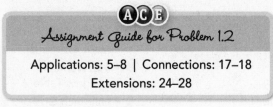

ⒶⒸⒺ
Assignment Guide for Problem 1.2

Applications: 5–8 | Connections: 17–18
Extensions: 24–28

Answers to Problem 1.2

A. 1. (See Figure 1.)

  2. Answers will vary.

   a. Data seem to cluster around 10–12 letters. Possible explanation: More than half the values are between 10 and 12 letters.

   b. There are no gaps. Possible explanation: Each value between the maximum and minimum values has at least one dot above it.

B. 1. The mode is 12 letters.

  2. Opinions might reasonably vary about this. There are almost as many student names with 10 letters as there are student names with 12 letters. Even though 12 letters occurs the most, it is not necessarily typical.

C. 1. The minimum value is 7 letters, and the maximum value is 14 letters; the range is 7 letters ($14 - 7 = 7$).

  2. The ranges from the three sets of data indicate that the U.S. class data are slightly more variable than the others and that the Chinese class data varies the least.

Figure 1

Lengths of Japanese Names

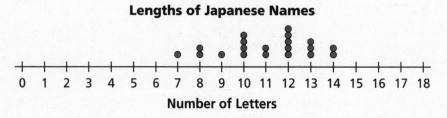

Number of Letters

At a Glance   Problem 1.3   Pacing 1 Day

1.3 Describing Name Lengths: What is the Median?

Focus Question How do you identify and use the median? How can you compare two distributions of data using the medians?

Launch

As students make connections to the median in Problem 1.3 and to the mean in Investigation 2, they should realize the mode is rarely used to describe the central tendency in quantitative data because it may be unstable.

The median is a more important measure of center given its position at the midpoint of a distribution. Its *position* depends on the order of the data values in a data set, so it is sensitive to *the number of data values*. Its *value* is determined from the actual data value (or average of the two data values) at the midpoint.

Suggested Questions

- *The median is another way to describe what is typical. You need to find the* position *and the* value *of the median for these data. To find the median, first order the data.*

Have students work in pairs on writing each name length in size order on a strip of grid paper, then folding the grid paper strip in half, to find the position of the median.

- *If you put the ends of the strip together and fold the strip in half, where does the crease fall in the list of numbers?*
- *How many numbers are to the left of the crease? To the right?*
- *What is the value of the median for these data?*

Explore

Some students will find it difficult to believe that the median may not change when additional data values are added.

Suggested Questions

- *Why did the position and the value of the median change when you added 3 names but not when you added 2 names?*
- *Why should you say that half the name lengths are greater than or equal to the median of 12, not just greater than 12?*
- *How can you find the medians for the U.S. class and Chinese class data? Is the table of data or graph helpful?*
- *How do the medians of the data sets help you compare class name lengths?*
- *When there is an even number of name lengths, the position of the median is between the middle two data values. Does this mean the value of the median of an even number of name lengths will always be a fraction, such as $11\frac{1}{2}$?*

Key Vocabulary
- median
- summary statistic

Materials

Labsheet
- Half-Inch Grid Paper

Accessibility Labsheet
- 1ACE: Exercise 20

Assessment
- Check Up 1
- sticky notes
- Data and Graphs Tool

Summarize

Be sure to discuss how to calculate the median when there is an odd number of data values and when there is an even number of data values.

Suggested Questions

- *Earlier, you found a different measure of center called the mode. How does the median compare with the mode in this data set? Is it possible that the median and mode may not the same?*

- *If you had several data values, folding a strip of paper to find the position and value of the median would be ineffecient. How else might you find the position and value of the median?*

- *What general rules can you use to find the position and value of the median when there is an odd number of data values? An even number of data values?*

Ⓐ Ⓒ Ⓔ

Assignment Guide for Problem 1.3

Applications: 9–14 | Connections: 19–23
Extensions: 29–30

Answers to Problem 1.3

A. 1. There are now 22 observations. The median is still located between 11 and 12. Its value is still $11\frac{1}{2}$. This is because one data value was added to either side of the midway point, keeping the data set in balance.

2. There are now 23 observations. The median's position is now on the last number 11. The value of the median is 11. Adding one data value smaller than the original median shifted the midway point to the left.

3. a. The position of the median does change. Of the data values added, more of them are greater than the original median; therefore, the location of the median shifts to the right.

b. The median is now 12 since the location of the median shifted to the right (which is a different data value).

c. When there are repeated values in the middle of a data set, the median might fall between two data values that are equal. In the case of the Japanese class names, the median value is 12 letters; half the class (15 people) has names

with lengths 12 letters or more, and half the class (15 people) has names with lengths 12 letters or less. Eleven people have names with exactly 12 letters.

B. 1. Chinese: median 7 letters, range 5 letters, data vary from 4 to 9 letters; Japanese: median 12 letters, range 7 letters, data vary from 7 to 14 letters; United States: median 12.5 letters, range 8 letters, data vary from 9 to 17 letters

2. Answers will vary. Possible answers: The U.S. class and the Japanese class have similar medians. The Chinese class has a smaller median, so the name lengths of the Chinese students are shorter than those of the other two classes. The range of number of letters in Chinese names is 5, so the name lengths for Chinese names are less variable (i.e., less spread out) than the other two classes.

C. 1. the 5th value from the top or bottom of the ordered list; the 10th value; the 500th value

2. between the 5th and 6th values, counting from either the top or bottom of the ordered list; between the 10th and 11th values; between the 500th and the 501st values

3. When there is an even number of data values, the median is located between the two middle data values; when there is an odd number of data values, the median takes its value from the middle data value.

2.1 What's a Mean Household Size?

> **Focus Question** How do you go about finding a number that is a good estimate of typical household size based on the given data?

Launch

Measures of center (mode, median, and mean) help describe data distributions.

Have your students construct the physical model in small groups by building a tower of cubes for each student's household. Have them arrange their cube towers in order from smallest to largest.

Suggested Questions

- *What is the attribute being investigated?*
- *How can you use the cube stacks to find the median of these data?*
- *How can you use the cube stacks to find the mode of these data?*
- *How much do the household sizes vary?*

Now turn to the focus on the new concept: *mean.*

- *How can you determine the average number of people in a household for these six households?*
- *These students decided to find the average by "evening out" the number of cubes in each tower. Try this on your own.*

After students work with their towers, discuss what they found. The towers are "evened out" by moving cubes from taller towers to shorter towers. Since each tower was originally a single color, students will be able to see from which towers the "moved data" came.

- *We call this "evened out" number the mean. How does the mean compare to the median for this set of data?*

Note: Using the terminology of "4 people per household" is a way to help students realize that the mean can be used to describe the number of people in each household if each of the six households had the same number of people. They have dealt informally with "per quantities" before in many sharing situations.

Tell students that they are going to see a new representation, an *ordered-value bar graph.* You might want to do Problem 2.1, Question A, part (1), as a whole class.

Explore

Suggested Questions

- *You made cube stacks and evened them out. What do you call the height of the stacks when they were evened out?*
- *How are the ordered-value bar graph and the cube stacks related? How are the ordered-value bar graph and the dot plot related?*

Key Vocabulary

- mean
- ordered-value bar graph

Materials

Labsheets

- 2.1: Household Size 1
- Blank Grid and Number Line
- Half-Inch Grid Paper

Teaching Aids

- 2.1A: Distribution of Household Size Table 1
- 2.1B: Mean Distribution of Household Size 1
- 2-cm colored wooden cubes

- *The dot plot keeps the original data about the 6 households. How does the location of the mean on the dot pot relate to the location of the individual dots?*
- *How does adding up the numbers and dividing by 6 relate to the cube stacks?*
- *For the two tables, the means are the same but the ranges are different. How is this possible?*

Note: The sets of data in this Problem are designed so that the mean will be a whole number. The cubes will all be the same height to indicate the mean. When you use more complicated data sets, the mean may involve a decimal or a fraction. When this happens, the cube stacks or value bars will have different heights.

Summarize

Suggested Questions

- *How does each model show the data before any evening out is done?*
- *How does each model show the data after the evening-out process is completed?*

Assignment Guide for Problem 2.1

Applications: 1–3 | Connections: 17–19

Answers to Problem 2.1

A. 1. Each dot on the dot plot represents an end point of the ordered-value bar graph. Since the bars are arranged horizontally, the ends of the bars line up with the locations of the values of the dots marking the size of the household on the dot-plot axis.

  2. Answers will vary. There are several moves that will even out the bars.

  3. Some students will physically move the cubes or use the ordered-value bar graphs; some may see that there are 24 people to share among 6 households/stacks. The final stacks/bars will have 4 people each.

B. 1.

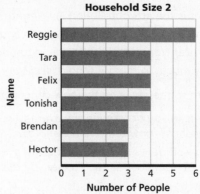

Household Size 2

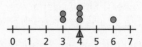

2. The mean is 4. Some students will even out value bars. Some will build the data values with cubes and even these out. Some will use an algorithm.

3. The mean is the same for both distributions (4), but the median is larger for Table 2 (4, as opposed to $3\frac{1}{2}$).

4. Once you have all the bars evened out, you have 6 bars, each 4 "cubes" long, so the ends of the bars line up vertically above 4 on the axis.

5. You can say that an average or typical household size is 4. Some are greater than this, some are less; 4 is an estimate that is not far from any of the original values.

2.2 Comparing Distributions With the Same Mean

> *Focus Question* How do you interpret, compute, and use the mean?

Launch

Refer students to the image of the rulers shown; it represents a "balance" model. **Note:** The image is meant to be purely a visual. This is not provided to suggest that you replicate this experiment. Because rulers have their own weights which would affect the balance, any replication would most likely not give accurate results.

Suggested Questions

- *What is meant by a balance point?*

Discuss the situations about household sizes from Problem 2.1.

- *Are there other sets of data with six households and a mean of 4 people that are different from the ones we explored?*

Explore

For Question A, if students are having problems finding a data set with a mean of 4 people per household, encourage them to explore through trial and error. If pairs are still having trouble, suggest they work backward moving from six towers of four cubes to six towers with different numbers of cubes in each but keeping the total number of cubes the same.

Students may struggle with the idea of a "half" of a person. Explain that the mean of $3\frac{1}{2}$ people does not have to be an actual or possible value in the data set.

Encourage students to connect the algorithm, "add up and divide" and the evening-out process.

Summarize

Suggested Questions

- *What are some quick ways to come up with different sets of data with six households and a mean of 4 people?*
- *What are some quick ways to make different sets of data with six households and a mean of $3\frac{1}{2}$ people?*

Ideally, students will see that if they know the number of households and the mean number of people in the households, they can determine the total number of people in the households. Then, they can work backward to identify a data set.

- *Why is the mean household size sometimes a fraction?*

Materials

Labsheets
- Blank Grid and Number Line
- Half-Inch Grid Paper

Accessibility Labsheet
- 2ACE: Exercises 4–7

Teaching Aid
- 2.2: Mean Distributions of Household Sizes

- 2-cm colored wooden cubes (optional)

At a Glance **313**

Answers to Problem 2.2

A. 1. Answers will vary. Possible example:
2, 3, 3, 4, 5, 7; sum is 24

2. Possible bar graph and line plot:

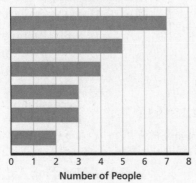

Household Size

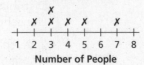

3. Answers will vary. Students may use the strategy of evening out.

4. a. Look at the length of the bar or at the data value below the ✗ on the axis.

b. Count the total number of bars or ✗s.

c. Add up the lengths of all bars or add up all data values on the axis below each ✗.

d. Even out the bars in the ordered-value bar graph. For the line plot, you can move each data value toward a central value as long as the number of moves for the values above the central value is the same as the number of moves for the values below the central value.

B. 1. Answers will vary. Possible example:
1, 2, 2, 2, 3, 3, 8; sum is 21

2. Possible bar graph and line plot:

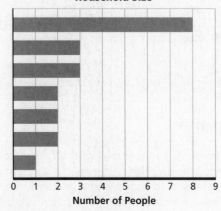

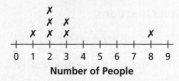

3. Answers will vary. Students may use the strategy of evening out.

4. Answers will vary. Students may imagine the cube scenario, rearranging household sizes so that the bar graphs and line plots spread out to the left and/or right of the original range.

5. See the answers to Question A, part (4).

C. 1. Answers will vary. Possible example:
2, 2, 3, 4, 5, 5; sum is 21

2. Possible bar graph and line plot:

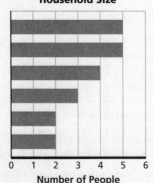

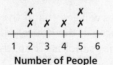

3. The mean does not have to be an actual or possible value from the data set.

D. **1.** The median is 4 people, the mode is 4 people, and the range is 8 people.

  2. Answers will vary. Guesses may be around 4–6 people.

  3. The mean is 5 people. The mean is affected by the large households which have to be added into the total. Comparisons will vary based on estimates.

  4. **a.** The median and mode are the same, the mean is not.

  b. It is possible to have all three measures be the same or all three be different.

  c. Answers may vary. At this point, students have not explored how to choose between using mean or median to describe what is typical.

E. Answers will vary. Most students will be ready to discuss the algorithm now. The mean is the number obtained by dividing the sum of all data values by the total number of data values. It is the value each data value would have if they were evened out.

Notes

2.3 Making Choices: Mean or Median?

Focus Question How do the median and the mean respond to the data in a distribution? How do you choose which measure of center to use when describing what is typical?

Launch

The mean, unlike the median, is sensitive to each data value. Every change in the data will impact this computation.

The position of median is at the midpoint of a distribution and so is influenced by the number of data values. The value of the median is not sensitive to extreme values. In general, with small shifts, the median keeps its value or has only a small change.

Suggested Questions

- *Compare the prices for skateboards in each of the four stores.*

Explore

Suggested Questions

- *Why do you suppose the medians are the same for Stores B and C, and the means are different?*

For Question B, ask students how they can use what they know about the current mean/median to figure out the new mean/median.

- *Look at Graph 1. Why are the median and the mean almost identical?*
- *Look at Graph 2. Why is the mean so different from the median?*
- *What do you think it means to be "resistant to change"?*

Summarize

Make sure students pay attention to how data influence the mean and the median.

Suggested Questions

- *When does the mean change in Question B? When does the median change?*

Use Questions D and E to summarize how the mean and median differ, and why you might choose one measure over another for particular distributions.

Students will begin to see that the mean overreacts to extreme ratings. They might still choose to use the mean as a measure of what is typical, perhaps because it does reflect all the data. Deciding which measure of center to choose requires some deliberation and sophistication. Let students share their reasons.

Key Vocabulary
- skewed distribution
- symmetric distribution

Materials

Labsheets
- 2.3A: Skateboard Prices
- 2.3B: Dot Plots of Skateboard Prices

Accessibility Labsheet
- 2ACE: Exercise 27

Teaching Aids
- 2.3: Symmetric and Skewed Distributions
- Data and Graphs Tool

Answers to Problem 2.3

A. 1. Store B: mean = $51.94, median = $50; Store C: mean = $64.61, median = $50

2. The median is the same for each distribution, i.e. the midpoint of each ordered set of data is $50 (for Store B, the ninth data value and for Store C, between the ninth and tenth data values). The means respond to extreme values; for Store C, a data value of $200 affects the mean. Since there are no extreme data values for Store B, the mean and the median are close in value.

B. 1. (See Figure 1.)

2. mean = $48.50; median = $50

3.

Store A's New Stock

New Stock Price	New Mean	New Median
$200	$56.47	$50
$180	$62.65	$50
$180	$68.24	$50
$160	$72.41	$50
$170	$76.65	$50
$140	$79.29	$55
Question B, part (4):		
$200	$81.79	$55

4. The mean would increase; the median would stay the same.

5. The mean will change with the addition of each data value. The median's position changes, but the value of the median may not change if there are repeated values; if the value of the median does change, it is not sensitive to the actual data value.

6. The median gives a better estimate of the typical prices of skateboards; students may want to add, "but there are some higher-priced skateboards, too."

C. 1. Graph 1: Skateboard Prices From Stores A and B; Graph 2: Skateboard Prices From Stores C and D. Possible explanation: Graph 2 has to show data from stores C and D because it contains values greater than 120. Stores A and B have maximum values of 120.

2. When there are extreme values, the mean will be more easily affected.

D. The mean is strongly influenced by any extreme observations that are included in the data set. The median is resistant to any extreme observations that the data set may include.

E. 1. Symmetric: mean = 5, median = 5; In the symmetric distribution, the two measures are (in this case) identical (in most cases, they are similar). The graph's values are balanced around the center.

Skewed-left: mean = 7, median = 8; The mean is less than the median. The long tail on the left shifts the mean to the left of the median. Both values, however, are higher overall.

Skewed-right: mean = 4, median = 3; The mean is greater than the median. The long tail on the right shifts the mean to the right of the median. Both values, however, are somewhat low.

2. Symmetric: the overall trend is in the middle: "It's okay." In the skewed-left distribution, the overall trend is a positive rating: "Thumbs Up." In the skewed-right distribution, the overall trend is a negative rating: "Thumbs Down." Because of the skewed graphs, it is probably best to report the median in all cases.

Figure 1

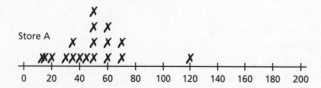

Skateboard Prices

At a Glance   Problem 2.4   Pacing 1 Day

2.4 Who Else Is in Your Household?
Categorical and Numerical Data

> *Focus Question* How do you distinguish different types of data? What statistics are used with different types of data?

Launch

Students do quite a bit of work with categorical data in the early grades, but they may not be familiar with the term "categorical data." In statistics, categorical data is of two types: nominal (naming of categories only) and ordinal (has an order or ranking like ratings given to preferences on a scale). Students will focus on nominal data for which the only measure of center to be used is the mode.

Suggested Questions

- *Look over the questions in the introduction and think about how you would respond to each. Which questions have words or categories as answers? Which questions have numbers as answers?*

Note: If you represent birth month with a number, "1" for January, and so on, then the answers to "In what month were you born?" are numbers that represent the months. However, these numbers do not represent numerical values; you would not order January < February, just because of this representation. Some care has to be taken in deciding if an answer to a question is categorical or numerical data.

Refer students to the Student Edition, which displays the tables and bar graphs. Work with students to make sure they can read the two tables and understand the data as they are presented. Discuss how to read the graphs, highlighting the information shown on the horizontal axis and the vertical axis for each graph. It is alright for students to move back and forth between the table and the graph. Just make sure they can locate information using both representations. You can ask questions, such as those below, to help students read the data, read between the data, and read beyond the data.

- *How many students chose a dog as their favorite pet?*
- *How many students have 6 pets?*
- *How many total students chose dogs or cats as their favorite pets?*
- *How many people have more than 6 pets?*
- *What do you know about how many pets each of the students has?*

Explore

Students may not understand that the height of each bar indicates how many students have that number of pets.

Suggested Questions

- *How many students chose cat as their favorite pet?*

Key Vocabulary
- categorical data
- numerical data

Materials

Assessment
Partner Quiz

- Data and Graphs Tool

- *How would knowing how many students chose each pet help you figure out how many students are in the class?*

- *How many students have 1 pet?*

- *How many total pets do the bars over "1 pet" represent? How do you know?*

- *How many student have 0 pets?*

- *How would knowing how many students own a certain number of pets help you figure out how many students are in the class?*

- *Can you compute a mode for categorical data like "favorite kind of pet"? Why or why not?*

- *Can you compute a median for "favorite kind of pet"? Why or why not?*

Summarize

Have a class discussion in which teams of students explain their responses to the questions. It is important for students to understand what they can and cannot know from a set of data, and which statistics they can apply to categorical data and which to numerical data.

To complete this activity, you may want students to work in pairs to write some questions about these data that can and cannot be answered. For questions that cannot be answered, discuss what information would be needed to answer them. Then have students spend five minutes writing a brief summary report of whichever set they choose.

Assignment Guide for Problem 2.4

Applications: 10–16 | Connections: 28–32
Extensions: 35–37

Answers to Problem 2.4

A. The Favorite Pet graph shows categorical data. The Number of Pets graph shows numerical data.

B. 1. 156 pets; Multiply each number of pets by its frequency and then add the results.

2. 21 pets; This is the highest number with a bar on top of it on the horizontal axis of the Number of Pets graph.

C. 1. 26 students; Add up the values in the Frequency column of either of the frequency tables. Or, you can add up the heights of each of the bars in either graph.

2. 4 students; the bar for *cat* in the Favorite Pet graph is 4 units high.

3. This question cannot be answered. The information is not collected.

D. 1. The mode is dog (it has the highest bar in the Favorite Pet graph); you can't compute the mean of categorical data.

2. median = 3.5 pets; range = 21 pets; data vary from 0 pets to 21 pets

E. 1. This question cannot be answered. There is no way to distinguish Tomas.

2. This question cannot be answered. There is no way to distinguish girls from boys.

F. Student reports will vary. For example, using the median as a measure of center, you can say that a typical number of pets owned by these students is 3 or 4. The mean might be overly affected by the student who owns 21 pets, an unusually high number. The range for the number of pets is 21; this shows there is a great variability in the number of pets owned.

3.1 Estimating Cereal Portion Sizes: Determining the IQR

> *Focus Question* What information does the interquartile range provide about how data vary in a distribution?

Launch

Read the introduction. A sample of an online survey question is given along with a graph of the results. The purpose of this sample is to help students think about designing their own surveys for the Unit Project.

Suggested Questions

- *What would happen if you asked: "What is your favorite cereal?" Why would you want to give respondents choices?*

Talk about the types of data (i.e., categorical or numerical) that are likely to be collected. Student surveys might only involve categorical data if teachers do not emphasize that students should also collect numerical data.

- *The data in the second row were not collected. How were the data entries found?*
- *Below the table is a dot plot. What data are plotted?*
- *How well do students estimate serving size when they pour Wheaty Os?*

Problem 3.1 gives students an opportunity to collect their own data.

Explore

You may want to complete Question A as a large group.

Help students to see that the middle 50% of the data are between Q1 and Q3. They can count all the data values (12) and then the number of data values between Q1 and Q3 (6) to see that half, or 50%, of the data are located here.

Suggested Questions

- *How is the IQR like or unlike the range?*
- *How will you find the IQR for servings of Raisin Flakes?*
- *How might you compare variability for the two sets of data?*
- *If the IQR were large, would the median be a good measure of center?*

Summarize

The purpose of determining the IQR is to be able to decide if one set of data is more variable than another set of data.

Key Vocabulary

- interquartile range (IQR)
- lower quartile
- quartile
- upper quartile
- variability

Materials

Labsheet

- 3.1: Serving–Size Estimates
- empty cereal boxes with different serving sizes (optional)
- Expression Calculator Tool

AT A GLANCE 3

Assignment Guide for Problem 3.1

Applications: 1–3 | Connections: 12–13

Answers to Problem 3.1

A. 1. The median (Q2) is midway between 1.04 and 1.07, or 1.055 servings.

2. Q1 is midway between 0.86 and 0.96, or 0.91 serving.

3. Q3 is midway between 1.32 and 1.54, or 1.43 servings.

4. The median is the midway point. Q1 is the midpoint of the lower half of data values. Q3 is the midpoint of the upper half of data values.

5. Student answers may vary. The middle 50% of the data values vary from 0.96 to 1.32 servings. Most are at or above the ideal 1 serving, so these servings are typical of what students poured for this cereal. However, the servings are not "about right," if that means "close to 1 serving."

6. IQR = 1.43 − 0.91 = 0.52 serving.

B. 1. (See Figure 1.)

2. (See Figure 2.)

3. The median is 0.94 serving.

4. Q1 = 0.79 serving; Q3 = 1.165 serving

5. Servings from 0.85 to 1.09 servings are in this middle 50%. Most of these are at or below the ideal 1 serving.

6. IQR = 1.165 − 0.79 = 0.375 of a serving.

C. 1. The IQR is smaller for the servings of Raisin Flakes poured. The servings poured are more variable for Wheaty Os.

2. The IQR by itself cannot answer the under-or overpouring question. It can tell you how clustered the data values are around the median. But if the median is already far above the ideal serving size, then having a small IQR only tells you that half of the data is clustered around a "too large" median serving.

3. A typical serving size for Wheaty Os is between 0.91 serving and 1.43 servings, with a median of 1.055 servings. The typical serving size for Raisin Flakes is between 0.79 serving and 1.165 servings, with a median of 0.94 serving.

D. 1. Wheaty's Os range: 2.11 − 0.71 = 1.4
Raisin Flakes range: 1.33 − 0.45 = 0.88

2. The range is the difference between the minimum and maximum data values. The IQR is the difference between Q1 and Q3. Both represent spreads.

3. Comparing ranges students still see that servings poured for Wheaty Os vary more than for Raisin Flakes (just as the IQRs indicated).

Figure 1

Pours of Raisin Flakes

Grams Poured	44	33	31	24	42	31	28	24	15	36	30	41
Serving Size	1.33	1.00	0.94	0.73	1.27	0.94	0.85	0.73	0.45	1.09	0.91	1.24

Figure 2

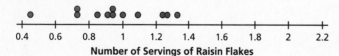

Number of Servings of Raisin Flakes

E. Seamus's report concentrates on variability. It is all correct. This report tells you for which cereal students had less variability in their estimated serving sizes.

Deanna's report concentrates on measures of center and what students typically pour. This report answers the question about under- and overpouring, but it does not address the issue of variability.

A combination of the two reports would give a clearer picture: students are more consistent at estimating an ideal serving size for Raisin Flakes than they are for estimating an ideal serving size for Wheaty Os. Also, for Raisin Flakes, their estimates tend to fall below the ideal, and for Wheaty Os, they tend to fall above the ideal.

Notes

3.2 Connecting Cereal Shelf Location and Sugar Content: Describing Variability Using the IQR

> *Focus Question* How is the interquartile range used to make comparisons among distributions?

Launch

In this Problem, students determine the IQRs for each of three distributions. They use information about variability to compare the three distributions, rather than focusing only on measures of center and what is typical.

Read or summarize the information on sugar content of cereals that is reported at the beginning of Problem 3.2. The data set of 70 cereals is shown only in graph form.

Suggested Questions

- *Is there anything that surprises you about the data and their distribution?*

When you work on Question A, highlight that each particular cereal is a case or example of the category being studied (cereals), and the information in the columns are attributes of a case. Highlight the attribute—grams of sugar. Attributes are variables; grams of sugar vary from one case to another, as would grams of sodium and calories. Look at the attribute of shelf location and discuss what the values of this attribute—bottom, middle, and top—mean.

Explore

Students will need to think about ways to compare the three sets of data, representing cereals on three shelves.

Suggested Questions

- *What would you say is a typical amount of sugar for cereals on each shelf? What measure are you using?*
- *Are there any characteristics that appear in one distribution and not in another?*
- *How else might you compare these data sets?*
- *What happens when gaps are included in the IQR?*

Summarize

Be sure to highlight how measures of center and spread can be used to help compare distributions. Have students consider what each kind of measure contributes to understanding a distribution.

Materials

Labsheets
- 3.2A: Distribution of Sugar in Cereals
- 3.2B: Cereal Distributions by Shelf Location
- 3ACE: Exercise 4

Accessibility Labsheet
- 3ACE: Exercises 17–18
- empty cereal boxes with different serving sizes (optional)
- Data and Graphs Tool
- Expression Calculator Tool

- *How might you compare these data sets?*

- *Using the median and IQR, how would you describe the distribution of grams of sugar for the cereals on the top shelf?*

- *Is there any other characteristic of the top-shelf distribution that you would like to note?*

- *What is the effect of the gap on the summary statistics?*

Students need to compare these groups of cereals to each other, with respect to the attribute grams of sugar. Make sure that students go beyond calculating statistics to using the statistics to make comparisons.

(A)(C)(E)

Assignment Guide for Problem 3.2

Applications: 4 | Connections: 17–20
Extensions: 26

Answers to Problem 3.2

A. 1. There are a number of data values located at 3 grams or 6 grams. Data cluster in the intervals 0–3 grams and 5–15 grams.

2. Work with students to locate points. When they locate, for example, Bran-ful with 5 grams of sugar, they will see that there are actually five such cereals, each having 5 grams of sugar in a serving. You can discuss if it matters which exact dot is the one for Bran-ful.

B. 1. For the cereals located on the bottom shelf, grams of sugar are clustered together. For the middle and top shelves, the data are more spread out. On the middle shelf, there are two gaps. On the top shelf, there are two larger gaps making 3 clusters of cereals. There appear to be three different kinds of cereals on the top shelf based on sugar content. To investigate the relation between placement of cereal and how sugary it is, students might compare measures of center. The medians are as such: top shelf, 3 grams of sugar; middle shelf, 11 grams of sugar; and bottom shelf, 7 grams of sugar.

2. a. The IQR for the bottom shelf is 4 grams of sugar (Q1 = 5; Q3 = 9).

The IQR for the middle shelf is 6 grams of sugar (Q1 = 7; Q3 = 13).

The IQR for the top shelf is 6.5 grams of sugar (Q1 = 1.5; Q3 = 8).

b. The top shelf has the greatest variability, but the middle shelf is similar in variability. The cereals on bottom shelf are the least variable in terms of sugar content.

3. A report should include a measure of center, such as median, and interpret this in a way that makes it clear that the typical amount of sugar is quite different depending on which shelf a cereal is located (See Question B, part (1)). Students already have the IQRs from Question B, part (2), so they might compare these and say that the top-shelf cereals show greatest variability. If they use range, however, then variability in grams of sugar does not differ much among the shelves. Students might also point out that some of the cereals on the top shelf have as much sugar as typical cereals on the middle shelf. They might point out the large gaps in the data from the top-shelf cereals. (These gaps affect the IQR and range for that data set.)

At a Glance

Problem 3.3 Pacing $1\frac{1}{2}$ Days

3.3 Is It Worth the Wait? Determining and Describing Variability Using the MAD

Focus Question What information does the mean absolute deviation provide about how data vary in a distribution?

Launch

Suggested Questions

- An amusement park advertises the average wait times for rides. However, people who have waited in line say that they can actually wait much longer (or wait much less time) than the advertised average wait times. What do you think?

- We are going to work thought Question A together. Describe the situation described in the introduction and shown on the dot plot.

- The dot plot and the ordered-value bar graph each show the 10 wait times of Scenic-Trolley riders. How are the distances from each data value to the mean shown on the dot plot? On the ordered-value bar graph? How do these distances help you describe how much the data values vary from the mean?

- How can you show direction on the graphs?

- You found the mean distance from the mean wait time was 7.2 minutes. Does this amount appear in the representations?

- Could Sally have waited more than 25 minutes + 7.2 minutes?

Explore

For Question B, help students to see that analyzing the Carousel data is related to what they did with the Scenic Trolley ride.

Suggested Questions

- Look at the data on the graph. How does the variability of the wait times compare to the variability of the wait times for the Scenic Trolley?

- How do you find the MAD for the wait times for the Carousel?

Summarize

Students should be able to complete these three sentences:

A person waiting in line at Scenic Trolley will wait a mean time of 25 minutes; however, the wait time could vary, on average, _____ minutes more or less. (7.2 ≈ 7 minutes)

A person waiting in line at Carousel will wait a mean time of 25 minutes; however, the wait time could vary, on average, _____ minutes more or less. (1.8 ≈ 2 minutes)

A person waiting in line at Bumper Cars will wait a mean time of 10 minutes; however, the wait time could vary, on average, _____ minutes more or less. (3.6 ≈ 4 minutes)

Key Vocabulary

- mean absolute deviation (MAD)

Materials

Labsheets

- 3.3A: Wait-Time Distribution for Scenic Trolley Ride

- 3.3B: Wait-Time Distributions for the Carousel and Bumper Cars

Accessibility Labsheet

- 3ACE: Exercises 14–16

Assessment

- Check Up 2

- Data and Graphs Tool

- Expression Calculator Tool

• *For the Carousel distribution, add the distances from each data value on the left side of the mean to the mean. Add the distances from each data value on the right side of the mean to the mean. What do you notice?*

ⒶⒸⒺ

Assignment Guide for Problem 3.3

Applications: 5–11 | Connections: 14–16, 21–25

Extensions: 27

Answers to Problem 3.3

A. 1. Determine the data values from the graph; find their sum (250) and divide by the number of data values (10) to compute the mean, which is 25 minutes.

2. Focusing on using just the ordered-value bar graph helps students notice distances. This is not new in this context; students explored changing data values on ordered-value bar graphs to locate the mean in Investigation 2. They should be comfortable using this model to complete this question.

a. Find the distance between each data value and the mean. Then find the average distance from the mean. This tells you how much the data values vary, on average, from the mean value.

b. The average distance is 7.2; this means that the MAD is 7.2 minutes. On average, wait times vary by 7.2 minutes from the mean of 25 minutes.

c. The total of the distances from wait times greater than the mean to the mean is 36 minutes. The total of the distances from wait times less than the mean to the mean is also 36 minutes. Since the distribution of wait times should balance around the mean you would expect these totals to balance each other. If you were to even out the ordered value bar graph, you would take the "extra" distances above the mean and add these to the wait times below the mean, so that you ended up with all wait times at 25 minutes.

B. 1. The MAD is 1.8 minutes

2. The MAD for Scenic Trolley is 7.2 minutes, a larger value than that of the MAD for Carousel. You might choose the Carousel over the Scenic Trolley. It would most likely have a lesser wait time than the Scenic Trolley because the wait time is more consistently close to 25 minutes.

Note: Some students may say that they would choose Scenic Trolley because there is a chance with Scenic Trolley that the wait time will be very short; this is not likely, but there is still a chance, because the larger MAD also means there are wait times for Scenic Trolley that are much less than 25 minutes.

C. 1. The MAD is 3.6 minutes.

2. The mean wait time for Bumper Cars is 10 minutes and for Scenic Trolley, 25 minutes. However, the MAD for the Bumper Cars is 3.6 minutes, which is half the MAD for the Scenic Trolley. You would want to wait for the Bumper Cars since both the average wait time and MAD are less than those for the Scenic Trolley.

D. If you choose the Zip Line you are likely to wait between 20 and 24 minutes, 2 minutes more or less than the mean of 22. On the other hand, if you choose Alpine Slide, then on average you will wait 6–30 minutes, 12 minutes more or less than the mean of 18. Wait times of 27, 28, 29, and 30 minutes may be typical for this ride, and all of these would cause you a problem. So, it is more likely that you will have time for one last ride if you choose Zip Line.

4.1 Traveling to School: Histograms

> **Focus Question** How can you use a histogram to help you interpret data?

Launch

Read through the introduction in the Student Edition.

Suggested Questions

- *Would a line plot or a dot plot display the travel-time data well?*

Have students work to answer this question for a few minutes before discussing as a class. As students begin to realize that dot plots or line plots are less effective for spread-out data, tell them that it is often helpful to group data into intervals. This might be true when the data are quite spread out or when there are few repeated data values.

Work carefully with students to build the idea of counting data values within a given interval. You may build the model histogram as a class.

- *What is the greatest data value? What is the least data value?*
- *You can graph this information using an interval size of 10 minutes. Locate the data values that are in the first interval from 0 to 10, but not including 10.*
- *How many observations fall within the interval 0 minutes–10 minutes? The interval 10 minutes–20 minutes?*
- *How might a frequency table help you construct the histogram?*
- *How is a histogram like a bar graph? How is it different?*

Explore

Students construct a histogram on their own and look at how data are organized in a histogram. Pay close attention to values on the border of the bars of the histogram.

Suggested Questions

- *If the interval size is 5 minutes, what values belong in the first interval? The next interval?*
- *Does this histogram give you any additional information about clusters or gaps?*
- *Can you make an estimate of where the median will be from the histogram?*
- *Will the mean be the same as, greater than, or less than the median?*

Summarize

Students should understand how are data organized and into which interval a "border" data point (one that touches two intervals) is placed.

Suggested Questions

- *Why is it useful to display the data in a histogram?*

Key Vocabulary

- histogram
- interval

Materials

Labsheets
- 4.1: Students' Travel Times to School
- 4ACE: Exercise 31
- Graph Paper
- Quarter-Inch Grid Paper

Teaching Aid
- 4.1: Student Travel Times— Dot Plots and Histograms

- calculators
- Data and Graphs Tool

AT A GLANCE 3

ACE

Assignment Guide for Problem 4.1

Applications: 1–9 | Connections: 27
Extensions: 31

Answers to Problem 4.1

A. 1. (See Figure 1.)

2. Answers will vary. Possible answers include: The first histogram shows larger intervals than the second histogram. That means that you can see more overall patterns for the data with the first histogram, whereas the second histogram shows more detailed data. Data cluster around 10–30 minutes in the histogram with an interval of 10. The histogram with 5-minute intervals unpacks these times a bit more so it looks like the cluster is actually between 15 and 25 minutes. There are no travel times less than 5 minutes, which is not clear from the histogram with 10-minute intervals. Both histograms show gaps and clusters.

B. Students whose travel times are 10 minutes or less are most likely to wake up the latest in the morning. You can find specific initials of these students in the table. Because they do not have to travel for as long, the students with a commute of 10 minutes or less can sleep longer.

C. Students whose travel times are 50 to 60 minutes are most likely to wake up the earliest in the morning. You can find specific initials of these students in the table.

Because they have to travel for a long time, the students with a 50-minute or 60-minute commute need to wake up earlier.

D. 1. The mode travel time is 15 minutes, the median travel time is 16 minutes, and the mean travel time is 18.975 minutes. The range is 55 minutes; the data vary from 5 minutes to 60 minutes. You find the mode by identifying the most-frequent data value. You find the median by ordering the data values from least to greatest (or greatest to least) and then finding the midpoint. You find the mean by adding up all the data values then dividing that sum by the number of data values. You find the range by taking the difference of the maximum and minimum data values.

2. The mode, the mean, and the median all fall within the interval 10 minutes–20 minutes (or 15 minutes–20 minutes for the 5-minute-inverval histogram).

E. There is a difference between the median and mean travel times of almost 3 minutes. The median separates the distribution of travel times in half; 50% of the travel times are less than or equal to the value of the median, and 50% are greater than or equal to the median. Both measures fall into the same interval of data. There are two travel times that are unusual—50 and 60 minutes. These two extreme travel times are probably the reason that the mean is greater than the median. While there is no set rule about which to use, it may be more reasonable to choose the median, since the mean is skewed by the extreme travel times.

Figure 1

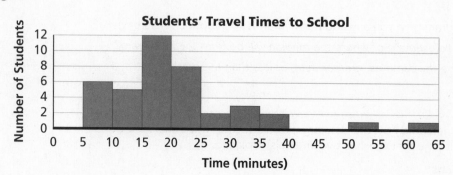

Students' Travel Times to School

4.2 Jumping Rope: Box-and-Whisker Plots

> *Focus Question* How can you interpret data using a box-and-whisker plot?

Launch

Students connect IQR to box plots during this Problem. They use this information to compare two or more data sets.

Suggested Questions

- *Look at the two tables of data. What question do you think was asked in order to collect this data? How was the data collected?*

- *Would using two line plots or two dot plots be a good way to show the data for the two classes? Why or why not?*

- *Mr. K's class claims they did better than Mrs. R's class. What evidence might they be using?*

You may want to construct the box plot of Mr. K's class data as a class. This gives students the opportunity to ask questions as they construct these new plots.

- *What are the positions and values of Q1, Q3, and the median for Mr. K's class?*

- *You need two other numbers to construct a box plot: the minimum data value and the maximum data value. Find these and mark them on the table.*

- *What percent of the data from Mr. K's class is in the box? What percent is on the lower whisker? The upper whisker?*

- *Why is the upper whisker so much longer than the lower whisker?*

Explore

Students should be able to find the five-number summary for Mrs. R's class.

Suggested Questions

- *What are the five numbers you have to look for?*

- *Mark the position of the median. How many data values are less than this? Greater than this?*

- *How do you find Q1? Q3?*

- *How can you use the five numbers to describe the distribution of the data from Mrs. R's class?*

- *How would a high IQR appear on a box plot? What would it mean?*

- *How do you know exactly which data values are outliers?*

- *The IQR is the length of the box. How can you check visually whether a data value is an outlier on a graph?*

Key Vocabulary

- box-and-whisker plot (box plot)
- outlier

Materials

Labsheets
- 4.2A: Jumping-Rope Contest Data
- 4.2C: Mr. K's Class Data

Accessibility Labsheets
- 4.2B: Mrs. R's Class Data
- 4ACE: Exercises 10–12

Teaching Aids
- 4.2A: Making a Box-and-Whisker Plot
- 4.2B: Mrs. R's Class Data—A Box-and-Whisker Plot
- calculators
- Data and Graphs Tool
- Expression Calculator Tool

Summarize

Ask students to describe the procedure for making a box plot for a set of data: order data from least to greatest, identify the five-number summary, and draw the box and the whiskers in relation to a number line.

Suggested Questions

• *How does the shape of the box plot give you information about the distribution?*

Applications: 10–16 | Connections: 28–29

Answers to Problem 4.2

A. (See Figure 1.)

B. Initially, the evidence using graphs and the table suggests that Mr. K's class performed much better because of the higher-scoring students. In addition to the median being greater than Mrs. R's class, the mean is also greater (reflecting the few higher numbers of jumps). Some students may point out that Q1, Q2, and Q3 are similar for both classes, though slightly higher for Mr. K's class.

C. 1. Anything higher than 137 is an outlier: 151, 160, 160, 300.

   2. There are no outliers in Mrs. R's class.

D. 1. The mean without the outliers is about 36.58. The median is 30. The mean with the outliers is 57.4 (and the median is 40.5, as indicated in the graphic).

   2. The outliers pull both the mean and the median to the right, but they have more of an effect on the mean. The mean of the data including the outliers is 20.82 greater than the mean of the data not including the outliers. The median of the

data including the outliers is only 10.5 greater than the median of the data not including the outliers.

3. Students are likely to want to discuss how much more similar the graphs of the two data sets are without the outliers included in the whisker. However, Mr. K's class's data is higher at three of the summary numbers, Q1, median, and Q3, so students can still say Mr. K's class is slightly better in this competition.

E. 1. If a distribution is symmetric, the median will be in the center of the box; if it is skewed, it will be closer to either Q1 or Q3. The median may even fall on Q1 or Q3.

   2. For Mr. K's class, the box indicates a more symmetric distribution even though there are some extreme values (outliers). Once the outliers are identified, the remainder of the box plot does suggest a more symmetric distribution.

   3. For Mrs. R's class, the distribution does seem slightly skewed to the right; the median is a little off center, located more to the left in the box.

   4. Once the outliers are marked in Mr. K's class, it is easier to see how to compare the two classes' data. They are more similar than different without consideration of the outliers.

Figure 1

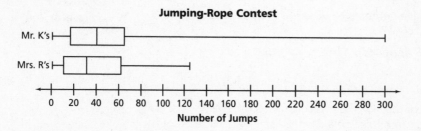

4.3 How Much Taller Is a 6th-Grader Than a 2nd Grader? Taking Variability into Consideration

> **Focus Question** How can you compare and contrast data represented by dot plots, histograms, and box plots?

Launch

Students consider different graphs of the same data sets and reflect on how each displays data. They also connect measures of center and measures of spread to the graphs to answer questions.

The data distributions are represented using dot plots, histograms, and box plots. Have students review how each graph is made.

Explore

Suggested Questions

- *What do you notice about the shape of the data?*
- *How can you answer, "How much taller is a 6th grader than a 2nd grader?"*
- *How does knowing that there is more variability in the 6th-grade data influence how you will decide how much taller a 6th-grade student is than a 2nd-grade student?*

Summarize

It may be helpful to set up a two-column table with one column labeled 6th Grade and the other labeled 2nd Grade. Then, for both, fill in observations. Fill in comments about shape. Continue with spread. Compare categories.

Materials

Labsheets
- 4.3: 2nd- and 6th-Grade Heights
- 4ACE: Exercises 17–19

Assessments
- Self-Assessment
- Notebook Checklist
- Unit Test
- calculators
- Data and Graphs Tool

ACE
Assignment Guide for Problem 4.3

Applications: 17–26 | Connections: 30, 32

Answers to Problem 4.3

A. 1. 84 students; Sample explanation: I counted all of the dots on the dot plot. There were 84 dots, so 84 6th-grade students must be represented.

2. The shape of the dot plot and histogram mirror each other in terms of shape, probably because the interval sizes in the histogram are each 2 inches. In the dot plot, each data value is shown on the number line; in the histogram, data are grouped so the heights of the bars are taller than the dot plot stacks. There is an outlier that is marked on the box plot.

3. The cluster at 62 is clear on the dot plot. Without the detail from the dot plot, the histogram can only tell you there is a cluster in the interval from 62 inches to 64 inches. From the histogram, you cannot tell whether there is an equal number of dots at 62 and 63, or if there are more dots at one axis label than the other. There are no gaps but you cannot tell that from the histogram or box plot. The dot plot shows there is no data value at 72, but that is not a real gap.

4. All three graphs show the range as 17 (56 to 73). The box plot tells you the middle 50% of the data is between 61 and 66. The other measure of spread, MAD, is not visible on a graph. The data are not spread evenly around the center. The data on the right of the graph is more spread out than the data on the left. You can see this most clearly from the box plot: both the right side of the box and the upper whisker are longer.

5. The dot plot and histogram are similar except that the histogram groups data in intervals of 2. The box plot seems the least like the other two graphs, but it does show the same cluster of data from 61 to 66 inches as the other graphs do.

B. 1. 84 students; Sample explanation: I found the height of each of the bars in the histogram. I added all of the heights together. The sum was 84, so there must be 84 students represented in the histogram.

2. The 2nd-grade data seem less spread out than the 6th-grade data. There is one outlier at 60 inches, but the IQR of the 2nd-grade data is 2 inches less than the IQR of the 6th-grade data. The graph is mainly symmetric around the median, but slightly skewed to the left.

3. The data cluster between 47 and 56 inches. There are really no gaps, unless you count the lack of data values between the outlier and the rest of the data. All three graphs show this gap clearly.

4. The distribution is much less spread out than the 6th-grade distribution. The IQR is only 3 inches, as compared to the IQR of 5 inches for the 6th-grade data. The mode of the 2nd-grade heights is 52 inches, but 53 and 54 inches are also frequent data values. Heights less than 50 inches and greater than 55 inches occur infrequently. The graphs are more symmetric than the 6th-grade distribution. All graphs show this: the data to the right of the graph has a similar shape to the data on the left of the graph in both the histogram and the dot plot. In the box plot, the whiskers are about the same length, as are the left and right sides of the box.

5. The dot plot and histogram are similar except that the histogram groups data in intervals of 2. Their shapes are very similar. The box plot shows the five-number summary of the dot plot and the histogram, which helps you pick out important summary statistics as well as outliers.

C. 1. Sample answer: The mean of the 6th-grade heights is 63.1 inches, and the mean of the 2nd-grade heights is 52.21 inches. This means that 6th graders are about 11 inches taller than 2nd graders. If you used the medians (62 inches and 52 inches), then 6th graders are, on average, 10 inches taller than 2nd graders. The difference of the means is about the same as the difference of the medians, so either calculation works well. The dot plot also shows that 6th graders are about 10 inches taller than 2nd graders. The mode of the 6th-grade data is 10 inches more than the mode of the 2nd-grade data. Also, the maximum and minimum values are close to 10 inches apart for the 6th-grade data and the 2nd-grade data. 2nd graders range from 47 inches to 60 inches in height, and 6th graders range from 56 to 73 inches in height.

2. The mean and median comparisons will be the same as for part (1). Possible comparison of the histograms: The most frequent range of data values for the 6th-grade data is 62 to 64 inches. The most frequent range of data values for the 2nd-grade data is 52 to 54 inches. Again, this shows that 6th-graders are about 10 inches taller than 2nd-graders. As in part (1), you can also analyze the maximum and minimum values (or ranges of values) by looking at the histograms.

3. The mean and median comparisons will be the same as for part (1). Possible comparison of the box plots: The medians are clearly shown on the box plots, so the 10-inch difference between 6th-grade heights and 2nd-grade heights is clear in the box plots. The minimum values also show about a 10-inch difference (56 and 47). The box plots, however, show a greater distance in the maximum values. Since the maximum value of the 2nd-grade data is an outlier, you may want to disregard that value. Then, comparing the right-hand whiskers of each box plot, the difference of the greatest 6th-grade height and the greatest 2nd-grade height is 73–56, or 17 inches. On all other measures (minimum values, Q1, median, and Q3), the difference between 6th-grade height and 2nd-grade height is about 10 inches.

4. Answers will vary. Some students may choose box plots. This type of representation clearly shows comparisons of medians, Q1s, Q3s, minimum values, and maximum values between the two groups. There is one outlier in the 2nd grade. Otherwise, all the 6th grade students are taller than all the 2nd grade students. Generally, students could say that the 6th-grade students are about 62 inches tall (the median) and 2nd-grade students are about 52 inches tall. So, 6th-grade students are about 10 inches taller than 2nd-grade students. If students use histograms or dot plots to display the data sets, they will most likely focus on mean, median, and skew of the data.

D. On all the measures of spread, there is greater variability in the 6th-grade heights.

E. Answers will vary. Sample response: I already have data on 84 6th-grade students. So I would just need to collect data on 8th-grade students. I would try to find data on 84 8th-grade students so that my graphs have about the same number of data values. If I couldn't find 84 8th-graders, though, some similar number would be fine. I would find the mean and median of the data from the 8th-grade students and compare them to the mean and median of the data from the 6th-grade students. I think I would choose a histogram or a box plot to display the data values. Since there are so many data values, displaying a dot plot would take way too much time.

Notes

Data About Us   At a Glance

At a Glance

Pacing ☐ Day

Mathematical Goals..

_____

_____

_____

_____

Launch...

_____

_____

_____

_____

_____

Materials

Explore...

_____

_____

_____

_____

_____

Materials

Summarize...

_____

_____

_____

_____

_____

Materials

Notes

Applications

1. **Name Lengths of Korean Students**

Number of Letters	Frequency
4	0
5	0
6	3
7	4
8	5
9	6
10	3
11	6
12	3

(See Figure 1.)

2. shortest: 6 letters; longest: 12 letters

3. The shape is uniform; there are no clusters or gaps.

4. Answers may vary. The typical name length could be 9 or 13. They are the most frequent name lengths.

5. **a.** Graph A; Korea (it matches the graph in Exercise 1); Graph B: the United States (they have a name length of 17 letters); Graph C: China (they have fewest letters); Graph D: Japan (there is a large number of names with 12 letters) .

b. Answers will vary. Four statements could include: The U.S. graph is the most spread out because it has the biggest range. Both the Korean and U.S. data have two modes, whereas the others have only one. Chinese names are shortest with the data values displayed to the left of the others on the scale. U.S. names are longest with the data values displayed to the right of the others on the scale.

c. Although the graphs are not wrong, the scales are truncated. It is difficult to compare the data sets if the scales are not aligned.

6. 15 letters; mode

7. 30; The bar for each number represents the number of students with that name length, so adding the bar heights $(2 + 3 + 5 + 3 + 6 + 5 + 2 + 1 + 2 + 1)$ gives the total number of students.

8. The data vary from 11 to 20 letters; the range is 9 letters $(20 - 11 = 9)$.

9. 15 letters; There are 30 student name lengths, so the median is between the 15th and 16th data values, which are both 15.

10. **a.** Half of all rats live less than or equal to 2.5 years, and half live longer than or equal to 2.5 years.

b. Knowing the maximum and minimum ages for rats would be helpful.

Figure 1

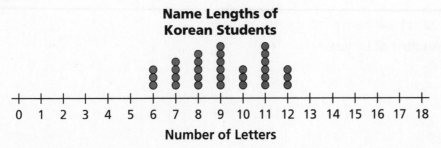

Name Lengths of Korean Students

Number of Letters

11. Possible answer:

(See Figure 2.)

12. Possible answer:

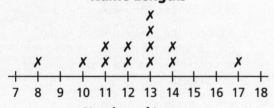

Name Lengths

13. Possible answer:

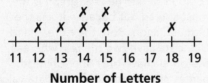

Name Lengths

14. Possible answer:

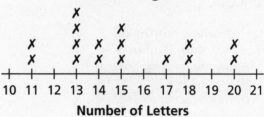

Name Lengths

Connections

15. a. The numerator tells you that 14 of the pets represented in the graph are dogs. The denominator, 24, gives the total number of pets owned by the class.

   b. It is not possible to determine the exact number of students surveyed. Some students may have more than one pet; some may have no pets.

16. a. numbers divisible by 5; multiples of 5

   b. odd numbers

   c. square numbers

   d. prime numbers

Figure 2

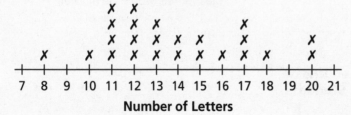

Name Lengths

17. (See Figure 3. Figure 3 provides a snapshot of the full graph from which you can identify patterns.)

   a. Prime numbers; they each have 1 in common as a factor; the other factor is the number itself.

   b. Numbers that end in 0, 2, 4, 6, or 8 are even; all have 2 as a factor.

   c. i. The greatest factor for any number is the number itself.

   ii. The least factor is 1.

   iii. The second-greatest factor is the number divided by its least prime factor. In particular, if the number is even, then the second-greatest factor is the number divided by 2.

   iv. Answers will vary given students' own observations.

18. a. The graph is trying to show sunglasses sales from a certain store for two months. The graph has a deceptive y-scale because it does not start at 0.

This makes it look like sunglasses sales plummeted, when in fact they dropped by only a small percentage.

   b. The graph is trying to show how many friends are made during each month in a new school. In the graph, the y-scale is not marked in equal increments.

   c. The graph is trying to show how many people own a certain type of pet. The lengths of the lines of animals are deceptive. The different animals have different sizes, even though each animal represents the same number of pets. For example, the line for cats is about the same size as the line for horses, even though there are many more cats represented than horses.

19. a. Answers will vary: Possible answers: Trevor grew least between 8 and 9 years. Trevor more than doubled his birth height by the age of 4.

   b. Answers will vary. Possible answers: Trey was 18 inches at birth; he grew fastest in the first two years.

Figure 3

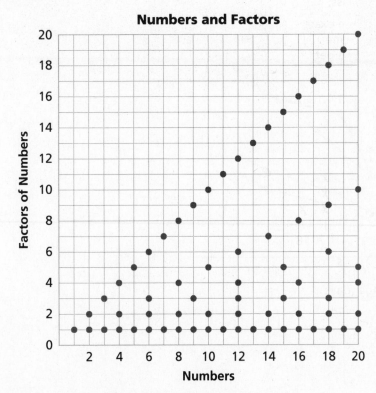

c. Answers will vary. Possible answers: Trevor was longer at birth than Trey was at birth. Trey was always shorter than Trevor when comparing them at the same age.

d. Suzanne is correct that Trevor is taller than Trey, at least up until age 8. After age 8, Trey's data is not collected, so a comparison cannot be made. Suzanne is incorrect that Trevor is growing faster than his brother Trey. Between ages 2 and 4, Trey grew at a faster rate then Trevor.

20. a. (See Figure 4.)

b. Answers will vary. Sample answers: Fuzz Ball grew the least from Day 11 to Day 27. Sleepy grew the most from Day 18 to Day 27.

c. Answers will vary. One could say the following: Gerbils grow very quickly, approximately doubling or tripling their weights from week 2 to week 4.

21. Possible answer: Graph A and Graph B are labeled 1 through 12 on the horizontal axis. However, the distribution in Graph A is unlikely for this data since few families have 7–8 children. Graph B is unlikely since few families now have 10 or 12 children. Graph C is most likely the graph that shows the number of children in the students' families.

22. Possible answer: Either Graph A or B could show the birth months. Graph C is unlikely since it would be unusual for no students in the class to have been born in November or December.

23. Possible answer: Graph C is the most likely answer. Some students may like only one topping. Twelve toppings seems excessive.

Figure 4

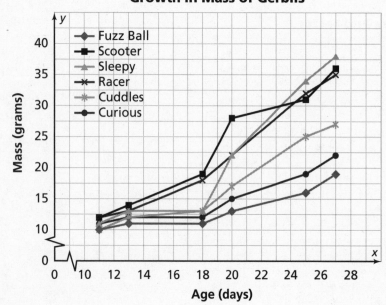

Extensions

24. The bar height, 7, represents the number of stickers left. Because there were 12 to begin with, 5 have been sold.

25. The bar height, 4, represents the number of street signs left. Since there were 12 signs to begin with, 8 have been sold.

26. Stickers are more popular. The bar graphs show that the number of stickers remaining (48) is less than the number of street signs remaining (66). Students may want to debate this because of the "peaks" in the data. You will want to remind them that the bar graphs show the number remaining, not the number sold.

27. The store has taken in $144 on the sale of 96 name stickers.

28. The most stickers, 12, have been sold for Amanda. The fewest stickers, 2, have been sold for Ava.

29. For Amy, the bars for stickers and signs are the same height. This shows that equal numbers of stickers and signs have been sold for the name Amy.

30. The stacked bars allow you to look at the data for stickers and street signs together. For example, Amanda has 0 stickers and 11 street signs left, while Alex has 7 stickers and 4 street signs remaining. These names have the same total number of items remaining. This is indicated by the stacked bars, which are the same height. Students will see that Allison and Amber are the most popular names, while Ava is the least popular.

Applications

1. a. The median is 3. Order the data from least to greatest. The median is the value that separates the data into two parts with an equal number of data values in each part. For 16 households, the median is located between the 8th and 9th data values. Both have a value of 3, so the median is 3.

b. Yes, six of the households have 3 children. This is possible because the median is located using the data values. The only time the median will not be equal to one of the data values is when there is an even number of data values, where the two middle values are not identical.

2. a. The mean is 4. You add the data values together and divide by the number of data values to get the mean; (64 ÷ 16 = 4). Or, you find the mean by making an ordered-value bar graph, showing the data for each of the households, and then evening out the bars so there are 16 households, each with 4 members. The mean tells you the value that each data item would have if they all had the same value.

b. There are no squares over the number 4 on the line plot, which means there are no households in the data set with four children. This is possible because there are households with more than four children and households with less than four children to balance each other.

3. Answers will vary. The mean (4) is influenced by the high data value of 11. So, the median (3) may be a better measure of a typical size.

4. D

5. Possible answer:

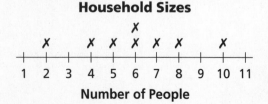

Household Sizes

Number of People

6. Possible answer:

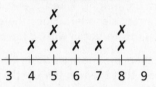

Household Sizes

Number of People

7. Answers will vary depending on the distributions in Exercises (5) and (6). It is possible for the medians to be different when the means are the same.

8. Possible answer:

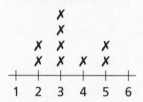

Household Sizes

Number of People

For nine households to have a mean of $3\frac{1}{3}$ people, there would have to be a total of $9 \times 3\frac{1}{3}$, or 30 people.

9. Possible answer:

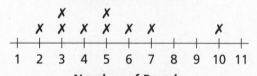

Household Sizes

Number of People

For nine households to have a mean of five people, there would have to be a total of 9×5, or 45 people. If one household has ten people, that leaves 35 others to distributed between the remaining eight households.

10. numerical

11. categorical

12. categorical

13. categorical

14. numerical

15. categorical

16. numerical

Connections

17. a. $\frac{3}{4}$ hour

    b. G

18. a. 32 ounces per player; 1,152 ounces ÷ 36 (two teams of 18 players) = 32 ounces.

    b. The mean; it represents the total amount of water evenly-shared among the 36 players.

19. a. Sabrina and Diego danced $3\frac{3}{4}$ hours and Marcus danced $2\frac{1}{4}$ hours.

    b. The mean is less than the median. The median is $3\frac{3}{4}$ hours; the mean is less than $3\frac{3}{4}$ hours because the low data value of $2\frac{1}{4}$ hours decreases the average amount of hours each person danced.

20. a. The mean tells Jon that if all the rabbits in the data set that was used to find the mean lived to be the same age, that age would be 7 years. What actually happens is that some of the rabbits don't live to 7 years and some of the rabbits live beyond 7 years.

    b. Knowing the maximum age, minimum age, and median age would give Jon more information about the possible lifespan of his rabbit.

21. If the typical price of a box of granola bars is $1.33 and there are nine different brands of granola, the total price for the nine boxes is $11.97. You would have to price the boxes so the total price would be $11.97. You could have the nine brands all priced at $1.33, or have just a few priced at $1.33, or have no brands priced at $1.33. Here is one possibility: $1.35, $1.39, $1.49, $1.17, $1.29, $1.35, $1.25, $1.29, $1.39.

22. No; some children may have spent 39 minutes but, overall, there were children who spent less or more time than this.

23. about 66%

24. about $\frac{3}{4}$ or 0.75 of an hour

25. $2\frac{1}{3}$ hours or 2.333. . . hours

26. a. Mayor Phillips determined the mean income. The total of the incomes is $32,000; dividing by the number of incomes, 16, gives $2,000 per week. Lily Jackson found the median income. There are a total of 16 values, so the median is between the eighth and ninth values. The eighth value is 0 and the ninth value is 200, so finding the median results in $100 per week. Ronnie Ruis looked at the mode income, which is $0 per week. Each of their computations is correct.

    b. No; no one earns $2,000 per week.

    c. No; no one earns $100 per week.

    d. Yes; eight people earn $0 per week.

    e. Both $200 and $100 are reasonable answers. The median of all incomes is $100. Supposing those who earn $0 are children, you could find the median of the remaining values, which is $200. You could also make an argument for using the mode as the typical income, $200, if you exclude the $0 data values; the mode is what most people earn. The mean, however, is greatly affected by the one large income value; it would not be a good choice for what is typical.

    f. The mode would be $200. The median would be $200. The mean would be $1,640.

27. **a.** Possible answer: Half the data values are grouped in the interval of 1–5 or 8–17. One quarter of the data values are grouped in the interval 8–13.

b. The range is 29 movies. You may find it by taking the maximum value (30) and subtracting the minimum value (1).

c. The mean is 9 movies. Add to find the total number of the movies watched (225), and then divide the total by the number of students (25).

d. The range is 29 movies and the mean is 9 movies. Since the mean is more toward the minimum than the maximum, more students fall in the low end of the data values.

e. The median number of movies watched is 8. The mean is larger than the median because the large values pull the mean up but have less influence on the median.

28. Numerical; the answer to the question "How many juice drinks do you drink in one day?" is a number.

29. No; the median is the number that separates the ordered data in half. The number of people that drink 5 juice drinks in one day is near the upper end of the data, so 5 cannot be the median.

30. No; there are 100 students, so the median is between the fiftieth and fifty-first ordered data values. A total of 39 students drank 0 or 1 juice drink in one day. This means the median is greater than 1 juice drink, because the fiftieth value will be in the next column—2 juice drinks in one day.

31. The total number of juice drinks is determined by evaluating each bar of the graph:

7 people $\times$ 0 = 0 juice drinks

32 people $\times$ 1 = 32 juice drinks

29 people $\times$ 2 = 58 juice drinks

16 people $\times$ 3 = 48 juice drinks

6 people $\times$ 4 = 24 juice drinks

5 people $\times$ 5 = 25 juice drinks

3 people $\times$ 6 = 18 juice drinks

1 person $\times$ 7 = 7 juice drinks

1 person $\times$ 10 = 10 juice drinks

So, 100 people drank a total of 222 juice drinks in one day.

32. **a.** Possible answers: grape, cherry, and mango juice drinks

b. The data are categorial. Flavors of juice are not numbers.

c. The graph for the categorical data could have a horizontal axis showing the names of the Juice Drinks and labeled "Kind of Juice Drinks." The vertical axis could display the number of students that said they liked each type of juice drink and be labeled "Frequency." The title of the graph could be "Favorite Juice Drinks Consumed by Students." Each bar of the graph would show how many people had chosen that particular juice drink. The height of the bar would be the frequency of that choice.

Extensions

33. Answers will vary. Pay attention to the students' reasoning. Generally, data reported in newspapers use the mean.

34. There are 365 days in a year. This means the average student spends about 3.2 hours in front of a screen per day.

35. Possible answer: (See Figure 1.)

The challenge for students will be developing the scale for the vertical axis. Because of the range of the data (9 to 303 pets), the scale probably needs to be numbered by at least tens or twenties.

36. Possible answer: Fish occur the most frequently as pets owned, followed by cats and dogs. In Problem 2.4, dogs occur most frequently, followed by cats, but with a definite difference in numbers. The remaining pets are not like those of the students in Problem 2.4. Many of these pets are "indoor" pets. In Problem 2.4, many of the pets were "outdoor" pets that would live on a farm or in more rural areas.

37. Answers will vary. Some students may immediately respond that 841 people were surveyed, indicating that each person surveyed had one pet. Other students may note that this response does not take into account that it is likely that some people surveyed had no pets or had more than one pet. This may lead students to look back at the data from Problem 2.4, in which they know both the total numbers of pets and the number of people surveyed. From this data, students might find the median number of pets a person has (3.5) and use it as a basis for looking at the new data set, dividing 841 pets by 3.5 per student to get the possible number surveyed (about 240 students). Some students may raise a concern that the data from Problem 2.4 may reflect a special group of students who live in the country and therefore often have more pets; perhaps this particular data do not reflect the kinds of people surveyed for Problem 2.4. Students may have other strategies as well.

Figure 1

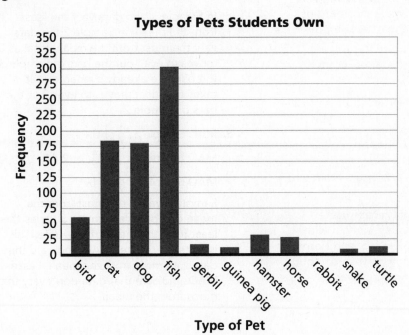

Applications

1. a) The range is $1.75.

b) Each server receives $15.65.

c) Since Yanna's amount is higher than the mean, they will each receive more. If Yanna receives the mean ($15.65), then the remainder of her tips ($.45) is shared among the five people. Each receives an additional 9 cents.

2. The mean is an average of all the data values, so it is entirely possible that no one received the actual mean.

3. a. Yanna could have made a low amount of tips, but the other servers made high tips, so the result would be a mean of $15.25.

b. The information is incomplete, but we know that Yanna has a smaller amount of tips than the mean, so this suggests that there must have been larger tips to offset this amount in order to make the mean $15.25.

4. a. IQR Korean names: 3 letters (from 8 to 11 letters)

IQR U.S. names: 3 letters (from 11 to 14 letters)

IQR Japanese names: 2 letters (from 10 to 12 letters)

IQR Chinese names: 2 letters (from 6 to 8 letters)

b. Both Japanese and Chinese name lengths are the least spread out with the smallest IQRs. The U.S. and Korean name lengths are the most spread out, so they have greater variability.

5. a. Sample 1: 2 moves

Sample 2: 11 moves

b. The mean household size is the number that each household would have if the people were distributed so that each household has the same number. The evened-out bar graph shows the households as having an equal number of people, so it shows the mean.

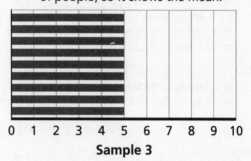

Sample 3

c. In Sample 3, the data vary the least from the mean; in Sample 2 the data vary the most from the mean. It takes 0 moves to even out the bars of Sample 3; the bars are already evened out. It takes the most moves to even out the bars of Sample 2.

d. MAD Sample 1: $\frac{4}{9}$ or 0.44;

MAD Sample 2: $\frac{22}{9}$, $2\frac{4}{9}$, or 2.44;

MAD Sample 3: $\frac{0}{9}$, or 0.

Sample 2 varies the most from the mean of 5 people; Sample 3 varies the least from the mean of 5 people. This is because greater MADs indicate that data vary more from the mean. Lesser MADs indicate that data don't vary that much from the mean.

6. a. (See Figures 1 and 2.)

b. Jeff: median: 80, IQR; 7.5;
Elaine: median: 80, IQR: 20

c. Jeff: mean: 80, MAD: 3.75;
Elaine: mean: 80, MAD: 10

d. Jeff; Both have the same median and mean scores; however, Elaine's data show greater variability, so that means that she is less likely than Jeff to receive an exact score of 80.

7. a. Ride 1: mean is 15 minutes

Ride 2: mean is 18 minutes

b. Ride 1: MAD is 2.4 minutes

Ride 2: MAD is 8 minutes

c. The data vary more for Ride 2. Ride 2 has a greater MAD, which indicates greater variability.

d. Answers will vary based on the data sets that students use.

8. Distribution A: MAD is about 1.49, and IQR is 3.
Distribution B: MAD is about 2.2, and IQR is 3.
Distribution C: MAD is 0.96, and IQR is 2.

9. C has the least variation from the mean. B has the most.

10. A and B have the same spreads. C has the least spread.

11. a.

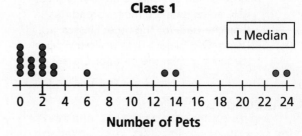

Class 1

Number of Pets

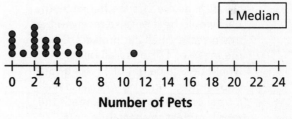

Class 2

Number of Pets

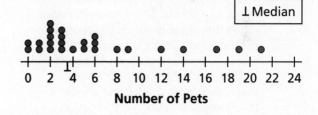

Class 3

Number of Pets

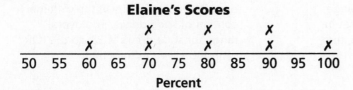

Figure 1

Jeff's Scores

```
                X   X
                X   X
                X   X   X   X
   50  55  60  65  70  75  80  85  90  95  100
                    Percent
```

Figure 2

Elaine's Scores

```
            X       X       X
        X       X       X       X       X
   50  55  60  65  70  75  80  85  90  95  100
                    Percent
```

ACE Answers

b. Class 1: median: 2 pets, IQR: 4 pets; Class 2: median: 2.5 pets, IQR: 2.5 pets; Class 3: median: 3.5 pets, IQR: 6

Possible answers: The medians are close for all classes, but Class 3 has the largest median. Class 3 has the highest IQR, so its data are more spread out than the data for the other classes. Using IQR, Class 1 data is slightly more spread out than the data for Class 2.

c. Possible answers: Class 3 has the largest mean. The distribution of number of pets for Class 3 is more spread out than for the other two classes.

Connections

12. a. Malaika would need a score of 19 on her fourth project. Students might say that the mean is the height all the bars would be if Malaika received the mean score on all her projects. Given the mean of 17 points, all four bars would be at a height of 17, for a total of 68 points. Right now, Malaika has a total of 49 points, so she needs the fourth project to score 19 points.

b. The spread is 15 to 19 points, for a range of 4 points. Some students might argue that there is not much variation in her scores. Others may convert scores to percentages (i.e., 15 points is 75%, and 19 points is 95%) that they interpret as grades and decide that there is, indeed, more variation, as the impact on final grades definitely matters.

13. a. Her mean score would be 20 points; 15 points.

b. If Malaika has a total of 80 points, then she must have scores of 20 on each project. For a total of 60 points, there are many options, such as 20, 10, 10, and 20.

c. For a total 80 points, each project will have a score of 20, so the range is 0. For a total of 60 points, the range depends on the student's data set in part (b). For the example above, the range would be 10 (20 − 10).

d. For a total of 80 points, the range is less variable (no variation) that her first set of scores. For a total of 60 points, the variability depends on the student's data set in part (b) compared to the answer for Exercise 12, part (b).

14. a. mean = about 26.4, median = 26

b. mean = about 37.8, median = 25

c. Other drinks most likely have more variability since the mean and median are further apart. The ranges also indicate that there is more variability in other drinks than in soda drinks.

d. Possible answers: There is a larger range of caffeine in other drinks than in soda drinks. The medians of soda drinks and other drinks are almost equal. Since the mean is larger than the median in the other drinks, the line plot of the other drinks data would probably be skewed to the right, whereas the line plot of the soda drinks data would most likely be symmetrical.

15. a. true

b. false

c. false; 50% have 25 mg or less

16. a. MAD = 5.16 mg and IQR = 10 mg best describe the variability in the caffeine content of soda drinks. The overall range for soda drinks is 23, so the IQR cannot be greater than that.

b. MAD = 25.93 mg and IQR = 59 mg best describe the variability in the caffeine content of the other drinks. The range of the caffeine content in the other drinks (81 mg) is much greater than the range of the caffeine content in soda drinks. So, the other measures of variability will be greater for other drinks as well.

17. Both the mean and the median name length for female names is greater than the measures of center for male names. So, female names are longer.

18. a. Student answers may vary. Sample dot plot:

Name Lengths—Females

Number of Letters

b. The change in data values will shift the median to a smaller value.

c. The change will affect the mean; the higher values being removed and the four values that are less than the mean being added in will cause the mean to be less than it was originally.

19. B

20. J

21. A

22. a. The mean is approximately 8.267.

b. The mean is multiplied by the same factor as the individual scores. So, The means are about 16.53, about 5.51, and about 1.65 for the given situations.

c. The response of the mean to multiplying each score by the same factor is an application of the distributive property. For example, if the 6 scores are a, b, c, d, e, f, then the mean $M = (a + b + c + d + e + f) \div 6$. If you multiply each score by a factor X, then the scores are Xa, Xb, Xc, Xd, Xe, Xf, and the new mean is $(Xa + Xb + Xc + Xd + Xe + Xf) \div 6 = X(a + b + c + d + e + f) \div 6 = XM$. The mean grows by a factor of X.

23. J

24. D

25. G

Extensions

26. Yes; since the definition of mean implies that you should divide the sum of the scores by the total amount of scores. This shows the Distributive Property of Multiplication Over Addition. Rather than multiplying the sum by one half or one third, Mark is multiplying each addend by one half or one third.

27. a. mode = 14, mean = 12.2, median = 13, IQR = 7, MAD = 3.6

b. mode = 17, mean = 15.2, median = 16, IQR = 7, MAD = 3.6

Since all values are shifted the same amount, the measures of center all shift by the same amount. For example, if you add 3 to each data value, you will add 3 to the mean, mode, and median. However, the measures of variability remain the same.
The IQR measures how different Q1 and Q3 are. Since both are 3 more than before, the difference stays the same. The MAD measures each data value's distance from the mean and then finds the average. Since each value is 3 higher than before, and the mean is also 3 higher, the distances from the mean are unchanged, so the MAD is unchanged. The distribution has just been moved right on the axis; it has the same shape as before.

c. mode = 28, mean = 24.4, median = 26, IQR = 14, MAD = 7.2

Since all values are affected by the same multiplicative values, the measures of center and variability will feel the same affect. If you multiply each data value by 2, you will multiply the mean, mode, median, IQR, and MAD by 2.

Applications

1. 1 student

2. You can use the histogram with 5-minute intervals to determine the number of students that spend at least 15 minutes traveling to school. To find the number of students, identify the number of students in the 15-minute to 20-minute interval, the 20-minute to 25-minute interval, the 25-minute to 30-minute interval, the 30-minute to 35-minute interval, the 35-minute to 40-minute interval, and the 45-minute to 50-minute interval. Sum these numbers together.

You cannot use the histogram with 10-minute intervals to determine the number of students that spend at least 15 minutes to travel to school. The interval size is 10. Within the 10-minute to 20-minute interval, it is impossible to know which of those students spend less than 15 minutes traveling to school and which spend more than 15 minutes traveling to school.

3. 26; You can add the heights of the bars in either histogram to find the total number of students.

4. The median time is 18.5 minutes; you can find the median by finding the two data values located in the middle of the dot plot. The two middle values are 18 and 19, so the median is halfway between those two values.

5. **a.** Juice F has the greatest percent of real juice. Juice G has the least percent of real juice. You can use Graph A. Possible explanation: Graph A identifies the individual drinks. If you use Graph B, you can't identify specific drinks represented in the graph.

b. Juice F has 34% real juice. Juice G has 9% real juice. You can use Graph A. It is the only graph in which you can identify exactly which juice has exactly what percent of real juice in it.

6. **a.** Possible answer: Graph A; you can even out the bars in the bar graph until all the bars are even. This would give you the mean. Alternatively, you can find the median by listing the data values in numerical order. Find the data value with the middle position; this is the median. Graph B is a histogram. You can only determine how many occurrences there are for intervals of data values. There is no way to determine exact data values. Because of this, you cannot find any exact measures of center, and therefore, it is difficult to find the typical percent of real juice in a juice drink.

b. Possible answers: 19.8% (mean); 18% (median)

7. Possible answers:

Graph A: The title could be Percentage of Real Juice in Juice Drinks. The horizontal axis could be labeled Juice Drinks and the vertical axis could be labeled Percent of Real Juice.

Graph B: The title could be Percent of Real Juice in a Sample of Juice Drinks. The horizontal axis could be labeled Percent of Real Juice and the vertical axis could be labeled Number of Juice Drinks.

8. Yes; from Graph A, you can count how many juice drinks have a percent of juice in each interval to make Graph B.

9. No; the specific data values cannot be identified from Graph B; to make Graph A, you need detailed information.

10. a. (See Figure 1.)

   b. The value of Quartile 1 is 11, and the value of the minimum data value is 4. This means that 25% of the data values are greater than or equal to 4 and less than or equal to 11.

   Looking at the data, the values that make up the first whisker are between 4 and 11, including both 4 and 11. The whisker is short in comparison to the other sections of the box plot because the distance between 4 and 11 is comparatively small. One fourth of the data is included in this whisker, so there is a cluster of data values within this small interval.

   c. The value of Quartile 3 is 95, and the value of the maximum data value is 213. This means that 25% of the data values are greater than or equal to 95 and less than or equal to 213.

The distance between Quartile 3 and the maximum value is 118. This is a large portion of the entire box plot, so the last whisker is long. This means that the upper fourth of the data values are spread out over a wide distance.

   d. The median is 50. This means that half the distances are less than or equal to 50 miles and half the distances are greater than or equal to 50 miles.

   e. The mean is about 67.47 miles, which is larger than the median. This tells us the distribution is skewed to the right (it has a long tail on the right with more data clustered on the left).

11. a. (See Figure 2.)

   b. 5 weekends; find the height of the bar in the interval of 20 to 40 miles. This is the number of weekends Jimena drove at least 20 but less than 40 miles.

Figure 1

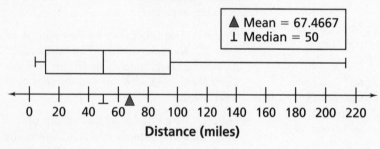

Weekend Travel

▲ Mean = 67.4667
⊥ Median = 50

Distance (miles)

Figure 2

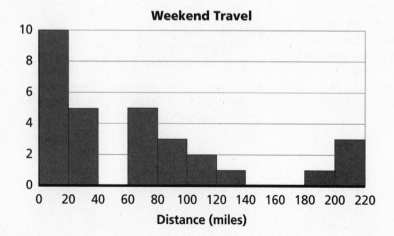

Weekend Travel

Distance (miles)

Data About Us   ACE Answers

c. 7 weekends; find the heights of all the bars from 100 miles to 220 miles. Add these heights together to find the total number of weekends Jimena drove more than 100 miles.

d. The median falls in the interval 40 miles to 60 miles. The median marks the midpoint of the distribution of data values. Of 30 data values, 15 are less than 40 miles; the remaining data values are greater than 60 miles. So, the median marks the halfway point between 40 and 60 miles, or 50 miles, even though no data points are near 50.

12. a. The histogram highlights 3 clusters in the data: 0 to 40 miles; 60 to 140 miles, and 180 to 220 miles. The box plot does not show these clusters. Instead, the quartiles suggest spreads of data values. Both distributions do, however, show a skew to the right.

b. The first bar in the histogram is tall. It suggests that many values cluster there. The length of the first whisker in the box plot is short, which suggests that there is little variation within that first whisker. These indicate the same pattern in the data.

c. The histogram shows the four highest data values, which relates to the last whisker in the box plot. The right-hand whisker includes these four data values as well as some of the values within the center cluster of the histogram. Additionally, the histogram shows more spread on the right side of the graph. This also relates to the last whisker in the box plot.

13. Both sets of box plots are shown below.

Possible answer: The girls in Mrs. R's class appeared to have performed better than the girls in Mr. K's class. The median for Mrs. R's class is 80 jumps. The upper 50% of the data is contained within 80 to almost 100 jumps. The median for Mr. K's class indicates that half the data values at or above the median (57) are more spread out than those below or at the median. (See Figure 3.)

Possible answer: The boys in Mr. K's class appear to have performed better than the boys in Mrs. R's class. The median for Mr. K's class is 27 jumps. The median for Mrs. R's class is only 16 jumps. (See Figure 4.)

Figure 3

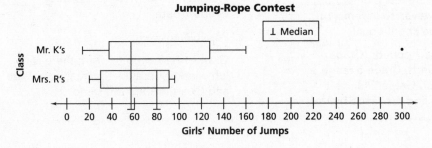

Figure 4

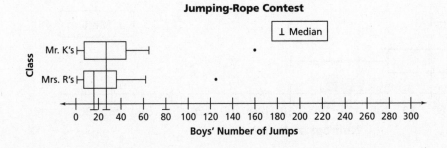

14. The box plots below compare the performance of the girls in both classes to the performance of the boys in both classes. The girls performed better than the boys. Both groups have outliers: the boys have outliers at 160 and 125 jumps; the girls have an outlier at 300 jumps. The boys' maximum value (not including the outlier) is equal to the median of the girls' data values. The median for the girls is 65 jumps, and the median for the boys is 18.5 jumps. Also, the minimum number of jumps for the girls appears to be almost identical to the median number of jumps to the boys. (See Figure 5.)

15. D; The mean is not used to construct a box plot.

16. Students can reasonably agree with either Tim or Kadisha. Their explanations determine whether or not they understand the box plots. Possible explanation: From the box plot of the number of raisins per box, you can see that about 75% of the boxes of Brand X raisins contain more raisins than any of the boxes of Brand Y raisins. From the box plot of the mass in grams per box, you can see that the brands are quite similar; the medians only differ by about $\frac{1}{2}$ gram. In terms of which is a better deal, if a consumer wants more raisins, Brand X is a better deal. It may be that Brand X raisins are less plump than Brand Y raisins, however, so in terms of mass, they would be about equal.

17. a. Grade 1 range is 7 pounds, Grade 3 range is 7 pounds, Grade 5 range is 19 pounds, and Grade 7 range is 36 pounds; you find the range by subtracting the minimum value from the maximum value.

b. Grade 1 median is 4 pounds, Grade 3 median is 7 pounds, Grade 5 median is 11 pounds, and Grade 7 median is 19 pounds; you find the median by identifying the value in the middle position in a set of ordered data.

c. Possible answer: Grade 7 appears to have the greatest variation in backpack weights. The data's range (36) is the greatest of the four grades. The data are quite spread out.

d. The data for Grade 1 data are clustered at the lower end of the distribution, but the data for Grade 3 are clustered near the median. The medians are different for the two grade levels.

18. a. C; Possible explanation: There are no values greater than 10. So the only box plot that could match is C.

b. A; Possible explanation: The greatest value shown on the dot plot is 11. The matching box plot must be A.

c. B; Possible explanation: The only box plot that shows a maximum of 23 (Grade 5's maximum) is B.

d. D; Possible answer: The only graph that shows the value of 39 (Grade 7's maximum) is D. This must display Grade 7 data.

e. Possible answers:

Grade 1 is skewed to right; there is no left whisker because the minimum value and Quartile 1 are the same.

Figure 5

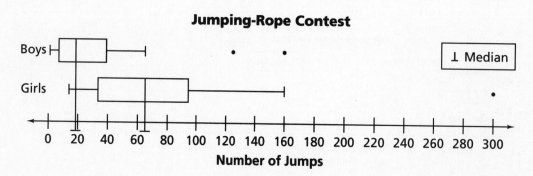

Jumping-Rope Contest

Number of Jumps

Data About Us   ACE Answers

Copyright © Pearson Education, Inc., or its affiliates. All Rights Reserved.

Grade 3 is skewed to the left; the median and Quartile 3 are the same. Also, there is an outlier.

Grade 5 is symmetric; the median is in the middle of the box and the whiskers are about the same size.

Grade 7 is skewed to the left; the median is shifted to the right side of the box. There is also an outlier and the distribution is very spread out.

19. **a.** C; Possible explanation: This is the only graph that has more than half its data values in the interval 0 pounds to 5 pounds.

b. A; Possible explanation: All but 4 dots on the dot plot belong in the interval 5 pounds to 10 pounds. This is the only graph where the histogram has that much height from 5 pounds to 10 pounds.

c. B; Possible explanation: The only histogram that has an even amount of data values in the 5 to 10 and 10 to 15 intervals is Histogram B. Additionally, this graph has no outliers.

d. D; Possible answer: This is the only histogram that shows a data value within the interval 35 pounds to 40 pounds.

e. Possible answers:

Grade 1 is skewed to right; the histogram has a high bar at the left, and the bars keep decreasing in height.

Grade 3 is symmetric, with a high bar in the interval 5 pounds to 10 pounds, and very short bars in the intervals to either side.

Grade 5 is slightly skewed to the right. It has values in intervals 15 pounds to 20 pounds and 20 pounds to 25 pounds that outweigh the 0 pounds to 5 pounds interval on the left.

Grade 7 is fairly symmetric. It has similar bar heights to the left and to the right of the most frequent interval, 15 pounds to 20 pounds.

20. Possible answer: You can compare medians. Both box plots are fairly symmetric, even though the 7th-grade data is more spread out. So while the shortest 8th-grade student is much taller than the shortest 7th-grade student, the Grade 8 median (65.5 inches) is 2.5 inches greater than the Grade 7 median (63 inches).

21. By using the medians of the Grade 5 and Grade 8 data, students should expect to grow about 6 inches (or $\frac{1}{2}$ foot) in height from Grade 5 to Grade 8.

22. The Grade 6 distribution is slightly skewed. The median is not in the center of the box. Also, the right-side whisker is longer than the left-side whisker. The distribution is slightly skewed to the right.

23. The Grade 8 distribution appears to be symmetric; the median is in the center of the box, and the two tails are about the same length.

24. Answers will vary; Possible answer: about 37 cm; looking at the measures of center, the typical height for a student in Grades 6–8 is about 162 cm. The typical height for a student in Grades K–2 is about 125 cm. Thus, the students in Grades 6–8 are about 35 cm taller than the students in Grades K–2.

25. Answers will vary; Possible answer: about 18 cm; looking at the measures of center, the typical height for a student in Grades 6–8 is about 162 cm. The typical height for a student in Grades 3–5 is about 144 cm.

Thus, the students in Grades 6–8 are about 18 cm taller than the students in Grades 3–5.

26. The K–2 heights seem symmetrical with a few heights at the lower end. The 6–8 heights seem symmetrical with a few heights at the upper end. The 3–5 heights seem to have clumps. One clump is found at 130–145 cm and then another clump occurs from 155 cm to 160 cm. The differences in their heights are due to different rates of growth at the different ages, some of which may be affected by factors such as gender.

Connections

27. a. The number of data values in the set must be 250 ÷ 25 (or 10). One possible set of values is 15, 10, 18, 7, 34, 26, 21, 19, 57, and 43.

   b. Any set of 10 values with a sum of 250 will work, so other students probably gave different data sets. **Note:** This helps students understand that some problems have more than one answer. It also points out that the mean may be a measure of center for many different sets of values.

   c. The median and the mean don't have to be close in value. If there are some very high or very low values, the mean might be quite different from the median. In the data set in part (a), the median is 20. The mean is affected by the relatively high values of 43 and 57.

28. a. (See Figure 6.)

   b. The numbers are not equally likely to be chosen. According to this data set, when people choose a number between 1 and 10 "randomly," they choose the number 7 over other numbers. The number 1 and the number 10 are not chosen frequently.

   c. 7 is the mode.

   d. If nine students chose 5 as their number, that means nine students are 10% (or one tenth) of the population surveyed. To figure out how many students were surveyed, multiply 9 by 10 to get 90. There are 90 students in Grade 7.

29. 72; The sum of her six scores with x, the score of the missing quiz, is $82 + 71 + 83 + 91 + 78 + x = 405 + x$. To get an average of 79.5 for the six quizzes, divide $405 + x$ by 6. So the question becomes "405 plus what number gives 79.5 when divided by 6?" or equivalently "79.5 times 6 equals 405 plus what number?". The answer is 72 since $(79.5 \times 6) = 405 + 72$.

Figure 6

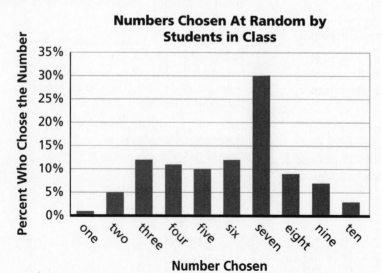

Numbers Chosen At Random by Students in Class

30. a. Springfield Yellows: mean: 23.$\overline{6}$ years, median: 23 years

Charlestown Spartans: mean: about 27.85 years, median: 27 years

Below are both dot plots and box plots for these data about ages. (See Figures 7, 8, 9 and 10.)

The Springfield Yellows appear to be a young team. The majority of players' ages vary from 20 to 26 years, with one outlier at 30 years old. The mean and median are both about 23 or 24 years.

The Charlestown Spartans appear to be older than the Springfield Yellows.

The median and mean are about 27 or 28 years. These data are more spread out.

Looking at the box plots, the Springfield Yellows seem to have a more symmetrical distribution (the median is in the middle of the box); the Charlestown Spartans' ages are more variable; the median is located closer to Q1 than to the middle of the box, which suggests an asymmetrical distribution.

b. Springfield Yellows:
mean: 198.25 centimeters,
median: 200.5 centimeters

Figure 7

Ages of Charlestown Spartans Players

Years

Figure 8

Ages of Springfield Yellows Players

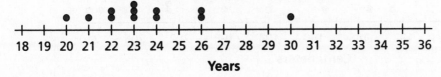

Years

Figure 9

Ages of Charlestown Spartans Players

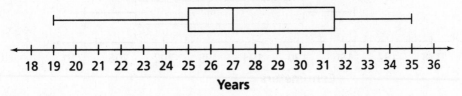

Years

Figure 10

Ages of Springfield Yellows Players

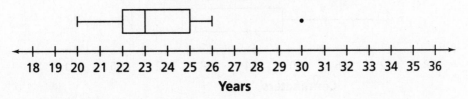

Years

ACE ANSWERS 4

Charlestown Spartans:
mean: about 196.46 centimeters,
median: 198 centimeters

Below are both dot plots and box plots for these data about heights. (See Figures 11, 12, 13, and 14.)

The heights of the teams display similar distributions. Both distributions are a bit skewed to the left. The Springfield Yellows, however, are slightly taller than the Charlestown Spartans. This can be seen by comparing their means, medians, and upper and lower quartiles.

c. The ages and the heights do not appear to be drastically different based on the statistics reported. A typical age might be about 25 years. A typical height may about 200 centimeters. Only two teams were compared, however, and it is not wise to generalize these statistics to the entire professional basketball league. The ages and heights for the Springfield Yellows and Charlestown Spartans may not be typical for the rest of the professional basketball league. You need more data from other teams to make an informed generalization.

Figure 11

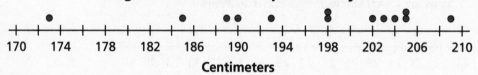

Heights of Charlestown Spartans Players

Figure 12

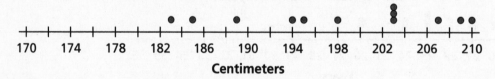

Heights of Springfield Yellows Players

Figure 13

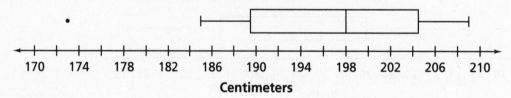

Heights of Charlestown Spartans Players

Figure 14

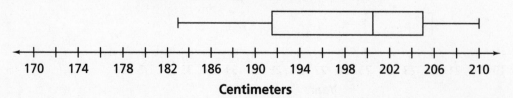

Heights of Springfield Yellows Players

Data About Us   ACE Answers

Extensions

31. a. The graph could be titled "Lengths of Baseball Games," with a horizontal axis label of "Game Length (minutes)" and a vertical axis label of "Number of Games" or "Frequency."

b. The distribution is skewed to the right. There is a tail of large data values on the right side of the graph. This means that the mean will be higher than the median. There are no gaps in the data, however, and no discrete clusters. Most games are between 140 and 190 minutes long.

c. About 147 games are represented.

d. Estimates will vary. Sample estimate: The lower quartile is between 140 and 150, the median is between 160 and 170, and the upper quartile is between 170 and 180. These numbers indicate that approximately 25% of games last less than 150 minutes, 25% last between 150 and 165 minutes, 25% last between 165 and 180 minutes, and 25% last more than 180 minutes.

32. Possible answer: The middle box plot is symmetrical. So if the median is 4, then Q1 could be 3, which would mean Q3 should be 5. The minimum data value could be 1, which would mean the maximum data value would be about 8 (since the right-hand whisker is slightly longer than the left-hand whisker). You could use these five values as your data set, or you could provide an infinite number of other data sets.

For the top box plot, Q3 and the maximum data value are close to the same summary statistics for the middle box plot. So Q3 would be 5 and the maximum data value could be 7. Q1 is between the minimum data value and Q1 of the middle box plot, so the top box plot's Q1 could be 1.5. The minimum value might be −1. You could use these five values as your data set, or you could provide an infinite number of other data sets.

For the bottom box plot, the entire left-hand whisker is within the left-hand whisker of the middle box plot. So the minimum value for the bottom box plot could be 1.5 and Q1 could be 2.5. Q3 could be 7, and the maximum value could be 11. You could use these five values as your data set, or you could provide an infinite number of other data sets.

Index